MUNICIPAL
COPING STRATEGIES

MANAGING INFORMATION
A Series of Books in Organization Studies and Decision-Making

Edited by **AARON WILDAVSKY,** *University of California, Berkeley*

What impact does the computer have on organizations (both public and private), and the individual decision-makers within them?

How can "data" be converted into "information for decision"?

Who produces (and who consumes) such data? with what effects? under which conditions?

What are the sources of error—and the means of overcoming them—in contemporary management information systems (MIS)?

What is the state of the art in MIS theory?

How can we increase our understanding of information and its management, as well as the surrounding organizational environment?

These are critical questions in an era of information overload, coupled with the need for decision-making by managers and policymakers dealing with finite resources. The **Managing Information** series meets the need for timely and careful analysis of these vital questions. Studies from a variety of disciplines and methodological perspectives will be included. The series will analyze information management from both public and private sectors; empirical as well as theoretical materials will be presented.

Jay D. Starling

MUNICIPAL COPING STRATEGIES
"As Soon as the Dust Settles"

Volume 7
MANAGING INFORMATION:
A Series of Books in Organization
Studies and Decision-Making

Series Editor: **AARON WILDAVSKY**

SAGE PUBLICATIONS
The Publishers of Professional Social Science
Beverly Hills   London   New Delhi

For information address:

SAGE Publications, Inc.
275 South Beverly Drive
Beverly Hills, California 90212

SAGE Publications India Pvt. Ltd.
M-32 Market
Greater Kailash I
New Delhi 110 048 India

SAGE Publications Ltd
28 Banner Street
London EC1Y 8QE
England

Printed in the United States of America

Library of Congress Cataloging-in-Publication Data

Starling, Jay D.
    Municipal coping strategies.

    (Managing information; v. 7)
    1. Oakland (Calif.)—Politics and government.
I. Oakland Project. II. Title. III. Series.
JS1248.2.S72   1985   352.0794′66   85-11867
ISBN 0-8039-2512-3

FIRST PRINTING

CONTENTS

PREFACE

THIS IS THE FINAL volume of a long-term, multi-faceted study of urban problems in the city of Oakland, California.[1] The Oakland Project began as an effort to use social science to help solve urban problems. But, in the end, it has been social science that has benefited from the opportunity to observe urban decision makers at close quarters. Among many other insights gained from the experience, particularly illuminating was an appreciation of the profound uncertainty under which local officials frequently must act. This volume analyzes their responses to conditions of uncertainty and explains why and how social science must integrate these findings into improved theories of decision making and public administration.[2]

Urban political and administrative leaders have suffered painful blows in virtually every arena of local government and politics for more than two decades. Well-to-do citizens, retail tradesmen, and manufacturers have fled from the core cities. Idle land and inflation have seriously eroded local governments' tax base while the commuters, the elderly, the poor, and the handicapped need and demand more services. Neither traditional nor innovative political or management solutions have successfully meliorated this situation. There is anger, resentment, and fear among citizens, political leaders, and public administrators alike.

NOTES

1. Earlier reports of the Oakland Project were made by Pressman and Wildavsky (1973a) and were documented in a variety of other books and articles, including Meltsner (1971) and Pressman and Wildavsky (1973b).

2. I rely primarily on the common language meaning of the term "uncertainty" and on the sense the reader should pick up in Chapters 2 through 8. But see the Appendix at the end of Chapter 1 for a more thorough definition.

ACKNOWLEDGMENTS

THIS RESEARCH IS drawn from practitioners, scholars, and participant-observers who were part of very ambiguous administrative situations and were interested in developing a more complete understanding of how decision makers cope with such ambiguity. Many individuals are responsible for the information and insights that are contained in this volume. Much of the data was collected unobtrusively from public documents, memoranda, and other written materials, while still other information was gathered from carefully drawn questionnaires and intensive interviews administered by the members of the Oakland Project. However, each case was enriched by having at least one of the contributing researchers serve an apprenticeship in the focal organization. For example, Donald Tamaki, coauthor of Chapter 3, was a leader of the low-resource pressure group examined in that case. The point is that the following studies are thorough and detailed. The members of the Oakland Project expended a great deal of time and effort to document the arguments so that they do not rest only on personal observation and anecdotal evidence.

Although the germ of the idea was mine, as is the responsibility for the analysis, many individuals contributed time, effort, and valuable insight to this volume. Particularly, Aaron Wildavsky, Arnold Meltsner, and Jeff Pressman from the Oakland Project offered support and valuable criticism, and freely shared their ideas. My colleague Ned Woodhouse deserves special mention; he labored long and hard to help clarify both thought and language.

Attempts to resolve the dilemmas of much needed services and insufficient financial reserves have had little effect other than to increase hostility and distrust between leadership and the citizenry and, ironically, to cost more. Despite increasing concern for efficiency and effectiveness in the provision of public services and a seemingly endless supply of analytically based panaceas like PPBS, ZBB, Productivity Analysis, and Cutback Management, it appears that citizens pay more and more for diminishing services. In addition to analytic cure-alls, there also seems to be an unending number of programs—usually originated by the federal government—to remedy urban problems. Model Cities, Community Action Programs, Drug and Alcohol Diversion Programs, Summer Jobs, and CETA Programs have come and gone and had little lasting effect other than to increase anger, resentment, and fear. Tax bases still erode, the well-to-do flee, and retail centers as well as light and heavy industries increasingly locate in the exurbs.

Why have these problems been so resistant to a bewildering variety of attempted solutions? Is it because local problems cannot be solved by local actors? Perhaps local leadership is not sufficiently talented, concerned or trained for their jobs. There is nothing to be gained by conceding defeat at the outset and assuming that nothing can be done by locals to solve their problems. Moreover, there is strong evidence that urban leaders today are well trained, honest, and committed to the community and professional service delivery.

Perhaps the difficulty is not with particular individuals or with institutions that provide public services. The argument put forward in this volume is that in the past two decades, local public decision-making processes have become increasingly outmoded. Decision methods— including style, form, reasoning processes, and substance—that may work acceptably in relatively quiescent political and administrative arenas are not adequate for situations marked by persistent problems, numerous changes, and social, economic, and political complexity. The basic understanding of, approach to, and methods for making decisions in arenas characterized by complicated, potentially explosive problems must be altered or citizens and leaders alike will continue to find themselves confronted with personal, professional, and institutional failure.

This volume examines citizens', citizen activists', elected officials', and professional administrators' responses to public policymaking in difficult, confusing circumstances—or stated somewhat more precisely, under conditions of moderate to high uncertainty. The setting is Oakland and the focus is on local government. The plan of the volume is that each succeeding chapter moves more deeply into the public policy process, with the penultimate chapter depicting a city's elected and appointed leadership wrestling with a problem that is completely beyond their understanding and that threatens to overwhelm them.

An unorthodox thesis is offered in this work. It argues that the way public officials avoid decisions and otherwise protect themselves when faced with confusing problems is not nearly as pathological as is commonly believed. Such behavior is at least normal and perhaps even healthy. The great error in common perceptions of bureaucratic behavior has been the assumption that public officials should always do their best to fulfill the stated mission of their agency or organization. In fact, society may be served better when officials do not try to fulfill their perceptions of ideal behavior. Instead, public officials ought to follow their natural inclination to protect themselves even if the prevailing view is that the organization's goals and programs appear to suffer as a result.

The basis for such a counterintuitive notion will become clear in later chapters. Chapter 1 simply introduces the argument. The first section of Chapter 1 describes the setting for the research. The second section explains how social scientists and practitioners commonly think about good administration and points to several key problems with the reigning view. The third section develops a theory of how public officials actually behave when confronted with moderate to high levels of uncertainty. The fourth section describes the structure of the rest of the volume. An appendix to Chapter I discusses the concept of uncertainty.

Chapter 2 analyzes Oakland's citizens' perceptions of city hall and their reactions to its policies. Chapter 3 carefully scrutinizes a low-resource pressure group's attempt to influence public school policy in Oakland. Chapter 4 observes the other side of this process: a policymaking body—the city council—reacting to a low-resource pressure group. In Chapter 5 attention is turned to professional administrators, as the police department, a hierarchically structured department that relies heavily on routine, is observed grappling with the uncertainties in its budgeting process. Chapter 6 examines the planning department's adaptation to considerable ambiguity about its purpose, and Chapter 7 chronicles a newly reorganized parks and recreation department's struggle to establish itself with few guidelines. Chapter 8 presents a graphic analysis of elected and professional policymakers laboring with a technology they did not understand and, like the "tar baby," could not subdue.

As suggested by James Thompson in his work on bureaucratic organizations, uncertainty emanated from the citizens', group leaders', elected officials', or administrators' respective environments, in each case analyzed in this volume. In Oakland, as elsewhere, there are elaborate rituals for diminishing personal or intraorganizational uncertainty, including religious beliefs, cultural myths, laws, rules, standard procedures, and many others. None of these methods succeeded in controlling the uncertainties induced by the external environment.

1
RESEARCH SETTING

BEFORE THE TURN of the century, elected officials and administrators in most city halls were confident of their ability to govern their cities. Old, well-established cities such as New York, Philadelphia, Boston, or Chicago have had turbulent histories. But many, such as Los Angeles, Houston, Oakland, or Orlando, have only recently encountered burgeoning problems that threaten to exceed elected and administrative decision-makers' capabilities for resolving them.

The situation in Oakland, California, was no different from that of many American cities after World War II. It had grown from a small to a rather large city on the crest of a large in-migration during the 1940s. Many, especially blacks and browns, had come to work in the shipyards during the war. Oakland also experienced the rapid development of a constraining suburban ring in the postwar years. Despite a magnificent setting, it became increasingly blighted, shabby, and dull. Industry and retail trade no longer settled within its borders. Suburban commuters drained city services and returned little revenue to the city.

In the late 1950s and early 1960s several factors combined to produce unusual burdens on city hall. These pressures were the product of a complex process that is difficult to explain through crisp, causal sequences. But the main factors are well known. After the war, 20 years of unprecedented prosperity and development, abundant cheap energy, rapidly spreading road networks, and ample quantities of cheap motor vehicles had a cumulative, unhappy effect on the American city.

Prosperity and mobility encouraged people, in ever-increasing numbers, to move to newly developing neighborhoods at the city's edge. In this same period, generous federal housing subsidies (particularly VA and FHA loan guarantees) further increased the number of persons able to move out of cramped, inner-city housing to low-density, single-family dwellings in suburban areas.

As the population around cities began to spread out, the central city—now very likely constrained by a solid ring of "independent" suburban communities—also began to lose hegemony over the commerce and manufacturing in its region. Tax advantages and ready-access roads for supply and distribution encouraged manufacturers to move away from the central city. Retail stores branched out to serve large suburban populations, and by the late 1960s the shopping center had become the regional center of retail trade. Such multifaceted withdrawal from the central city increased its decay rate so that blight spread faster than the city could be rejuvenated. Those persons who were left behind, together with those who moved into blighted areas to acquire cheap housing, demanded the same services as their well-to-do neighbors who had moved out of the city to more desirable neighborhoods.

This outmigration and spreading blight began to sap the city's ad valorem tax base. Roads, parks, parking facilities, and other public projects used up large chunks of taxable land; it is now common for 40% or more of a city's land-area to be used for public, nontaxable purposes. The result was increasing strain between the central city's income (revenue) and outgo (service costs). City officials and community leaders began earnestly looking for ways to increase revenue and to hold down increasing costs. In addition, the plight of those trapped in a blighted inner city was not improving; in fact it was worsening relative to that of its suburban counterparts. In many urban areas, moreover, inner-city dwellers were becoming noticeably restive. In short, the economic, social, and political condition of the American city for the most part was not good and was getting worse. Consequently, state governments and federal agencies were beginning to formulate new or expanded aid programs for large cities.

Socioeconomic and political factors combined with many hastily fashioned federal and state programs caused surprise and confusion among many municipal officials. It seemed that in a few short years, unemployment in the central cities was spiraling upward; development stopped; and no one wanted to live or work in the city except the few very rich and the numerous very poor. Problems that had plagued policymakers in a few "impossible" cities like New York for more than a century were now affecting most American cities, and municipal officials were not prepared for them. Many city officials were trying for the first time to cope with and adapt to persistently ambiguous situations arising from newly fashioned aid programs, unexpected demands from citizens' groups, and the adoption of little understood management support techniques that were supposed to save money.

No sooner had cities like Oakland developed workable relationships with their respective federal and state program administrators, and learned to use the new resources, than the situation changed. City leaders who for 15 or 20 years had privately and publicly generated programs and monies literally foisted on them were confronted with completely different conditions.

In the early 1970s the nation increasingly was beset by inflation combined with a depressed economy. This condition hit the federal government, and particularly its social programs, like powerful combination punches. Budget demands increased more rapidly than normal while revenues could not keep pace. Deficits increased, and the programs, both public and private, providing aid to cities became ever more constrained.

In short, finances in many cities were affected by decrements in federal support as well as noticeable diminution in revenue increases (Clark and Ferguson, 1983: 43-74).

As this so-called stagflation continued through the decade of the seventies, the political mood of the country also changed. One of the characteristics of this new mood was a push by the executive branch to reduce sharply federally supported programs for the social and physical rehabilitation of cities.

Many cities like Oakland have been riding a fiscal roller coaster since the late 1950s. First, there was a burgeoning number of programs, characterized by confusing rules and rapidly changing players with new interpretations of the already confusing rules. Next, tantalizing amounts of money became available for long-term social and physical development. Last, the past decade has been one of diminishing programs, dollars, and possibilities for places like Oakland.

Today, after more than 20 years of being pulled up and down on this programmatic roller coaster, Oakland has survived. There have been marked changes in the cityscape that demonstrate the direct or indirect influence of the programs developed for cities by such agencies as the Economic Development Administration (EDA), Housing and Urban Development (HUD), or the Department of Transportation (DOT).

As a result of these agencies' programs as well as those of others, Oakland today is serviced by the Bay Area Rapid Transit system (BART); there is a convention center downtown flanked by a new hotel and high-rise office buildings; the major thoroughfare through the Central Business District (CBD) has been revamped into a stylish boulevard, and many old neighborhoods near the CBD that 15 years ago were vacant slums are being restored and occupied by professional offices, pleasant restaurants, and elegant shops.

Similarly, social programs developed for cities like those administered by Health, Education, and Welfare (HEW, now separated into the Office of Education and the Department of Health and Human Services) and the Office of Economic Opportunity (OEO) have left an imprint on cities like Oakland. For example, Oakland today has a black mayor, a black city manager, and the majority of city council members are black or brown.

Such changes notwithstanding, in recent years the programs that helped to add vitality to Oakland's physical and social character have been markedly reduced or terminated. The result is that Oakland again is stalled; several developments proposed for the CBD have been slowed or cancelled; many ghetto areas yet remain; and high rates of unemployment continue. It may be that city support programs were cut before Oakland had achieved a self-sustaining level of development or it may be that the city professional leadership, though much changed over the past 25 years, has yet to develop a vision of and programs for building Oakland into a preeminent American city.

The following example may be illustrative of the present state of mind of the elected and appointed officials in Oakland. One city official recently interviewed reported that the city leadership had sold the new convention center, museum, and municipal auditorium on a lease-back basis. This is an unusual and innovative strategy that could be invoked in order to acquire cash to maintain the momentum of downtown redevelopment after federal and private program money had been reduced to a trickle. The sale and lease-back tactic provided Oakland with a great deal of cash. However, the city has earmarked most of this money to purchase the Raiders professional football club and thus return them to Oakland from Los Angeles. The city officials apparently believe that the Raiders are more important to Oakland's image and future as a city than continuing downtown redevelopment or rehabilitative social programs.

The studies in this volume are drawn from this particularly turbulent period in Oakland's development, the two decades between 1960 and 1980. The city leaders that we have studied are squeezed between blight, lackluster commercial activity, and increased demand for city services from poor residents and suburban commuters. To combat these problems they are looking for ways to reduce unemployment, attract new business, reduce blight, increase revenues, and level increasing service costs. But the programs, policies, and techniques employed to reach such objectives often are beyond the experience and expertise of local elected and professional decision makers. The result is that they are confronted by surprising problems that they do not understand.

RATIONALITY UNDER UNCERTAINTY

There is a widely shared, multirooted conception in our society that, though we are fallible creatures, we ought to strive toward an ideal of rationality, particularly with respect to decision making in formal organizations. Moreover, there are strands in this shared cultural concept that encourage us to believe that by study, work, and practice one can more closely approximate an ideal, almost objective rationality. The roots of this belief are very deep. They probably began in ancient, highly bureaucratized civilizations like those of China, Egypt, or Phonecia and continued through the development of Western civilization. Regardless of their roots, these ideas became more well defined beginning with the enlightenment and continuing through the past century, a period widely referred to as "the age of rationality."

The direct, recent antecedents of our normative beliefs about rationality can be traced to the work of Max Weber nearly 100 years ago. The beliefs were strengthened and dispersed by the preeminence of time-motion specialists and their intellectual heirs, industrial engineers, in this century and by many journalists and scholars who extended and applied Weber's work on modern bureaucracy. To be sure, more than 50 years ago some scholars and practitioners began seriously to question the practicality, utility, and wisdom of pursuing a kind of total rationality.

Today, the intellectual and scholarly communities have all but dismissed these beliefs as unsatisfactory conceptions. But the fact remains that such conceptions have been and continue to be a strong cultural force in advanced industrial societies.

An idealized conception of rationality leads decision makers to try to reach the best possible decisions in order to solve problems and to provide services that their agencies are supposed to provide. In contrast, the natural tendency is for decision makers to protect themselves first, even if urban problems thereby go unsolved. Neither public officials nor scholars have completely worked out how decision makers act when cross-pressured by their natural tendencies and the normative thrust of the ideal type.

Uncertainty in public life is hardly a phenomenon discovered by the Oakland Project. Risk-avoidance tactics are common fare in descriptions of both public and private decision processes. James Thompson's classic work on organizations, for example, argues that coping with uncertainty is the essence of the administrative process (1967: 159).[1] More generally, contemporary students of administrative choice processes agree that (1) one cannot escape completely from uncertainty and (2) administrators typically seek shelter from uncertainty in standard operating routines, rules of choice, the chain of command, and other institutional practices. In fact, modern bureaucracies often appear to function as if they were designed to minimize threatening uncertainties for their employees. Some early writing about management techniques was based on the assumption that administrators could and should behave according to norms established from formalized, rigid, and unrealistic ideas about rationality (Gulick and Urwick, 1937; Mack, 1971: 82).[2] Decision makers were encouraged to rank order all relevant values to be served by a decision, survey all possible policy choices, and choose the option that would do most to promote desired values. Uncertainty would be minimal, these writings implied, if administrators followed a few simple decision rules to render a decision process selfless and completely rational.

This early work has been discounted among professional students of government and administration. Such demanding decision techniques have been shown to be beyond human cognitive capacities. And it has been argued that satisfactory decisions often can be obtained without such superrational techniques (Braybrooke and Lindblom, 1963; Lindblom, 1963; Simon, 1976).

So it is now taken for granted among social scientists that political decision makers cannot and do not abide by norms prescribing strictly rational behavior. But how do administrators behave when faced with uncertainty or other difficult problems? Considerable progress has been made in understanding the organizational routines and standard operating procedures that often govern decision making in bureaucratic organizations (Allison, 1971). There has also been increased attention to cognitive and other barriers of evidence-based perception and choice (Etheredge, 1978; Holsti, 1976; Janis, 1972; Jeruis, 1976; Lerner, 1976). However, relatively little progress has been made in specifying the coping behaviors that political actors actually tend to adopt when confronted specifically with decisions characterized by great uncertainty (Steinbruner, 1974). In regard to how public officials *should* behave there is even less literature.

Students of administration have not done a good job, then, in providing organizations and their members with a prescriptive model of how to go about making decisions that will serve both the individuals' interests and those of their organizations. Partly as a result of this defect in scholarship, the (impossible to achieve) goal of optimizing each decision by employing objective-rational techniques lives on in the norms of most organizations. These espoused norms are in perpetual conflict with the actual operating norms, and very serious problems in organizaional performance result (Argyris and Schon, 1978; Bateson, 1972).

Decision techniques that are based on idealized rationality are not appropriate for decision-making processes characterized by high uncertainty. Consequently, because most officials are not fools, superrational techniques are not much used in the Oakland decision settings. But there was nevertheless a widespread belief in selfless rational behavior, or at least frequent lip service to it. This led to confusion, frustration, guilt, and duplicity for many Oakland decision makers. In sum, a cultural belief in complete rational action lives on even when it is inapplicable; this serves to complicate an already difficult situation and to mislead those caught in contemporary urban dilemmas.

If the techniques developed to promote rational behavior do not work well under conditions of great uncertainty, what does work? Are the choices made in these situations chaotic or nonsensical? Many of the methods for coping with uncertainty that are analyzed in this volume are not "rational" in the sense of an objectively best choice to reach a particular end. They are, however, sensible from a subjective perspective in which the best choices are those that minimize the probability of unhappy surprises and other forms of psychological pain for the decision makers.

Starting from an assumption that individuals can and should make choices under uncertainty following a methodology or decision technique that respects personal concerns will have a high priority in many decisions. Starting from such a premise, it should be possible to improve the coping procedures urban administrators employ to protect themselves and to improve organizational outputs. Further analysis of these opportunities for blending personal concerns, environmental demands, and organizational needs is deferred until Chapter 9. The core of the volume, beginning in Section 3 to follow, is devoted to understanding how public officials actually did respond to uncertainty in Oakland decision settings.

DECISION MAKERS' RESPONSES TO
HIGH-ORDER UNCERTAINTY: A TREE
OF COPING TACTICS

Oakland decision makers' strategies for coping with unfamiliar problems turned out to be remarkably similar despite different persons, purposes, experiences, beliefs, and values. In fact, their tactics in the face of uncertainty were so regular that they can be charted as a sequence of adaptive coping behaviors that vary with parameter conditions and available resources. Figure 1.1 depicts this Guttman-like response sequence based on the assumptions outlined above predicting that decisions made under conditions of great uncertainty do not follow the model implicit in concepts of formal rationality. The surprisingly similar behaviors observed across the cases suggest that, under conditions of great ambiguity, a uniform response pattern exists. The evidence also indicates that such response behavior is logically connected. Certain easy or passive responses are chosen first; more sophisticated or difficult coping tactics are adopted only when insufficient resources or a breakdown in screening processes forces active coping.

The initial reaction to a poorly understood decision problem is to avoid it. This response is so common that "passing the buck" has become a truism in descriptions of bureaucratic reaction. The irony is that a decision maker nearly always is chastised for choosing the avoidance path. It is widely considered pathological administrative behavior, yet avoidance is at worst normal and can even be a tactic that mitigates overreaction or needlessly quick choice. In short, one tends to avoid that which one is not prepared to engage. The argument is not that avoidance is always good; it is that there will be a strong tendency to pass the buck under conditions of great uncertainty and that avoidance is not always a poor strategy (Peterson, 1981: 178-182).[3]

For example, in Chapter 6 the planning administrators consistently avoided confronting the manager and the planning commission with problems of role ambiguity. Although the uncertainty about their role in Oakland was difficult for them, pressing for clarification from their superiors might have increased their frustration and further crippled their activities. If subjective rationality, as presented in Figure 1.1, is a normal state for individuals faced with great ambiguity, fewer policy choices appear anomalous than when viewed through a cognitive filter shaped by the tenets of an ideal rationality. This is not an apology for all avoidance of tough questions by decision makers. But it does suggest that, despite the frustration and antagonism that often is engendered by avoidance tactics, avoidance may yield a less disruptive solution than the available alternatives. Avoiding a problem can be viewed as sensible, thus it need not be confounding or crippling, and certainly need not be treated as pathological.

After avoidance, *delay* is the predominant reaction in the face of high-order uncertainty. Like avoidance, delay is normal and usually wise in conditions of great ambiguity, though objectively it is often pictured as indicative of timidity and weakness. In difficult circum-

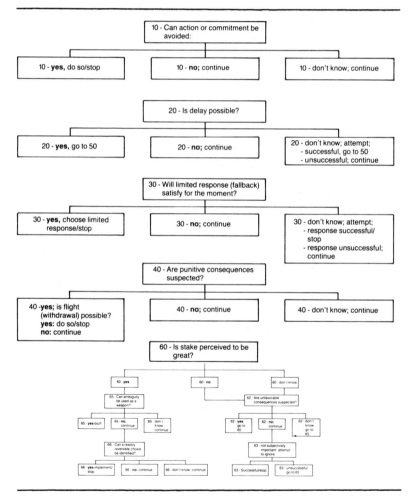

Figure 1.1

(continued)

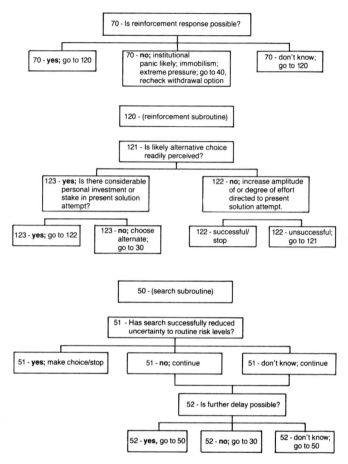

NOTE: The research in Oakland suggests that responses to conditions of middle to high uncertainty can be constructed. Choice problem penetrates from environment; it appears nontrivial and is not familiar.

Figure 1.1 Continued

stances, he or she who hesitates is not lost, but is usually in a tactically advantaged position. There was evidence of delay in virtually all the cases studied.

The difference between avoidance and delay may be principally one of time or the degree to which a problem is perceived to require a solution. Very few pressing problems can be avoided forever. If responsibility cannot be yielded completely, the problems ultimately must be settled less passively. Specifically, delay implies that a decision maker needs more time in order to implement further tactics that will enable him or her to cope better with or to reduce his or her uncertainties. The next most often adopted tactic is that of *limited response*, which is based on professional education, training, or on-the-job experience. This, too, is more of a passive than active response. In this mode, the decision maker attempts to muddle through an ambiguous problem by limiting himself or herself to those actions that he or she can explain, understand, and thus justify in terms of accepted codes, previous experience, or education. This also is normal under subjective assumptions and can be a helpful interim tactic when, for example, experienced administrators find themselves confronted by choice problems in an environment in which familiar operating rules and guides have been suspended or do not apply. But it can bring frustration and surprising consequences to the decision makers if they fall back on a routine that irritates rather than meliorates the problems facing them. Such is the case in Chapter 8 when the finance department administrators limited themselves to narrow, traditional criteria to judge a new, problem-laden technique.

The more active the coping tactic the less likely it is to be chosen, as a commitment to action is psychologically more difficult than inaction and is more likely to engender offensive results. Limited responses are found less often than avoidance or delay, for example.

After limited choice, the response pattern under highly uncertain conditions becomes more complex. If decision makers do not have professional education, training, or on-the-job experience, they may not have sufficient capacity to "fall back" to a limited response. If this is the case or the limited option is not working, the choices become increasingly difficult. If decision makers fear punishing consequences, they naturally will withdraw from the arena if possible. Withdrawal was observed among the citizens, officials, and administrators in each arena of Oakland politics.

If withdrawal is not possible or decision makers believe their stake to be great, the tendency when facing considerable loss is to look for weapons in order to fight. The same high-order uncertainty that confounds decision makers can become an effective weapon. Under subjective norms, the one who appears to be relatively more certain has the advantage. Relative uncertainties can be manipulated and bluffing tactics can be employed by leaders in order to negotiate successfully a decision sequence. For example, in Chapter 3 the leaders of the students' movement were quite effective in their use of ambiguity as a tactical weapon to win concessions from the school board. In short, these tactics helped them to survive in the organizational sense despite great ambiguity and possible professional or personal reprisals.

In conditions in which stake is great but personal or institutional resources like money, friends, power, or legitimate authority are not plentiful, the basic coping tactics such as delay may not be available. The predominant response is to employ methods such as study to reduce one's own ambiguity, combined with tactics designed to increase others' sense of uncertainty.

If a bluffing tactic is not possible because the decision maker thinks he or she cannot carry it off or because the conditions of a particular decision situation do not lend themselves to it, the tendency is to select a course of action that is readily reversible. Some of the administrators studied did not bluff; rather, they chose responses that, for most situations, could be easily changed. For instance, the planners in Oakland were faced with considerable ambiguity about their role in Oakland and therefore chose roles that were easily shed.

Similarly, giving away opportunities in the form of programs or policies also can be seen as wise actions, while attempting well-worn choices again and again even though they do not work is understandable, even normal, from a subjective perspective. The electronic data processing (EDP) controversy detailed in Chapter 8 suggests that the auditor was wise when he decided to give control of the city's electronic data processing operations to the manager. It was also understandable that the finance officer and the manager, who did not understand EDP equipment and operations, and were confronted with one confounding situation after another in the city's EDP operation, could do nothing but spend more money for ever bigger, more sophisticated machinery. This condition, which usually leads to a reinforcement response, and the consequences of which can be devastating, is all too common at every level of government (Lerner, 1976). This particular strategy is a surprisingly frequent outcome of decision processes in an environment of high-order uncertainty. We see policies that are attempted time and again with increasing intensity when the expected results are not realized. A notable example was that of the United States' policy toward Vietnam. Although of lesser magnitude in Oakland, this type of coping resulted in outcomes similar to those in Vietnam (i.e., compounded expense, confusion, frustration, and anguish).

As suggested at the beginning of this section, these coping strategies are not chosen arbitrarily by harried, unsure political and administrative actors. In fact, there is a logic to the basis for the choices made under conditions of great uncertainty; but it is a logic rooted in concerns about outcomes, consequences, and self, rather than in an ideal optimizing strategy.

In many instances, however, the clear logic of a subjective response is masked by powerful institutional, culturewide norms that specify that administrative and political leaders must strive to make choices that are selfless and totally rational. The coping tactics outlined in Figure 1.1 are not considered acceptable, responses in institutional settings adhering to the tenets of idealized rationality. This suggests that decision makers in such settings, confounded by a choice-problem, move only to the most natural, elementary responses. Then, cross-pressured, confused, and anxious, they are not likely to use these first, most instinctive subjective responses to move to more complex, yet potentially useful, coping tactics. The research in Oakland offers many examples of administrators who attempted to avoid and/or continued to delay when a different tactic clearly would have resulted in a better experience and more satisfying outcome for all concerned (Meltsner and Bellavita, 1983: Chap. 1).[4]

THE OAKLAND CASE STUDIES

Each of the arenas of Oakland politics displayed several of the coping tactics in the model presented above. But it is possible also to view each in terms of a predominant coping strategy. This section introduces the plan of the book and discusses briefly some prominent examples of coping tactics that run through several of the cases in order to alert readers to some of the similarities and differences among the studies. These cases, taken as a whole, suggest that few individuals are comfortable acting under conditions of high uncertainty. Although officials strive to avoid doing so, the policy process in an urban center is complicated and those who would influence or guide policy increasingly must learn to cope with disquieting ambiguities.

This work depicts those living in Oakland and those responsible for the public welfare struggling for clarity and developing strategies to cope with amorphous, changing conditions. Commenting about coping with urban change, Richard Rose claims that there are at least four types of change: nil, incremental, threshold, and qualitative. It can be inferred from his argument that the difficulty of adaptation increases with each level of greater change. Generally, the degree of induced uncertainty in the policymakers will increase with each more comprehensive change, though, as Rose indicates, the time available for "forethought" or preparation can be an important intervening variable. Many of the Oakland studies, such as those of the parks and recreation department and electronic data processing in city hall in Chapters 7 and 8, are examples of qualitative changes. They focus on changes of kind rather than degree. New organizational structures, personnel changes, new routines, and services resulted from the policy decisions examined in these chapters. In some of the other cases—for example, the studies of police budgeting and the planning department in Chapters 5 and 6— there were aspects of the city's policy process that the administrators were not able to clarify to their satisfaction or to alter.

The research is diverse and each study is rich. Despite the differences among them with respect to choice behavior in ambiguous conditions, there was considerable similarity. In each chapter, for example, avoidance or delay tactics are manifest. There are also instances of search, limited response, withdrawal, easily reversible choices, and reinforcement *across* the cases.

If this research were to be characterized in terms of a predominant coping tactic, one would conclude that most citizens in Chapter 2 stop at avoidance, though some indicate they would follow the tactical path to withdrawal (at 40 in Figure 1.1). The student leaders in Chapter 3 at first are screened out by the school board and school administrators' protective tactics; this forces them down the path (to 65) where they demonstrate the effectiveness of ambiguity as a weapon. In Chapter 4, the city council is forced by low-resource, antipoverty activist groups beyond its normal, well-screened routines into a set of coping tactics common under conditions of high-order uncertainty. They are forced down the path to immobility (at 70 in Figure 1.1) where, under extreme pressure, they loop back and withdraw.

The police administrators, detailed in Chapter 5, demonstrate their preference for avoidance under conditions of ambiguity, but if forced to adopt further tactics, withdrawal appears to be the most common. If withdrawal is not an available choice, however, they demonstrate facility, with ambiguity as a weapon. The planners in Chapter 6 display a clear tendency to rely on the limited response and reversible choices. In Chapter 7, the parks and recreation administrators also demonstrate a preference for the limited response; when forced beyond that level, the easily reversible choice is common for them. Lastly, the finance administrators depicted in Chapter 8 find themselves in an uncomfortable reinforcement loop (subroutine at 120 in Figure 1.1).

These studies provide initial support for two hypotheses. The first is that a subjective logic is dominant in administrative decision problems characterized by great ambiguity. The second is that decision makers' behavior, guided by subjective concerns, will follow a relatively predictable sequence despite widely varying contexts and differences in subject matter, personalities, and other factors.

To recapitulate from the perspective of the administrative decision maker, choice normally is guided by routine, past experience, and training. When confronted by a problem that is not readily understood in terms of these guidelines, the most natural thing is to avoid it. When it appears that the particular problem cannot be avoided, the tendency is to delay choice in order to search for information that can reduce one's puzzlement about the situation. But if the search is unsuccessful within the constraints of time and effort available or if delay is not possible, how can administrators choose? The evidence in these studies suggests that they tend to choose alternatives that can be understood in terms of their education and experience. However, if the limited response will not suffice and choice is still required, the natural tendency is for the decision maker to consider his or her particular circumstances. Consideration of personal costs resulting from a choice will be relatively more important when "professional" criteria are not available to defend the decision. Under the circumstances, if he or she suspects personally costly consequences, a decision maker will attempt to withdraw or flee from responsibility for an unfamiliar decision or situation.

Generally, the tactics in the lower part of the "tree" depicted in Figure 1.1 are less frequently encountered and may be characterized as active. Active coping tactics normally are forced by insufficient resources for screens or a breakdown in the screening process. The active mode includes such tactics as search and the employment of ambiguity as a weapon. This suggests that, though most everyone's natural inclination is to avoid high-order uncertainty, it can be turned to one's advantage, and this research indicates that a few actually thrive on it.

Passive and active tactics both are influenced by intervening variables that affect the likelihood that either set of modal tactics or both combined will enable a decision maker to cope successfully with uncertainty. These variables, which can influence individuals or organizations, include perceived stake in the choices, staying power, and substantive scope of the uncertainty. In other words, values, investments, resources, and the areas of responsibility touched by high-order uncertainty partially determine the tactical process in conditions of great ambiguity. If one believes that the investment is great, then he or she has considerable incentive to wrestle with uncertainty to protect his or her interests (Wildavsky, 1975: 138-140).[5] But such engagements, as subsequent chapters vividly portray, are expensive. To subdue high-order uncertainty requires effort, intelligence, skill, courage, and time. Those who have or can buy these commodities are more likely to reduce their ambiguity than those who do not.

CONCLUSION

In summary, behaviors that have been widely viewed as pathological or "bureaupathic" by scholars and administrators alike are more than just understandable; they are natural. Until such behavior is understood to be normal under conditions of high uncertainty, prescriptions for and entreaties to policymakers to avoid such responses will have slight effect. It can do no good to chastise decision makers for not being better optimizers. Once the normal coping behaviors are understood, however, the foundation is laid and thought may be given to aids that actually could help those in public bureaucracies and political areas cope better with the strain of uncertainty.

The Oakland studies provide support for the utility of analysis on risk-avoidance from the perspective of normal inclination and lead to a set of specific suggestions about how public decision makers might selectively abandon unproductive avoidance tactics without abandoning either their public duties or their personal concerns. The result can be a significant improvement in public or administrative choice with rather slight increases in political or personal risks. The bulk of this volume explains and illustrates how administrators act when confronted with great ambiguity. The concluding chapter offers a set of organizational and policy aids for decision makers confronted by high-order uncertainty.

APPENDIX

In order to develop a useful understanding of uncertainty, it is necessary to cut through considerable conceptual and lexical variety. It will be helpful, therefore, to condense the discursive scholarship that directly or indirectly addresses uncertainty.

There are many citations one can enumerate. For the now classic formal treatments, see John Von Neumann and Oskar Morgenstern (1944); Leonard J. Savage (1954) or Duncan Luce and Howard Raiffa

(1957). For less rigorous formulations, see Anthony Downs and Ruth P. Mack (1971). Three basic notions appear in the literature concerning uncertainty that easily confuse the reader if the context or use of uncertainty is not carefully specified.

In the first place, absolute certainty is an intellectual artifice; in order to be completely certain in regard to the outcome of a situation, complete knowledge must be present. Obviously the limitations of the human mind make it impossible even to know in what ways knowledge is limited. However, assumptions of relative certainty are useful for day-to-day living.

Second, the idea of risk pervades the decision-making literature. Many students of decision processes commonly equate risk and uncertainty. But it is not particularly useful to link the concept of formal risk with that of uncertainty. If someone flips a "fair coin," he or she does not know whether it will land heads or tails. One does not have perfect knowledge, but neither is one basically uncertain about the act; he or she is sure that it will land heads or tails because there are no other possible outcomes. Moreover, it is absolutely certain that heads is just as likely to turn up as tails. In other words, the idea of formal risk assumes complete knowledge about possible outcomes and the likelihood of their occurrence. Although the concept of risk has demonstrated its value in strategic planning, simulation, and network scheduling among other activities, common sense decrees that in day-to-day experiences and problems the assumptions necessary to frame a situation in terms of formal risk rarely—if ever—can be met.

The word "risk" also is ambivalent in meaning. Risk can mean whimsical speculation in one sense and taking a specific, well-under-stood gamble in another.

A third concept found in the scholarship on decision making is uncertainty. Formally, uncertainty assumes inadequate knowledge about alternatives and their consequences. This seems a more useful construction than that of formal risk for those making choices in a public or administrative setting.

In the broadest sense, the ideas of certainty, risk, or uncertainty do not connote a single condition of unknownness but a continuum of such conditions. There is no certainty; however, the lower boundary of the uncertainty continuum is as close as one can get to certainty when involved in a choice problem. The upper boundary of the continuum is at the point of complete ignorance that allows no alternative formulation or prediction. This space divides into three broad typologies. The first or "low" type of uncertainty exists when all possible outcomes or consequences are identified and the probability of each occurring can be confidently assigned so that their summation equals one. Obviously, such an assignation process implies that the consequences—and the likelihood of each occurring—are clearly and reliably mapped. This means that collecting more information cannot affect the relative probabilities. Stated more formally, it is a distribution for which the marginal effect of an additional piece of information is consistently negligible and there is slight chance of unintended or surprising consequences.

The middle part of the continuum or "midlevel" uncertainty exists when a reasonably complete alternative set can be specified, most outcomes or consequences identified, and tentative probabilities assigned. In situations of this kind, added information can have a considerable effect on the provisional probability estimates. This idea parallels but is not necessarily the same as Bayesian analysis (see, for example, Mack, 1971). Under conditions of mid-level uncertainty, there is a strong incentive to begin searching for more information and to continue the effort as long as the marginal return is consistently greater than the marginal cost. At the midlevel, then, delay and search are likely tactics in order to reduce ambiguity.

The fact that technical and staff assistants are widely employed and extensive files or technical libraries maintained suggests that decision makers often face questions that can be clarified for them by information search. Administrative and/or professional guides, rules, established procedures, and experience also help the decision maker determine tentative probabilities. Thus under conditions of middle-level uncertainty, delay and search activities can pay substantial dividends, greatly reducing the likelihood that a decision maker will be confronted with surprising or unintended consequences of his or her choice. The research in Oakland indicates that municipal policymakers frequently confront this type of uncertainty.

In the upper area of the continuum, high-level uncertainty, there is little confidence that alternatives have been accurately identified. The universe of possible outcomes is not complete or accurate. Under these conditions a decision maker is not likely to feel confident that he or she can assign probability estimates. Decision making under these conditions is obviously difficult and has not been widely studied. Despite carefully organized attempts to thwart activities that are highly uncertain, scholars acknowledge that in the administrative processes, high-level uncertainty is encountered. Again, the research suggests that politics and administration in cities like Oakland increasingly are characterized by high-level uncertainty.

In the middle area of the uncertainty continuum, a decision maker can have some confidence in first estimates that can be checked or improved with relative ease. In the high area of the continuum it is unlikely that information can be obtained that will markedly improve a decision maker's understanding of the situation unless he or she undertakes an extensive self-education and research regimen that is formidable given the limitations of time and energy in the life of most people. Moreover, routines, training, experience, and readily available expertise by definition can but rarely yield either a complete set of possibilities or reliable information about choices. Thus unintended consequences and painful surprises are likely to result when high-level decision makers rely on the foregoing criteria as the basis for choice.

Acting under conditions of high uncertainty presents a painful paradox to an administrator. He or she naturally wants to reduce his or her uncertainty level; the possibility that he or she can do so under these conditions in a short period of time is slight. Furthermore, it follows logically that the longer uncertainty prevails, the greater his or her discomfort. In situations of this kind, creativity, judgment, and inspiration must take the place of careful attention, study, and calculation.

NOTES

1. The literature on this subject is voluminous and may be found in many disciplines. However, beyond the work of Crecine, Meltsner, or Pressman and Wildavsky, I am not aware of any research that speaks to the problem of municipal officials' response to high-level uncertainty.

2. Ruth Mack (1971: 82) points to an interesting wrinkle in this regard when she suggests the difficulty of discriminating, in a natural setting, between uncertainty about outcomes and uncertainty about utilities. This is indeed an intriguing problem, but I do not think that it is relevant to the problem of high-level uncertainty beyond the obvious proposition that the more difficulty one has identifying the range of possible outcomes and the less his or her confidence in the probability assignments, the more difficulty one will have judging which choice is most self-serving and, thus, the more one will resist choosing.

3. Peterson (1981: 178-182) perceptively notes that delay or avoidance is not always straightforward. He argues that city leaders will make false promises in order to buy time or will respond to specific complaints while ignoring the underlying problem.

4. One important limitation to making more generalizable statements about adaptive or coping behaviors is raised by Meltsner and Bellavita (1983). They contend that language is an intervening variable and often has an effect on the particular strategies adopted. In other words, when mutual understanding is low, uncertainty is correspondingly higher and the types of strategies that appear available or useful might be different.

5. Wildavsky's (1975) work raises an interesting issue with respect to the effects of and responses to high-order uncertainty. Wildavsky asserts that uncertainty is more important in poor countries than in rich because the division of very scarce resources matters more. Are the consequences of inadequate knowledge greater for the poor than the rich? Probably, but the anxieties raised by high-order uncertainty are likely to be greater for the rich because they have more at stake and more to lose.

THE KALEIDOSCOPIC CITY
Citizens Talk About Oakland

with
Mari Malvey
Aaron Wildavsky

HOW DO CITIZENS cope with the complexities of urban life? There is more than a little evidence that many, if not most, do so passively, becoming active only to flee. The well-worn phrase is that they vote with their feet; they are dissatisfied with the character of their lives; and they plan to leave the central city environment as soon as possible. For many this will not be possible and they must fight to make an accommodation to a changing city. Relatively few are confident that they can play a part in alleviating those conditions that trouble them. Some trust others, particularly the elected and administrative leadership of the city, to act for them. Some have no such faith in the leadership and fight to bend the collective will of the officials toward their particular needs.

Most citizens of Oakland, however, don't know much about their government, its operation, or its effect on their lives—until it's too late. A new freeway has been cut through, their home has been condemned for urban renewal, their taxes have been increased, utilities have gone up again, a cabaret license has been issued for their neighborhood, and a bar is opening soon, or their neighborhood has been rezoned and a new industrial park is planned. The list of ways that city hall commonly touches our lives is very long while our information about it is slight.

The evidence suggests that most citizens respond by doing nothing, even when such governmental actions directly touch their lives. Eventually they become frustrated, cynical, and fatalistic regarding even those units of government closest to them.

Part of the trouble seems to be that a good bit of the information most citizens hold about local governments is untested and just plain

fallacious. Any move based on inaccurate understanding and information is likely to be quickly frustrated so that the citizen feels he or she
has had no effect and has received no satisfaction. This then reinforces
the tendency toward inaction and provides no incentive to correct
inaccuracies and to become more fully informed. Thus things are always
happening *to* most of the citizens; they make very little happen *for* them
and are able to avoid very little. Their uncertainty, tendency toward
inaction, and frequent subsequent frustration remain high.

Despite the increasing interest in American urban life, there is a
paucity of studies that have asked a broad-based sample of citizens how
they feel about the cities in which they live. Although there are several
investigations of racial conflicts and specialized works that touch on
specific areas like housing, none seek to place citizens in relation to their
neighbors, their fellow urbanites, their government, and beyond—to
their thoughts about remaining or moving, even to their hopes and fears
for the future. We shall make a beginning, for it is with the lives of its
inhabitants that our concern for the city begins.

Our proposition is a simple one: People's feelings about a city depend
on how well they do in it. Richer is better; poorer is worse. The rich can
afford better housing; the poor cannot. Across the railroad tracks in
Oakland are the hills, surely one of the most scenic residential areas in
America. The higher up you are, literally, the better you like your
neighborhood. Variations on this theme are provided by differences in
generational experience and by race.

Our hypothesis curls at the edges; it is good in the middle but bad at
the extremes. The very poorest live chaotic lives. They are really outside
the political process. They can follow no interests of their own because
they are preoccupied with sheer survival. A portion of the rich also lead
disordered lives. They have too much. They don't know what to do with
it or with themselves. They reject the achievement norms that motivate
others. They've been there, they think, and they want something new
and better. They are seekers of causes. Their interest lies in being
interested. If they can keep motivated long enough (boredom is their
enemy), they can provide fuel for political change. Despite their
extremely limited numbers, they have the resources—money, time, and
education—to make an impact.

There is not, as some people claim, a vast disparity in values among
the mass of people in the city. On the contrary, homogeneity of values is
the norm. Most people—black and white, rich and poor, young and
old—adhere to similar American values: work, family, individual effort.
The difference is that circumstances make it easier for people who are

richer to make these values work for them than it is for those whose initial disadvantages are greater. They all want the same things—the house, the lawn, the good schools; they just don't all get it. Another trait they have in common is the low priority they give to political activity.

The rational man or woman does not spend much time on political activity because the cost is likely to be higher than the gain or because the opportunity costs, the advantages of using the time and effort elsewhere, are too high. They may vote (unless the registration laws or affairs of the moment make it marginally inconvenient) because the effort required to salve civic conscience is so small. But going beyond that into campaigning for office or seeking to affect a decision by the city government is likely to cost more than it is worth. Ordinary people are far more likely to make more money by working extra time on their jobs and to gain more personal satisfaction by spending time with their families or hobbies. Consider the situation of a person who wishes to live a certain kind of life. To assure the existence of desired civic services, they can run for office, serve on local recreation committees, become a member of the water district or sewer commission, join the PTA, and so on. But the demands on their time and energy would be enormous. They would be much better off to "vote with his feet" by moving to a place that already approximated the mix of services they desired for themselves and their families. The additional income they need for this move (if, indeed, they did not gain financially by it) could be obtained in less time and with greater certainty of reward than extensive participation in political life would give.

The poorest are under a double handicap: They need the most from the government but are least able to get anything at all. People who are already well off may be content with small favors. Their demands are small and they have ample resources with which to pursue them. The poor want government to help improve their life chances. They make large demands, but the resources they can devote to them are slight. As political participation seems more essential, the possibility of acting effectively appears to recede further into the distance.

Under what conditions, then, does intensive participation take place? Imagine a private or public act that threatens an individual or a neighborhood, a change in a zoning ordinance or a move to locate a business in a residential area. If individuals feel aggrieved, if they know their neighbors, if they know where to complain, and if they have reason to believe they may be efficacious, they will be disposed to act. City employees or those who depend on (or hope to receive in the future) government benefits also have a special motivation to act. They join employee unions, seeking to gain city approval or ward off its hostility, in order to enjoy benefits from the federal government. Their income, if nothing else, depends on public political activity, and they act accordingly.

Oakland is a city of parts, and the geographic terrain precisely circumscribes its demographic neighborhoods. The flat neighborhoods nearer to the bay, the flatlands, are the primary commercial areas and encompass the poorest residential sections. The second ring is higher terrain, the gently rolling foothills, that hold the older residential areas of the city that now house the lower middle class. The outer ring rests on the hilltops and houses the more well-to-do citizens who are often called "hill people."

The lower middle class, symbolically placed in the foothills, follow a politics of flight. They do not want to slip back to the flatlands and they are not rich enough to aspire to the hills. The values on which their mobility depends—home, family, church, work—mean a great deal to them. It makes little sense for them to defend these by direct political action. They lack the education and the communication skills. Besides, their work and their church (hence the designation "Bible Belt") take up most of their time. It is far easier for them to follow the freeway and pick a suburb where they can pause with their own kind until they try to make the next move up.

How do the hill people know what goes on in the rest of the city? Their level of formal schooling is as high as their houses, and with it comes a distant awareness of problems in the city. To the extent the schools are integrated (Oakland has voluntary busing), they are also made directly aware of its racial tension.

For most hill people, avoidance is easier than action. They do not need help. For others more disposed to act, there is the vexatious problem of how to do it. The nation's parties are just becoming active in Oakland; there have been no evident channels for participation. A few of the more conservative ones may have personal contact with a council member or some individual connected with city government. How about the liberals? In another city they would be in the local Democratic clubs; in Oakland, they go off into congressional politics or they languish in boredom and frustration.

The hill people, we hypothesize, play three different kinds of politics. There are the politics of avoidance: We have it good; don't bother us with what happens elsewhere. There are politics of amelioration: These are the people who are plugged into action in Oakland. Mild liberals or concerned conservatives, they reinforce the status quo when they sense extreme behavior and seek changes, such as minority representation on governing bodies, to alleviate felt strains. The avoiders are many, the ameliorators few. The avoiders have gotten as far as they can go or are striving to improve their positions. Either way, they want to enjoy what they have or be free to devote their energies to enhancement of the self. The third group, also a small one, follows the politics of noblesse oblige: Hello down there, all you unfortunates; we're rooting for you up here. These "hill radicals" seek to give added meaning to their lives by being altruists for special interests. They are looking for underprivileged masses who need leaders. They can write; they can talk; they can organize. They want to help, and that means finding people who need to be helped. It is a question of supply and demand: They are willing to supply a certain kind of leadership only if they can help generate the demand.

The politics of noblesse oblige are distinguished by its absolutism. Its adherents want systemic change. The political system is not merely defective in part; all of it is bad and must go. The holistic quality of their rhetoric stems from two sources: The first impels them to seek followers by offering more than any conceivable competitor; the second flows from their almost total lack of success (given their perspectives) in securing their aims. The city has been far more conservative than they have, and their response has been to call for a radically different system, one that would have a place for them. They also want something out of politics, just like the others.

The leading quality of hill politics when confined to neighborhood affairs is its tangible and concrete quality. The demands are specific; the channels of influence are mapped out; and the outcomes are known. These are people who are used to acting effectively to help themselves. They expect to be successful and often are.

The outstanding quality of hill politics of all kinds when concerned with the rest of the city is its abstractness. The problems and the people they refer to are categories of analysis, subject to verbal manipulation, not people one encounters in real life. They may know black professionals who speak on behalf of (but who do not live among) the people of the flatlands. They have no contact with the older residents of the central city or the foothills unless, by chance, they work in different parts of the same firm.

The survey begins with an exposition of the common values most Oaklanders share, deflected by their social positions into different conceptions of the problems that beset their city. It continues by showing how these citizens relate to their government, if at all, and how these relations breed satisfaction or dissatisfaction, depending on their ability to cope with life in Oakland. The chapter ends with a discussion of critical perspectives: Will they leave or stay? Would they encourage the city to do more or less in specific areas? Are they optimistic or pessimistic about the future of the city?

THE PEOPLE OF OAKLAND

On the surface it appears that Oakland has resisted contemporary change. The old demarcations—the hills, the foothills, and the flat-lands—continue to stave off fusion and remain the "great dividers" of economic position and philosophical stance. Accordingly, this section begins with a selection of descriptions about the city drawn from these different neighborhoods. In Oakland "neighborhood" still has a real and very vital meaning, certainly as arbiter of the urban perspective. But Oaklanders are less likely to actually know their neighbors than to know the aspects of society the neighbors represent. As a city, Oakland is not substantial to its residents. Most of them like it, but for reasons that touch only tangentially upon the city itself—the climate, the location, the nearness of other cities—all accidental features of geography. We then asked our respondents, What is real and alive in Oakland? What is happening in Oakland? About half told us they hadn't noticed anything at all happening the last time they looked. The other half had actually noticed changes, and we will discuss them and suggest what con-sciousness of change implies for the coping tactics of different groups within the city. Last, we extract from respondents and their neighbor-hoods the lifestyles that appear to describe the Oakland way of life.

A City of Parts: "A Black Ghetto in the Flatlands and the Well-To-Do in the Hills"

What's it like to live in Oakland? "It depends," a housewife told us, "on which part." Then she added, "My part is a very good part." She was describing the densely wooded slope running down from Oakland's northeastern boundary and forming part of the city's residential area called "the hills." Other people who lived in the same area—pro-fessionals, technicians, local mandarins, and hard core elites—were equally enthusiastic: "Oakland? I love it. There's nothing like being in the hills and having everything around you. . . . You get such a lovely view." "The location is ideal." "The hill area is as nice as any in the world." "It has," another man told us, "one of the best views in the Bay Area." By and large, hill residents can afford to wax enthusiastically about the views that fan out over Oakland from their large and widely spaced houses. These cherished views extend far across the bay to San Francisco and parts of the peninsula, neatly overlooking the rest of Oakland spread uncomfortably below. From the tops of the hills, Oakland is beautiful—and distant.

Beneath the view from the heights of Oakland are other parts of the city, and other Oaklands. People who live in the foothills are not so much looking across the bay as they are looking down at their small gardens. "Here," a retired Oaklander told us, "you can have a backyard you don't have to go through the house to get to." "Oakland," said another, "is a nice, comfortable place where you can have a garden." In the foothills, as well as in the immediately adjacent but more compact bible belt, many people have time to spend in their gardens because they are elderly or retired, as opposed to hill residents who range in age from their late twenties to mid-fifties and generally have growing families. To the retired Oaklanders the city had, of course, seen better days: "It used to be a very beautiful city. Now it's gone to pot." To residents in their middle years, Oakland "used to be a good place to raise children, but now the infiltration of these new types of people, the streets aren't safe." Or, "Well, it's a pretty nice city, all things considered." From the foothills and the Bible Belt, Oakland was "comfortable." The Bible Belt gets its name from its high density of churches. Bible Belt residents are churchgoers as well as gardeners, and we were not surprised that some of these residents would tell us that they lived "within walking distance of the church" or that almost everyone in the neighborhood went "to the same church." Of course, not all of the Bible Belt or foothills is exclusively stable and elderly. Many lower- and middle-class people living here are in transition—newly arrived or on their way out of Oakland. To them Oakland is a temporary location until circumstances send them elsewhere. In the meantime Oakland is neither good nor bad. It is simply "nothing special."

Another group of Oaklanders, generally young, single, career people, occupies the prestigious apartment area along the shores of Lake Merritt in the downtown area. To them Oakland was "an attractive city," one with "real potential," "a really nice place." They hadn't been around long and the future was indefinite. They added that they "didn't spend much time in Oakland." From the shores of Lake Merritt,

Oakland was a very nice place to be if you only looked at the lake—and spent your weekends in the country.

For the most part these are white Oaklanders who are describing their city. They are people who live very well in the hills or around Lake Merritt because they are young, highly skilled, fortunate, or live at least moderately well in the foothills and Bible Belt. They are people who could look to the future, look across, look up, look down at their gardens, or, failing all that, could at least look back on a city that, all things considered, is a pretty good place to live.

Moving from the center of the city toward the waterfront, there is another and far different Oakland, a place of the very young, the unskilled, unemployed, or underemployed. A small part of this area belongs to Mexican Americans, but, by and large, the majority of the population is black. Here in the flatlands there's not much of a view down or up. Oakland is "like a downgrade where the colored people live," where "even the dirt is dirty dirt," or as one young man said, "Oakland depends on the part you are talking about—some of it is a ghetto, some middle class, and some upper class. This is the ghetto." Yet to blacks who lived in other areas of the city, who were skilled or economically mobile, Oakland was the Oakland of the average white resident. They lived "in the good part," the city "was a fine place with a good future."

People described Oakland in terms of their own economic positions in the city. The more resources they had and the higher up geographically in the city they lived, the more attractive Oakland became and the more distance they could put between their homes and the dusty discord of the downtown and industrial sections. This does not mean they were unaware of others parts of the city that did not resemble their own; they were—vaguely. "I just never go into those parts of town," a hill housewife said. A young person in the flatlands said, "Everything, I mean everything, goes up there to the hills and the white people." The two ends simply never met, or if they did it was through the mediation of another group of Oakland residents, black professionals and educators who were very critical of Oakland. They themselves led satisfactory lives in satisfactory neighborhoods, but they described Oakland's political climate as "complacent as far as finding solutions to social problems" or "apathetic," "conservative," and "slow to change."

No Oaklander proffered a geographical description of his or her city or information about it that would distinguish Oakland from any other medium-sized American city. One woman said, in fact, "The only difference between Oakland and any other city around here is that the name is different." Some people ticked off the local landmarks: "There's Jack London Square, Lake Merritt, and the coliseum." But it appeared that the Oakland that lay beyond the doorsteps of its residents was a nebulous and uncertain place.

The City of Friendly Unknowns: "You Can Live Here All Your Life and You Will Be Years Getting to Know Your Neighbors"

Not only did we ask people what they thought of Oakland, we encouraged them to tell us something about what it feels like to live there and be a member of a community, a part of a neighborhood. Was Oakland a friendly place? Did the people in our survey know their neighbors? Their answers were somewhat perplexing. Yes, Oakland was a friendly place. No, they did not know their neighbors. Many were newcomers to Oakland, others worked, or the neighbors did, and they seldom saw each other. The longer people had lived in neighborhoods, to be sure, the more likely they were to know their neighbors. In some cases, however, the respondents had recently moved into their neighborhoods; in others, they were waiting out an unpleasant situation until they could move out. One man told us he didn't know his neighbors because "they weren't good people . . . left garbage laying around . . . the neighborhood was deteriorating," and he was moving away. A woman in the flatlands avoided her neighbors because "they spent all day doing nothing but running in and out of each other's houses and gossiping." One might expect to find people to be friendlier with their neighbors in areas where turnover is low because even if personal interaction was low, these people would at least see each other over the years and establish stable (even if minimal) communication. Furthermore, the longer people lived together in neighborhoods, the more likely they would be to share certain interests and concerns about their area. In fact, these expectations turned out to be true.

Oaklanders had widely assorted views of other Oaklanders. Most said that Oakland was a "friendly city compared to the east coast," or "as friendly as any city its size," or friendly "as cities go." A few newcomers lamented the lack of "small-town friendliness," "hometown atmosphere," or "midwestern friendliness" they were accustomed to elsewhere. Others had a more pragmatic view of friendliness: "If you're friendly, people are friendly to you." Or "You get what you give out." In general the casual atmosphere of Oakland was welcomed by people who

had moved to Oakland from larger cities; whereas people who had come
to Oakland from smaller cities and towns found Oakland less friendly
than their former hometowns.

Oakland's friendly atmosphere did not extend to the real-life
situations of the neighbors; most people said they didn't know their
neighbors beyond the "hello" of "waving" stage. Oaklanders who talked
to their neighbors talked to the ones next door or across the street—the
nearest ones. People who didn't talk to their neighbors said they had no
time or interest to do so. One man said he didn't know his neighbors
"because I don't put myself in their way"; another said that he kept to
himself. Still other residents reported similar operating rules of the game
such as, "We mind our own business and they mind theirs."

Generally, it turned out that people in neighborhoods of single-family
residences knew each other. Frequently, the people who told us that they
knew several or most of their neighbors and did indeed talk with them
also told us that they had lived many years in the same house. Older
people, housewives, and mothers of school-age children knew more
neighbors than single people, people who worked, or people who were
childless. People who lived in neighborhoods where there was little
changeover in homeownership also knew more people in the area.
Therefore, some people in Oakland do know and talk with each other
after all. These relationships, as we shall see, are important to Oakland's
political life.

Does Anything Happen in Oakland?
"This City Is Changing Fast"

Change in Oakland appears to be gradual but persistent. It is often
not possible to look back and identify exactly at what point a particular
change took place, even though it is obvious that things are different
now, that Oakland is "like any other big city" or is no longer "small and
comfortable." There is, for example, an entirely different mix of people
living there now than 10 years ago. There are more Mexican Americans,
more blacks, more young people, and more elderly ones. Often the
clashes between generations, races, and interests in the contest over
public resources has been brought to immediate reality by the public
media or simply by a heightened interest in a timely issue. Are
Oaklanders aware of the changes taking place that are inevitably
shaping Oakland's future?

We asked our respondents to tell us if they had noticed anything of significance happening in Oakland during the past year. Over one-half had not. They replied that "nothing had happened," they "couldn't think of [or remember] anything that had happened," or "nothing of importance had happened." These responses did not come from any particular group or area but were representative of a general response. Another quarter reported noticing some changes in the visible features of the city. They told us that the construction of the coliseum or the port was important to Oakland's future, for example, or that "the coliseum has been responsible for some progress in the city." Some had noticed something, such as "the BART tube," and were aware of "what it could mean to Oakland." They were hopeful that "the new art museum would be a nice place to visit." Responses of this genre often came from people in the middle level of Oakland life. They saw changes in the city's physical characteristics as pertinent and positive in terms of increasing opportunities for employment and attracting new investments to Oakland (for example, the port, the downtown convention center, and the coliseum) or as making the city more stimulating and interesting (the museum). Essentially, they linked concrete changes in the city's face to effects on the city's future. They felt good both about the changes and Oakland's future. The remaining one-quarter of the survey, in contrast, described changes not so visible to the eye: changes associated with the political and social aspects of Oakland. What most concerned this group were changes in the policies and institutions of Oakland. These responses generally came from people aged 30 to 35, hill residents, with an average of 10 years in Oakland, black as well as white residents, married people, and usually those who were professionally employed. They saw changes taking place that had the potential to alter significantly both Oakland's future and their own. They wanted things to get better in Oakland.

The foregoing has been a very general summary of three modal groups living in Oakland. Those who weren't aware of a changing Oakland, those who saw visible changes, and those who saw political changes. Basically three factors appear to be associated with the way people perceive what is going on in Oakland: interest, education, and amount of personal investment or stake in the city's future. On the whole, people who noticed changes in city policies and institutions were more aware and usually better educated than those who noticed no changes at all or those who noticed changes predominantly in the physical characteristics of Oakland. They were also interested in the way these changes could affect their lives because they had a greater stake in the future of Oakland than the other two groups. As could be expected, those seeking policy and institutional changes were mostly hill residents. The fact that they are the group least likely to leave the city despite their greater socioeconomic mobility gives emphasis to their interest in and commitment to Oakland. These people, particularly the younger hill residents with the most formal education, for example, talked of "the outcry over school board elections," "the difference the new housing developments make," or "progress in urban renewal." They plan to stay in Oakland but are uneasy about Oakland's future.

But it also turned out that a group of hill residents as well as a group of flatland residents—despite their possession (or lack) of resources and investments in Oakland—shared a common consciousness of changes *not* taking place in the city: "Oakland is backward—the city doesn't try to change." "It's a wonder that Oakland has kept its cool; it's a catalog of conditions for social disorder." "Sure, there's been some change in the housing picture and blacks have got into office, but this is only token change," they pointed out.

How do people react to the changes they see about them? Unless they are among the few possessing both interest and the resources to influence change, Oaklanders react by withdrawing into their own neighborhoods with others who are like themselves. So the neighborhood and the family become bulwarks against a city undergoing rapid and perplexing social change.

To the average Oaklander, social change essentially means that more people and newer groups are consuming the city's resources, particularly in the form of services like food stamps, housing, and health care. He or she feels that these new consumers are paying less for their share of public goods. The average Oaklander looks on these groups of people as being very different from himself or herself, as we shall see later when looking at the attitudes of blacks and whites toward each other.

As previously noted, Oakland neighborhoods are relatively homogeneous in that they contain people of similar outlooks and circumstances. This commonality makes Oaklanders suspect that people who do not live in their neighborhoods are different and are likely to have different views of life from their own. However, as we talked with Oaklanders in many neighborhoods, we discovered this view to be incorrect; despite different locations within the city and different economic positions,

Oaklanders hold many values in common that point to a general lifestyle shared by most Oaklanders even though they may not know it.

Of course, age, education, and economic status still define how well or poorly one does in life, but the dominant lifestyle that emerged from our interviews was broadly characterized by work, discipline, home, family, church, and self-sufficiency. Naturally, for people in the socioeconomic middle of Oakland life, the rules of the game for pursuit of prosperity and happiness are self-evident and unequivocal. People in the lower socioeconomic part of the city also affirm the same values; but within the constraints of their environment, the rules of the game are less certain. It is harder to be self-sufficient and disciplined when the neighborhood or the family is of dubious stability or jobs are not available.

At the other end of the scale, people with the most resources in Oakland do not differ in values very much from other people in the city simply because they have more money. They can, of course, afford more of everything, but family, church, and hard work are not less important. The dimensions of their values, however, are deepened by increase in formal schooling, particularly among the younger members of this group. Education, in addition, has increased social awareness. They may not go near the flatlands, for instance, except through the mediation of professional social planning, but they are acquainted in a general way with the problems of the economically disadvantaged and sympathize with their interests. We can learn more about the various ways in which Oaklanders view their problems by considering how their styles of life affect their opinions.

The Oakland Way: "It's a Pretty Good Life Here"

Much of middle-class Oakland's life, black or white, Bible Belt or foothills, is built upon expectations of slow and steady progression in the individual's ability to master his or her environment. That is to say, the government is expected to provide some necessary protection to its citizens—schools should be useful, streets should be safe, jobs should be available—but beyond this point the individual should be able to cope and the government should not attempt to arrange his or her personal options. A frequent theme from our middle-class respondents' stories was personal independence. They had worked hard to get what they had. The value of work thus emerges as an important part of social ethic: "Jobs are good for anybody who has the ability to work or the interest." "If a person's willing to work, he or she can find a job anywhere in the city." There was a relative convergence of opinions between blacks and whites on the values of work and self-sufficiency too: "I guess you might say I'm doing all right. I've worked hard but I'm doing okay." "I've got a good job . . . a good union job. I've got no complaints."

After work, the home and family occupy the central interest. Respondents talked about "a home-centered life," "a family," "a family life," and "just having a home with a backyard" or "one's own garden." Others were quick to point out that they lived where they did because of some particular feature that was important to their family, such as a good school, a safe neighborhood, or a convenient park. However devoted to their families Oaklanders may be, they are nevertheless firm with their children and are convinced that discipline and respect for authority are basic principles of both child rearing and good citizenship. "Children need guidance, inspiration, and an occasional kick in the pants." "People who lack a family-oriented life are those most prone to commit criminal acts." "Both blacks and whites alike have the same problem. If they paid more attention to the kids . . . taught them the art of self-respect and how not to be wild." "People should have respect for other people's rights."

The attitude of middle-class Oaklanders toward other groups is an extension of their attitudes toward themselves. They are convinced that work, responsibility, discipline, and respect for authority are the foundations of the way life should be for everyone, black as well as white: "Blacks should work within their own homes to change their situation." "All you can do is educate them—they've got to do it for themselves." "People have got to learn they can't get something for nothing." "It's what a person makes of himself." "The opportunities are there. People have a choice. It depends on the individual."

As one is confident of his or her own personal worth, middle-class Oaklanders generally think of others like themselves as trustworthy and cooperative. Consequently, they are more likely to view the government and its institutions with confidence. Although they may have little or no direct contact with the government, they ask little of the government and trust administrators and elected officials to make the kinds of choices that affirm the basic principles of their way of life. As long as policy does not impinge on home and neighbors, they are reluctant to venture out into the city's public life except through the mediation of church, clubs, and immediate community. They do not feel the need exists to increase the scope of political decision making. They may not have time or energy to familiarize themselves with current issues, so if politicians will stay out of their lives, Oaklanders are content to stay out of theirs. There is plenty of work to be done in their own backyards.

The lower middle class is different from the middle class because so much of it is in transit: People pass through it en route up the economic ladder or, as the result of personal or economic calamity, down the same ladder. Because there is a clash of interests and lifestyles in an environment of scarce resources, the rules have not been laid out for effective mastery of the environment as clearly as in the middle class. The juxtaposition of opposites—whites and blacks, the old and very young, the longtime and newly arrived resident—forms sharp centers of conflict and competition in which being different is dangerous. There are greater economic constraints in this environment; consequently, there is a lot of tension over who gets what resources. The implication is clearly that the wrong people are getting too much. "People should work for money." "All those blacks—they get welfare all over the place and all they know how to do is riot." "Oakland attracts a lot of welfare recipients.... They rot ... go downhill, and that doesn't help anyone—not themselves, not the city." If lower-middle-class residents can do so, they will move out of Oakland as soon as possible; if they can't they will try to defend themselves against what they consider as unfair invasions by other groups who want to share what they have.

We turn now to the extreme positions on the socioeconomic scale. We found that the values described to us by flatland residents (mostly black people with the lowest incomes in the city) were roughly the same as everyone else's in Oakland: "A lot depends on how a person starts out." "A child needs yards and exercise to keep him out of trouble." "You've got to go to school to get a job; it's just imperative." "I've never got nothing on a silver platter." "If they'd give young kids more to do, it would be a better place." It might have been expected that even though the same values (work, home, church, self-sufficiency, etc.) operate in the black ghetto as elsewhere, they would be subordinate to opinions that the "system," the established way of life, impaired their effectiveness. Generally, this opinion was not proffered, but rather its opposite—that people within the black community did have some degree of control over their destinies if only they chose to exercise it. This was reflected in the following comments from black residents: "Where I live, they receive their money one day and the next day they don't have any." "They drink, they have no respect for others or themselves, no pride, no self-respect. . . . They have the attitude, 'Live for today and let tomorrow take care of itself.' " "The white kids want to go to school; the black kids don't." "The majority where I live are on welfare. All they do all day is run in and out of each other's houses."

This is not to say that blacks in the flatlands were ignorant of the realities of economic existence. On the contrary, they almost unanimously pointed out: "If you're poor *and* you're black, everything is against you." "Poor people should be helped." "Employment is unfair to minority groups." "Blacks are underrepresented and underprivileged." But by emphasizing the importance of employment opportunities to enable self-help to operate, they were reinforcing their commitment to the dominant social ethos of Oakland.

Holding the other position in the economic scale are two major groupings in the hills: the older group, the town fathers who have been in Oakland for many years and who are the traditional backbone of the city's political life, and a younger, professional group who came out of colleges during the 1950s and gradually began to experience a rise in social awareness—an awareness that was to extend beyond their home, family, and neighborhood into the city, its policies, its institutions, and its issues. Both groups perceive themselves as important to the social-political life of Oakland, and so they are. They are confident of their ability to affect the government, just as they are confident of their ability to bend the environment to their own choosing. Their economic investments in Oakland work to deepen their commitment to the city.

High in the hills, although the elite of Oakland rarely mingle in other parts of the city, they maintain the strongest commitment to it. Despite their greater socioeconomic mobility, the hill residents are least likely to move away from Oakland now or in the future. The first and older group of hill residents have lived in Oakland for many years. Many of them own businesses and factories in Oakland or have served on public commissions or in public office. They do not differ significantly in value affirmation from the middle-class Oaklanders we discussed above; they simply have more money. If anything, this group might place more emphasis on self-sufficiency because they themselves began with small businesses or minor jobs and over the years worked slowly up the ladder to where they are now. This is why the older hill residents believe, for example, that "there are too many people on welfare who should not be on it," that "people should get tax incentives and low-cost loans for improving their properties," that "the city's main goal should be to attract new businesses to Oakland," and that "blacks and whites need to work together to make the city." They imply that improvements in the city's environment will bring benefits to all groups. They want to see the city upgraded for everyone.

The younger hill residents are less likely to own businesses in the city and are more likely to manage or head technical staffs of businesses or to hold professional positions in the city administration because they have more education than any other group. They have been in Oakland less than a decade but are familiar with the mechanisms of local government through their professional capacities or through public committees and board services. The values this group describes are those that reflect their interest in evoking rapid changes in policies and institutions that affect large groups of people in the city. These changes rarely affect themselves and most often affect others they have little contact with, such as the poor, the elderly, blacks, or other groups they feel the city has disenfranchised from the political process: "The city should get extensive federal funds to clean up West Oakland and put in low-cost public housing." "The city has not even tried to solve any of the problems of the blacks." "The city is favorable to moneyed conservative interests only." This group of younger hill residents is composed of both blacks and whites who, in effect, function as advocates for the city's other groups.

In the next section we will discuss some of the problems that Oaklanders feel affect their city and their lives. We will see that their feelings about the city closely follow their feelings and expectations about life in general.

THE PROBLEMS OF THE PEOPLE OF OAKLAND

In this section we will look at the city's problems as Oaklanders described them. It will be immediately apparent that these problems are not unique to Oakland, but describe problems of city life in general. Thus the headaches of urban miasma mark Oakland's transformation from "small town" to "big city." Also apparent in this discussion of Oakland's problems is the presence of a simple axiom: People who have money don't have problems, certainly not, at least, like those who have nothing. Problems like housing and unemployment, for example, are built out of such extremes. They are very easy for some of the city's groups and very difficult for others. However, the problem that affects everyone in one way or another is race. Oaklanders have a pronounced concern about being black or white, both now and in the future. We end this section with a report of some of these attitudes.

Several Well-Assorted Discords:
"This City Has a Lot of Problems"

The area with the most problems affecting the greatest number of people is the flatlands. There is greater poverty, poorer housing, inadequate schools, more unemployment, and a higher crime rate than anywhere else in the city. The flatlands are not only afflicted with multiple problems; but these problems are so complex and change is so costly to bring about that there is little likelihood that the problems will be solved now or in the immediate future.

In the hills there are fewer problems affecting fewer people. The school situation, for example, is of concern to people with school-age children only, and then only to those people whose children attend public schools. The people in the lower section of the hills may complain about crime, whereas those in the upper parts of the hills may not complain at all. Many problems are not only local but are purely minor. A barking dog may disturb a neighborhood, but very few people are likely to be troubled by unemployment or bad housing in the hills.

People in the Bible Belt and the foothills are just as likely to be plagued by both barking dogs *and* crime because they are in the center of the city. On the other hand, unemployment may affect only the young or the newly arrived, just as high taxes may be more troubling to the elderly or the retired than are other problems.

It may be recalled that Oaklanders liked Oakland mainly for physical or environmental features, such as the coliseum or the good climate. What Oaklanders dislike about Oakland, on the other hand, are problems that stem from human factors: The environment in Oakland is not deteriorating, but relationships between people are, and the quality of urban life is affected, as is the "good life" Oaklanders see for the city.

The major problems Oaklanders see for the city—schools, race, government—are complex and intricate. Naturally enough, there is little agreement among Oaklanders over which problem is most severe, the priority with which problems should be solved, or even how they can be ameliorated.

While there is little agreement about what people dislike in the city, respondents were even less clear about the cause of the difficulties. Some people complained that they disliked the crime situation in Oakland because the police were not forceful enough, for instance, whereas others complained that the police were overzealous in their treatment of minority groups. The only common agreement among Oakland residents, therefore, was that they all disliked something.

Walk at Night? "Are You Kidding?!"

The public transportation system in Oakland seems to be used mainly by the elderly, who complained that it was slow, expensive, tedious, and had poor connections. Although a few other respondents reported using BART or the bus system "sometimes," the majority of the respondents had regular access to private transportation. They added that driving in Oakland was easy: The streets were relatively uncrowded and parking was generally available. Only a few people in our survey said they walked anywhere in the city, and "only to the corner store." When we asked if they walked at night—in the city, in their neighborhood, or anywhere—the question elicited more heated responses than any other in the survey.

We asked about walking at night because we wanted to know if Oaklanders thought the streets of their neighborhoods were safe or if the streets in any one particular district were considered safer than those of any other district. The answers were overwhelmingly negative. With few exceptions, no one walked willingly or without trepidation. The range was from a few men who reported they "could go anywhere and not worry" to another extreme few who said they "didn't even drive after dark." All the women interviewed expressed concern because "the streets were very dangerous at night." Elderly people and small businessmen also reported "unsafe streets" at nightfall.

The areas rated least safe were the flatlands and the downtown areas, followed by the Lake Merritt district, that is, the areas closest to the poorer neighborhoods.

Where Are the Police? "As Far as I'm Concerned the Crime Rate Stinks"

About one-third of our respondents reported having been (or knew) victims of robberies, housebreaking, or muggings. A common complaint from blacks and whites alike was that police protection in Oakland was "slow" and "inadequate." Some people complained that police came only after a long wait and then "wasted time asking repetitious questions" or performed "unnecessary" functions such as fingerprinting or searching the premises. White respondents were sympathetic to the problems the police faced and felt the police "were doing the best they could under the circumstances." Most blacks thought otherwise: "The police can be as dangerous as any person I could run into." "I'm actually more afraid of the cops than of the people." "They'll search your bag on the slightest pretext." "They are often hostile."

It appears that attitudes toward the police in Oakland are aligned less along neighborhood and age lines than along racial lines. Blacks complain that police treat them unfairly. One woman reported that police stopped her and accused her of soliciting men when she was in fact a housewife en route to the corner grocery to buy a quart of milk. White respondents view the situation differently and blamed the black population for the high crime rate: "As more and more blacks have moved in and more and more whites have moved out or into the hills, the crime rate has gone up." "Negroes have a different set of moral values and they don't think it is wrong to steal." "The colored don't care. They grow up like animals." Blacks pointed to social causes such as unemployment, inadequate housing, and a society moving too fast and leaving too many behind as major factors contributing to the high crime rate in Oakland.

A point on which both blacks and whites agree is that there should be more police and that they should be more in evidence on the streets of Oakland. As one respondent put it, "Their presence alone would discourage crime." Other suggestions were that "police should walk beats," "there should be more street lighting," "stiffer penalties for offenders should be implemented," "the court system should be speeded up," and "police should be given training in psychology." Blacks also pointed out that more minority members should be hired by the police department and suggested that all police be better trained in how to get along with people. On the whole, most people were ambivalent toward the police. As one hill resident said, "When you don't need one, you don't care if you ever see one. When you want one, you want the biggest and meanest one possible, as soon as possible."

Respondents contacted the police department more than any other city service, not merely in cases of actual crime but also to request the police to send representatives to schools and clubs for teaching purposes, to silence barking dogs or noisy neighbors, to give directions, and even to round up children coming home late from school. Elderly people and the very young appeared to have more contact with the police department than other age groups.

Little Red Schoolhouses: "They Are All Incompetent"

Oakland citizens feel that their schools are of lower quality than those in other California cities and are not adequate to meet the demands of today's world. This response was given by people with children in city schools, by those with grown children, and even by the childless. About one-third of all respondents had a child (or children) of school age or about to enter the school system. An additional one-tenth had children attending private or church-sponsored schools. Those who used the public school system considered the best schools in Oakland to be those located in or near the hills. Reasons for these choices varied, but a common opinion was that "schools here [in the hills] are newer and get top-quality teachers."

Generally, hill residents gave an unflattering opinion of the entire school system even though they pointed out that their own schools were good: "The schools are totally uneven." "The quality of the schools depends on the area you live in." "Miller is a good school but the rest of them are bad, bad, bad." "The schools are poorly administered and good only in some areas, depending on how good the PTA is and how good the home is at supplementing the school."

People living in the flatlands discussed this question in terms of the children as well as the quality of the schools and teachers: "The children don't care about learning. . . . They aren't interested." "The children don't pay attention." "The schools are overcrowded and the teachers aren't interested." "The teachers are only interested in putting in time." Another kind of response from the flatlands was the following: "All the good things—teachers and equipment—go to the hill schools."[1] "These kids need teachers who are really good and care about them." "The teachers keep order; that's all." In addition to agreeing that the schools are bad, these respondents reported that schools were worse in the flatlands owing to "old buildings, broken windows," "inadequate playground facilities," "lack of supplies," "old teachers," and "overcrowding."

Many other Oaklanders, mostly people from areas outside the flatlands, felt that "the Board of Education did not respond to the needs of the people," "the city was not willing to take the initiative and provide leadership," or that "the curriculum hadn't been updated in years." They referred frequently to personnel ("Unless there's a more responsive superintendent [or school board] the schools will get worse"), curriculum ("The entire curriculum needs to be made relevant"), and government ("The city government and the Board of Education are simply not responding to people's needs").

Although everyone wanted changes in the Oakland school system, they did not agree on what kinds of changes. Comments frequently referred to concern about school disruptions due to tension between blacks and whites. Hill people with children in Skyline High School offered the opinion that integration had created trouble between blacks and whites that extended beyond the school room and onto the playground. Parents in other areas also reported racial disruptions and added that the problem had to be dealt with "in some way," but they had no possible solutions to offer.

A curious sidelight of the general concern over the school situation is that although so many people worry about the schools, few appear to do anything, even to the extent of bringing a complaint to the Board of Education (only six parents had gone to at least one meeting) or to the school PTA. As far as the PTA was concerned, there was a very uneven pattern of attendance. Some people suggested that the PTA at one hill school was good, whereas at other schools it was bad.

The few people who said they had attended Board of Education meetings were all hill residents. About one-quarter of all respondents told us they helped their children with their homework, and these were usually younger children attending hill and foothill schools.

Black and White Perspectives: "Listen, I Think
Black People Are Giving Us the Prejudice Deal All the Time"

At the heart of all the problems Oaklanders told us they confronted in their daily lives was the matter of racial conflict. A few respondents said outright that blacks were a problem and the city "shouldn't let any more in." Another thought the city "should be divided one-third white, one-third black, and one-third integrated" so that people "could know what was what and choose." Respondents linked racial conflict to problems such as lowered property values, increased crime rates, and high welfare costs, on one hand, or to conservative administration, racism, unemployment, substandard housing, and inadequate opportunities on the other.

One dimension to the problem of racial conflict that emerged from discussions with our respondents was that of proximity: The closer people lived to other races, the more negative they felt about the other race. Bible Belt and foothill residents who live in close proximity to blacks expressed angry feelings about them, whereas hill residents—who live in distant white neighborhoods—were less hostile. No lower-class black was close enough to threaten them. Some sample comments from foothill residents reflect the linkage of race to property values: "Oakland used to be a good place to live. . . . These people have come in and it's no longer the same." "One gets in and pretty soon you have to sell out." "They let their houses deteriorate. . . . Three families crowd into one place. . . . They just don't care." These responses were intensified by Bible Belt residents on the fringes of the flatlands who expressed anxiety over new groups in competition for scarce resources. Blacks in flatlands reported the following: "Everything is in favor of the white man." "Whites are doing much better than blacks." "We don't have nothing in common with those people."

Hill residents are, above all, similar in economic status; although a few blacks may live in the hills they are more likely to be similar to other hill residents than blacks and whites in the foothills or flatlands. The responses of white hill residents about black hill residents is altogether different: "There's a black man down the street. . . . He's a doctor and he's okay." "I don't think there are any black families in this neighborhood. Oh, maybe one or two—I don't know. . . . We never see them."

Another important factor affecting white attitudes toward blacks in the Bible Belt and flatlands is age. The median age of the white population in Oakland is steadily increasing while that of the black population is decreasing, which means that an older group of whites is living in close proximity to young blacks. The Bible Belt, in fact, contains the oldest group of white Oaklanders in the city.

Density is also a factor. The black population is densest in the flat areas and lowest in the hills. Moving up into the hills there is a growing abstraction in attitudes toward blacks; moving down from the hills, there is a conversion to concrete opinions. For example, some people in the foothills and Bible Belt told us that the racial situation was the direct cause of the Oakland crime rate or the inadequate school system: "It's easy for 'them' to get on welfare. . . . Those kind don't think it is wrong to steal." "I wouldn't drive in their neighborhood after dark."

Blacks in the flatlands did not feel that being black was as difficult a problem as being without resources or opportunity: "Jobs, unemployment . . . people should get together and work out the situation." "Poverty—the community should be mobilized." "West Oakland is a real mess." Whites told us that the *presence* of one factor (blacks) caused the city's problems; blacks told us that the *absence* of several factors (jobs, affluence, urban renewal) caused them. Blacks with improved economic situations—and concomitantly, residence in a better neighborhood—don't think about the city's problems from an economic perspective but in terms of civic improvement: "They really should do something about the downtown—it's a real mess." "This city needs to be fixed up and made to look attractive." "The schools are in really bad shape. There are too many problems in the ghetto schools."

We know now that almost everyone in Oakland feels there is a racial problem of major dimensions in the city—or so they told us indirectly when we asked what Oakland's problems were. At one point we asked a direct question on this topic: "Are the various groups in Oakland getting along?" A general response was to back off from the racial perspective and become wary and assume a noncommittal, or a "public," attitude: "As well as in most cities." "Compared to other cities, okay, I guess." "It's hard to say. . . . I don't know." "Fairly well, I guess." "They could improve." Because responses like this came from many people—both black and white—who had previously expressed outright hostility to each other, this reaction was somewhat puzzling until we realized that their interpretation of "getting along" was the absence of interracial violence. Sometimes they even followed up their first comment with comparative information: "There hasn't been any trouble yet." "At least things are peaceful here."

Do Oaklanders Think Things Will Get Better?
"All I Can Say Is That Oakland Has Seen Better Days"

The different opinions among Oaklanders about the future appear to be a function not only of economic position but of age as well. Obviously, young people have an advantage over older people. They can drop out, change jobs, or go somewhere else if they wish. Generally, people over 55 felt that relations between the races in Oakland would worsen: "There are those young radicals who might incite black people to riot more than they would otherwise." "Blacks are too ready to make demands." "The militants stir things up." "The situation is going to erupt one day." "They'll get a whole lot worse before they get better." People aged 35 to 55 felt relations would improve over time: "It's purely a matter of self-preservation." "People are gradually becoming a little more realistic about the needs of the other group." "The city government is becoming increasingly more interested in trying to solve problems before they explode." "More blacks will get into government." "We will have to learn to live together and put up with each other." People under 35 felt the same way: "Whites are being friendlier." "Communications will improve." "It is necessary to get to understand the other." "We will get to know each other and each other's problems better." These responses came from blacks as well as whites and range from pessimism to optimism. Do these responses also indicate directions in which possible political strategies could be developed?

Older people—particularly the elderly—have little stake in the city's future. They are looking backward, toward a past that has recently seen much in the way of turmoil and disruption. Changes in the residential character of their neighborhoods have come to them at ages most resistant to change. They have no reason to assume things will improve. Optimism about the future comes from people likely to stay and thus to link their own futures to that of Oakland. They anticipate development of various strategies that will contribute to easing that future. They suggest, "It's a matter of self-preservation" (or "we will have no alternative but to solve our problems"). "People are becoming more realistic" (or "are more willing to talk"). And then they suggest some other strategies that might have some effect: The government is looking for acceptable solutions; more blacks are getting administrative and political positions; reasonable discussion is possible.

Optimism also comes from young people. Whites under 35 had higher educational attainment than any other age group. Their comments reflect a strong emphasis on education, communication, understanding, and getting to know one another. In other words, they postulate education as a useful adaptive strategy, as did educated blacks in this age bracket. Their statements suggest a commitment of ending racism at the personal level.

Responses about the future of Oakland from flatland residents were conditional. It would improve if "the poor people were helped," "there were more jobs," and "there were more opportunities for black people." It would get worse if "something isn't done about West Oakland" and "the government doesn't pay attention to these problems." The strategies blacks advocated were economic improvements; however, another strategy was implicit—the threat of violence—if "something" wasn't done to ease the situation. The task of doing something public presumably belongs to government. How do citizens of Oakland relate, if at all, to their city government?

THE PEOPLE AND THEIR GOVERNMENT

The problems discussed in the preceding section were generated by the uneven impact of change upon the city and the lives of its citizens. In this section we will indicate some of the ways Oaklanders seek to influence the direction of change by political activity. The gap between feeling and action is huge, and few people in Oakland ever try to seek solutions to local problems by way of the political process. Many people feel there are no real problems—that everything is fine, thank you, they have their homes and churches to attend to. Others feel there are great problems, indeed, but how can they do anything? No, thank you—and they also have their homes and churches. A much smaller group of people both care intensely and work feverishly through political activity to effect or forestall changes—when they themselves are concerned. A still smaller group cares about and works intermittently regarding problems that seldom affect them directly.

Those people who do not engage in politics at all are characteristically unconcerned or ignorant of the public channels of opinion in the city: The government is an amorphous collection of anonymous individuals in a rather dingy building downtown, whose business is to funnel essential services out to neighborhoods in the city. A relatively well-structured core of information about whom to see in city government and what to say to get things done characterizes people who venture into political life. The function of the city government, they say, is politics—the granting of favors and election promises in exchange for support at the next election. The opinions of Oaklanders about their government will become more explicit as we explore them below.

The City Government: "I'll Never Forget What's-His-Name"

A three-part question asked respondents what they thought of (1) the mayor, (2) the city manager, and (3) the City Council. The majority of respondents could not differentiate between city manager and mayor. Typical responses were vague: "Who (or what) is the city manager?" "He's the same as the rest—they're all alike." "I don't know who those people are. My husband might." The mayor was said to be "a nice family man," "a typical politician," or, "He's just like the rest of the government"; "I don't hear much about him."

The mayor was more often identified correctly than the city manager, who was almost totally unknown except to some professionally employed respondents, some of whom worked in departments under his jurisdiction. Not surprisingly, the less aware respondents were about important happenings in Oakland, the less aware and informed they were of the functions and identities of city officials; they lumped them all together into anonymous collections of "politicians." Conversely, the more aware they were of what was happening, the more aware they were of the political actors involved; aware people could identify officials and their functions. These Oaklanders were more likely to voice firm opinions of approval or disapproval about the principal officials, such as "The mayor is too conservative and does not care about change"; "The mayor is doing the best he can with all the problems in the city"; or "The city manager is the man behind the scenes who really runs things." This is in strong contrast to "The mayor? He's okay, I guess," received from a respondent who told us "nothing" had happened in Oakland during the past year.

If Oaklanders are almost totally unacquainted with their city government, it might be due in part to the absence of visible personalities in the political arena, particularly in comparison with the strong personal appeal of San Francisco's mayor or Berkeley's vociferous City Council. But people who are unacquainted with the identities and functions of the local government would be sorely equipped to take part in the political process. Because some knowledge of the political actors, as well as the weight of general issues, would constitute the minimal information necessary for playing the role of active citizen and because about one-half of the survey respondents did not fulfill this requirement, we find an absence of groups in Oakland interested in "good government" as well as an absence of people likely to intervene or participate in the city's public affairs.

How Fair Is a Fair City Government?

Because Oaklanders appear to question the performance of the government in terms of what it does or does not deliver to the individual respondent, it is interesting to look at the survey responses concerning the fairness of the government toward all groups. Checking the satisfied and unsatisfied participating and nonparticipating citizens gives some idea of how directly most people interpret the idea of government in terms of their own position.

Satisfied nonparticipants answered that the government was "fair to everyone" or "as fair as any city government can be." Dissatisfied nonparticipants said the government was fair "to those they played golf with," and "to their friends only." Satisfied participants noted that the government "was more responsive to middle-class interests . . . but they try to be fair to all." "Naturally they [government officials] are more responsive to people who vote." Dissatisfied participants indicated a different attitude: "They pay more attention to conservative interests." "They are unfair to groups that challenge the status quo." "They respond to groups with the loudest demands." In other words, nonparticipants mostly offered amorphous answers with no political overtones, whereas participants answered in terms of political content (contrast "friends" with "conservative interests") and indicated they had thought about the reasons for the government's fairness or unfairness.

Whereas dissatisfied nonparticipants cited economic interests as monopolizing the government's attention, dissatisfied participants claimed political interests. Both groups are dissatisfied because they lack what they feel gets the city's attention: to the first group, money; to the second, power. This group possesses the personal resources to be influential but their demands are not widely shared, so they are not effective.

We asked all the respondents if they felt the current political situation, as they saw it, was likely to change much in the future. Respondents who participate were generally more optimistic than nonparticipants. The former felt the government was becoming more responsive: "They are beginning to. . . . People are expecting to be heard." "They are trying to get things done. More and more they are involving the people." "More blacks are getting into government and more groups are being heard from." But nonparticipants felt differently: "This city has always had its own little cliques and it always will." "The same people always run things." "It will take a riot to get them [the government] to understand anything." "They just don't care about anything but what the *Oakland Tribune* says."

We had expected respondents who participated and obtained results to be optimistic about the government, but why are the dissatisfied participants also optimistic about the political future of Oakland? Apparently the act of participation increases the belief that desired changes can be made, even when past experience has not been entirely salutary.

The more aware and better educated an individual, the more likely he or she is to extend political involvement from his or her family to his or her neighborhood and then to the city at large. But although political involvement on the neighborhood level appears relatively successful and, thus, satisfying, beyond the neighborhood both complexities and opportunities for frustration and dissatisfaction increase steeply, as do the conflicting criteria for evaluating government policy. A lot of people want the city government to do a lot of different things.

This survey offers a comprehensive composite of Oaklanders' feelings about, understanding of, and hopes for their city. For most, the Oakland beyond their doorsteps is a nebulous, uncertain place. The city is undergoing rapid and perplexing social change, and many respond by withdrawing to their own friends and neighborhoods; in short, one simply ignores that which is uncertain. Citizens, though they admittedly know little about it, expect their local government to simplify their lives: to protect, to educate, and to assure that jobs are available. If government can handle these often overwhelming problems for them, then they will manage the lesser, day-to-day difficulties themselves. Naturally, as the citizen perceives the city's problems to be more real, immediate, and threatening, the focus is close and the orientation pragmatic. For those who do not see the city's problems on a personal, day-to-day basis, the tendency is to view them more abstractly. The irony is that as uncertainty increases it seems to demand a more abstract focus for successfully coping with it, and those who have the greatest need are least able to find satisfying answers.

Actually, the individual citizens' problems, as we shall see in subsequent chapters, are not so different from those of organized groups or the local government itself. Everyone wants more for less; the individual is everywhere is search of the "good life"; and organized groups want more and better service for their dollar, while government officials struggle for efficiencies to meet such expectations. This is not to say that all have the same likelihood of achieving the better life either individually or in the context of an organized, collective effort. Quite simply the paths to success or satisfaction are of differing qualities and degrees of difficulty. Similarly, the abilities to traverse successfully any given path are not equally distributed. The conundrums then are the following: What is to be learned that will enable us to predict better who is likely to cope successfully? How will they do it? What will increase the likelihood of successfully managing the uncertainties of life in the city? From the individual's point of view, leaving the city may be the best way.

Who Will Stay? Who Will Go?

Almost half of the respondents said they might leave Oakland in the future. Some of their reasons suggested a desire to live an idyllic rural life: "To live in the country," "to own a small farm, raise vegetables, get away from the city." Others, primarily younger people, were dependent on changes in personal circumstances or simply had a desire for a change: "My husband's company might transfer him." "I was sent here for two years and I've been here five." "I'm engaged to a man in Arizona." "I'd like to see a different city." Removing these two groups, we have left a selection of people whose desires to leave Oakland are directly or indirectly related to the racial situation, constrained economics, or a combination of the two situations in which the racial situation was perceived as causing a change in the quality or assessed value of the neighborhood.

(1) Whites under 35 with families: They wanted to move from the city to the suburbs. Reasons given related mainly to superior school systems, fewer blacks, and better real estate values. "It's better out beyond the tunnel... better schools ... no problems with the colored." "You can get a better house with a yard [in Contra Costa County] for the same money you pay here." "We'll go if the school system doesn't improve."

(2) Whites and blacks, particularly those over 40, who wanted to leave because they felt there were more desirable communities with less racial strife than Oakland: "There's too much violence here. Cities breed discontent." "We can find a place where there isn't all this trouble between the races."

A third group of respondents wished to stay in Oakland but felt they would have to leave if forced to do so by large tax increases. More often, older (45-65 years) white residents of the foothills gave this response. "We will definitely have to move if taxes go up. . . . We just can't afford to pay more." "I don't know. . . . If there's a tax increase we'll move out of the city." Another reason that might make people reluctantly move would be if their neighborhoods' black populations increased. Again, these were older whites, likely to live in the Bible Belt. "There are just too many black people here, and the neighborhood is declining."

Most of the Oaklanders who plan to stay will do so because they are satisfied with their personal situation. Satisfaction is also related to the length of time they have already lived in the city; the longer people live in a neighborhood, the more likely it is they will stay. Owning a home or business or having relatives, in short having a stake in Oakland, also make people more likely to stay. The elderly plan to stay because of habit as well as their constrained finances, their restricted physical mobility, and (often) the presence of nearby children and grandchildren. Almost all of the hill respondents, irrespective of age, plan to stay (barring job transfers). Blacks in the flatlands want to leave the flatlands rather than moving out of Oakland, but, like the elderly, will stay in Oakland because of their constrained personal situations. Because most of those who plan to stay either have or will have families, their primary conditions for remaining center on their children. They want to see improvement in the school system. They also want more children in their neighborhoods as companions for their own—a number of respondents regretted they had "the only young children on the block." Black families wanted to stay if they could live in an integrated area. Overall, Oakland was "as good a place as any" to raise children so long as certain basic conditions were met, and these conditions stemmed from previously discussed values the respondents held as important for themselves and their families.

The elderly will remain in Oakland. The young will leave (Clark and Ferguson, 1983: 216-219).[2] The unattached will leave in search of their futures. Young families will leave for better schools, better jobs, better housing values, or to live in new towns with other young families like themselves. Older families will stay as long as the neighborhood stays the way they like it, as long as the school can do at least a satisfactory job of educating their children, and as long as the tax rate doesn't soar beyond their means. Many of these people, however, will find the kind of life they want at a lower cost just beyond the city limits, and so they will move out and join the throng of commuters who work in Oakland and live elsewhere. The poor will stay in Oakland because there is nowhere else to go. The rich will stay in Oakland for the same reason. When there is enough money to buy a comfortable life, why go elsewhere? But these groups are small in comparison to the other groups who are daily slipping out of Oakland and whose exits are leaving behind a city of elderly whites and young blacks. It is these people Oakland must find a way to retain. How might those who are needed in the city—the young who have a stake in their work, family, and the city—become more able to feel hopeful and satisfied about living and working in it?

One likely proposition would be that they must invest in acquiring knowledge about the city and its government so that they may participate more meaningfully and effectively. We found repeatedly that those who were informed about Oakland, whether satisfied or dissatisfied, were more likely to participate actively and to remain in the city. In the long run, it does not appear likely that the more common response, withdrawal into family and friends, will work either for the citizen or the city.

We next turn to a study of a students' organization—The Associated Students Union of Oakland—in order to examine this proposition more closely. In the late 1960s, many of the high school students in Oakland perceived themselves as a subset of citizens with a considerable stake in

Oakland's school system. They knew very little about how to change public attitudes and policies, but few dissatisfied students could choose simply to go to private schools or public schools in other neighborhoods. Dissatisfaction in a situation in which the natural choice—withdrawal—was not possible engendered action, investment, and learning as the students attempted to cope without resources. How did they do it?

NOTES

1. A second, quite recent but less comprehensive round of interviews was obtained. At this point, Oakland had a black mayor, a black and brown majority on the city council, and a black city manager. Moreover, downtown redevelopment had added a new hotel, a convention center, and office buildings. Some of the very old buildings in the CBD had been and were being rehabilitated to make office and retail space. Many of the streets in the CBD had received a much needed facelift, and the general impression is one of a charming central city emerging from a decaying, dowdy central city.

Surprisingly, many of those interviewed responded to our questions about Oakland very much like the citizens in the preceding set of interviews. Despite many obvious social, political, and physical changes in the past several years, many commented that "Oakland has not changed." More than one person voiced real disappointment that "government in Oakland is pretty much like it was before (blacks and browns achieved greater proportional representation in city hall)." "Oakland continues to suffer from unimaginative leadership."

In short, the consensus from the second set of interviews was that Oakland has changed, but the same old social, political, and fiscal problems remained. There was widespread disappointment, especially among the young professionals, that Oakland yet has not fulfilled its promise.

2. Clark and Ferguson point out that several variables effect urban migration, including tax rates and welfare levels as well as typical SES variables.

THROUGH THE LOOKING GLASS
The Associated Students Union

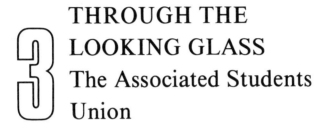

With
Donald Tamaki

PART ONE

This chapter is a rare personal study. It is a particular case of the more general difficulties, outlined in the previous chapter, encountered by citizens attempting successfully to cope with life in a complex urban center. There is stunning, intimate detail documenting the cost of public action or access when one begins with no resources. It is difficult to influence public policy when one begins with no organization, access, expertise, knowledge, information, or informal social network. In this case, then, we see high school students developing coping tactics, in some instances to the level of fine art forms, with few resources readily at hand.

Regardless of other resources, in order to act effectively, theory and information must be available or acquired either personally or vicariously. In the end, the pressure group leaders examined in this chapter had considerably more of both than when they had begun.

This study centers on the Oakland school system during what can be considered a "peak year" in terms of student politicization, unrest and activity. It was a time when heightened awareness and worldly events seemed to collide, producing a volatile situation (notably the widespread formation of high school black student unions coincident with the assassination of Dr. Martin Luther King, Jr.). The first part of this chapter will trace the formation of the Associated Students Union of Oakland and its relationships with the community and community organizations, the schools, the students, and the Oakland Board of Education. It is a study of confrontation, low-resource politics, that is

67

politics without power-intensive commodities like money or long-standing influence, using instead great numbers of people, publicity, and demonstrations to exert pressure and policymaking bodies. The second part analyzes the problems of groups whose survival and activity level rest primarily on a small nucleus. These include the problems of internal conflict and dissent, power struggles between leaders, leader-follower relationships, and the risks encountered in low-resource politics. It will become evident that we are not describing traditional student organizations or the typical student government. Rather, we are focusing on a group that more closely resembled a community pressure group, embroiled in serious and far-reaching issues and concerns such as potential riots, firebombings, the production of future unemployables, and so on.

As a final caveat to the reader, this chapter does not attempt to bring the objectivity of the observer to the analysis but, instead, the perspective of an active participant. When individuals are deeply and emotionally involved, detachment, even in retrospect, is difficult. One should read it knowing that it is not so much a description of events as it is an impression and an interpretation of unrest and a student organization's attempts to make meaningful changes in local school policies.

Investment to Increase Knowledge
Is Difficult, Frustrating, and Plain Hard Work

Toward the end of the academic year 1967 until the beginning of 1968, a new stage of student involvement in politics was dramatically marked by the formation of high school black student unions. It began, practically speaking, at a high school where the administration had refused to allow a black student union to be organized. Their refusal was followed by a general student boycott of the school. Responding to pressure from the protesters, the administration rescinded some restrictions on student activity. This set a precedent, and similar demands were successfully pressed in other Oakland high schools. Organizations of Chicanos and Asians would soon develop, following the black students' example.

For the first time in Oakland, students realized that it was possible to get and use power. This realization can be attributed mostly to the black power movement, fostered particularly in the young by the rhetoric and bold actions of the Black Panther Party. Notably, black students were to provide both the impetus for and leadership behind student organizations. The years 1967 and 1968 became more or less years of awakening to the injustices of the school system, discriminatory practices, racist textbooks and curricula, and so on. For students of color, the awakening led to discovery of a cultural heritage that became a source of pride, identity, and, ultimately, militancy.

The ASUO (Associated Students Union of Oakland) Is Born

In the spring of 1968, several black leaders began to form a black students union (BSU) at a large, central-city high school. At that time the school administration considered the idea of a BSU to be extremely radical, threatening, and hostile to whites. They viewed it as a step backward to separatism, incongruent in an era still strongly charac-terized by progress toward meaningful integration. The students countered the administrators' resistance by proceeding to plan a demonstration for their cause. The necessary ingredients were present; students were interested, discontented, and tensions between whites and blacks had been heightened. All that was required was a trigger to set it in motion.

On April 4th, 1968, a citywide student talent assembly at a central high school provided that spark. The show was to last precisely an hour, but because of technical difficulties, it ran behind schedule. The last act was a black vocal group from another high school. In approximately the middle of their performance, the dismissal bell rang, signaling the end of assembly and the beginning of class. The master of ceremonies attempted to close the assembly but the audience demanded that the group be allowed to finish. The black group continued singing, refusing to leave the stage as the curtains began closing on them. Several black students leaped to the stage to hold the curtains open. The adminis-trators then ordered the microphones turned off and announced that the assembly was over. The students were thoroughly angry. Because the white groups had been allowed to finish and only the black group was interrupted, it was taken as a racist insult. Word passed to congregate on the front lawn bordering the school. The black vocal group had already left to set up conga drums to attract people. Several hundred met and sat on the lawn to hear student speakers, mostly black and Chicano, while ignoring the principal's pleas to return to class.

Student leaders used the momentum generated by the spontaneous protest to demand the legitimation of a black students union and the inclusion of black and Chicano history courses in the curriculum. To avoid further trouble and to alleviate tension, the administration agreed to discuss these demands. School ended quietly that day; no one was aware of the earthshaking events taking place in Memphis, Tennessee.

On that same day, April 4, 1968, as he stood on an upstairs motel balcony, Martin Luther King, Jr., was shot down by an assassin's bullet. The shock reverberated through the nation, pent-up frustration and bitterness boiled over, touching off a flurry of major and minor riots throughout the nation. His murder cast a shadow of despair over many; for others it marked the end of the belief in nonviolent resistance of more militant and violent means. The aftermath was predictable; for several days, Oakland's high schools were shaken by disturbances, forcing them to dismiss early. Sit-ins were commonplace, fires set, white students pummeled in the halls, and teachers harassed. At this time, several Oakland high school students went to visit community leader and twice school board candidate Electra Price so that she might help assess the situation and determine what might be done about the troubles and tensions emanating from Oakland's school system. The problem seemed clear-cut to many; student government was obviously a farce, controlled and censored by school administrators. Appeals that were being made to the Board of Education by loose and fragmented community groups were regarded as virtually futile. The board had a long history of being nonresponsive to minority and liberal elements in the community. It was determined that a student organization was needed that was not attached to any particular campus, thus free from administrative intimidation and manipulation, to help organize a cohesive community effort to confront the Oakland Board of Education en masse. Seemingly this was the only way that a student community could be heard.

Those attending this informal gathering with Electra Price were to provide the initial core group of workers and leaders for the student organization. Actual organizing began in the summer of 1968; student leaders from each of the six high schools in Oakland were contacted by phone, the concept of an off-campus student union was tested on them, and they were urged to attend a meeting to discuss its formation. Those contacted—such as black student union chairmen, student body presidents, and Chicano leaders—were known to have status, power, or formal positions in their respective schools. The assumption was that if the core group convinced individual school leaders, they would be able to reach their followers, thus creating a mass student effort. In many ways the concept of a citywide student union was patterned after Community Organizations United for Progress (COUP), an Oakland organization incorporating many autonomous organizations into a unifying structure, enabling a concerted effort on selected issues. This organization of leaders loosely held together by a staff was later to provide us with invaluable help, including material and tactical assistance.

Approximately 15 (mostly white) students showed up at the meeting from four of the six schools. It was a small beginning. As time passed, the composition of the group changed to include a majority of nonwhite students, but the numbers remained constant. Small numbers, though initially discouraging, are a fact of life in most organizations without resources; masses of people become interested only after the group is established, has gained momentum, and made a name for itself. Group status and cohesion are resultant prizes to be won through the dedicated efforts of a few.

Our group met each week throughout the summer, discussing precisely what we considered the problems to be, formulating programs to remedy them, and building a future strategy for dealing with the Board of Education. Even within this small group, delegation of authority and work tasks was extremely difficult. Often the organization virtually degenerated to a one- or two-person operation; mailings, phoning, material printing costs, even transporting individuals to various meetings fell to two or three persons. What should have been a dynamic work force of many frequently became the vested interest of an individual. The ASUO never really resolved this problem.

About midway through the summer, the ASUO leaders realized that in order to be heard and to be regarded as a strong organization, a dynamic personality was needed to become the primary speaker and chief organizer. Howard C. Williamson, a black student living in West Oakland, stood out as the obvious choice for the position. A forceful and articulate speaker, skilled in the use of rhetoric, and a shrewd analyst of political and social situations in Oakland, he already possessed considerable experience from working with Model Cities, the West Oakland Youth Council, and other black community groups.

Some leaders met continuously, in addition to the weekly general meetings, to discuss questions of ideology and strategy. Although philosophical and ideological questions such as those having to do with the historical roots and effects of racism, the nature of power, action and repression, or the primary causes of urban unrest were not pertinent to specific issues and the current problems of organizing, discussing them was necessary to clarify convictions, to understand the situation, and to make the tactical plans and rationales for ASUO actions as lucid as possible.

By the summer's end, a solid list of demands had been developed to present to the school board. They included ethnic studies, adequate counseling, and remedial and tutorial programs. The history of the board, its actions and reactions, when confronted by low-resource groups demanding that the board attend to their grievances had been thoroughly studied. ASUO leaders had carefully reviewed the feasibility of each demand, the probable cost of implementation in relation to the actual funds for the district, and so on. It was all part of a preparedness, "doing one's homework," to avoid being tritely dismissed by the board—as so many groups in the past had been—for lack of appropriate knowledge and information.

In mid-September 1968 the Oakland Public Schools commenced their fall term. Soon after, the first outbursts of student violence occurred at a high school in the southern part of the district. This appeared to be the beginning of new conflict that some had been predicting for a long time. By October 1968 a public meeting for all organizations interested in education and the educational system, sponsored by the East Bay Council on Race, Religion, and Social Justice, was held at a college in Oakland. This was the meeting that the ASUO had been planning for all summer, both to present itself publicly as an organization and to solicit support for its program. However, the trouble that had just occurred added a more profound dimension. From the political perspective, events could not have moved in a more timely manner to generate interest and enthusiasm for a community organization. Citizen attendance at the meeting was unusually high, and the ASUO leadership was able to capitalize on this public concern. Significantly, the 12 ASUO members that attended the meeting were from a cross section of the high schools and were the only students present. Thus they became the unofficial spokesmen for the entire student population, a situation not unlike that of a lone black seated at a white-filled convocation on race relations. At the time, the ASUO was the only student group in the city politically organized with plans and tactics, and communitywide concern for minorities in the schools thrust it into the spotlight.

About 20 liberal, mostly white community organizations were present. That evening, after much argument, discussion, and debate, they resolved to form together as the Oakland Educational Coalition (OEC) to support the efforts of the ASUO and to develop alternative plans for reform. The OEC held general meetings every other week, with many leadership planning sessions between. The ASUO leadership found the coalition to be slow-moving and cumbersome because their demands and actions had to be explained in the simplest terms and with a great deal of tact, which was an absolute necessity. By this time, ASUO leaders were addressing three to four such groups every week. In order to obtain their active support for ethnic studies, for example, they had to be convinced of the historical roots of institutionalized racism in America, which dated back to early European culture. The two or three who were doing most of the speaking inadvertently developed stock speeches because each speaker began to anticipate arousal and response patterns in the audience. The ASUO leaders also found that there was a distinct delivery suited for different types of organizations: for moderate groups the presentation would be simplified and toned down; for militant groups and radical students the delivery was direct, rhetorical, and forceful. Diverse appeal was necessary if the mass movement strategy was to be realized.

It was extremely difficult for one speaker to address effectively, for example, both a militant ghetto organization in West Oakland and an upper-middle-class white liberal community in the hills. The level, language, demeanor, and even the kinds of information that were conveyed to persuade and communicate were entirely different, and rarely did a single individual possess the talent, tolerance, and insight that such differing styles demand. The ASUO managed this problem as best it could by dividing duties: one would address the young, the grass roots poor, or the militant-radical; another spoke primarily to white adult groups, laborers, concerned parents, PTAs, school community councils, church organizations, and the like.

For those speaking to the latter groups, there always seemed to be a bigot or racist in the audience who, often unconscious of his or her own prejudicial attitudes, would fire questions and criticisms concerning the facts and interpretations that were presented. There was usually one politically naive individual, unaware of inner-city problems, who was somewhat shocked by what was said and who looked upon the ASUO as militant rabble. Conversely, there were those who ostensibly supported every word; for them, students seemed to possess a sort of mystical access to truth. Naturally, there also were many who thoughtfully weighed and understood what was said, giving their physical and financial support whenever possible. These various individuals could be identified rather quickly, usually within an hour or so. Speakers soon learned to anticipate the critic's comments, and through predictable verbal give-and-take routine, the stock verbal trap was set, sprung, and the stock answer given. ASUO speakers found that if one listened carefully and waited for the proper moment, the diverse elements in the audience could be manipulated and pitted against one another. In this way strong attacks were neutralized and many were persuaded to support the ASUO. Those working among the more militant groups faced a series of different challenges. Again, there seemed to be a general pattern of audience reaction and response, some leading to attacks and condemnations. Many charges emanated from personal "hang-ups" and frustrations, factors that every political movement encounters.

Since the student disturbances at the beginning of the fall term, the ASUO meetings were increasingly well attended. The core leadership had been working diligently, attempting to generate publicity for the meetings and to explain the organization. Hundreds, eventually thousands, of leaflets were produced.

Some of the funding to pay for such expenses was received as donations from organizations and individuals, many of whom had been addressed by an ASUO speaker, but most of the money needed to cover expenses came from the pockets of the ASUO core membership.

About mid-October, the ASUO received its first significant newspaper coverage in the *Oakland Tribune's* "teen section," publicizing a general meeting that had occurred on October 20, 1968. Approximately 60 student leaders, from six city high schools, attended to discuss ASUO demands, rationale, and strategy.

The article, which appeared the following Saturday, was typical of what appears on a paper's "Teen Page"; ASUO members were characterized as sincere, if not wholesome, young people. The coverage was fair as an image builder for the moderate citizenry but detrimental in terms of the "goody" image that was projected to the students the ASUO was trying to reach. Nevertheless, the ASUO was identified for the general public, and many calls were received from interested community organizations requesting speakers to present the students' case.

By this time, the ASUO core workers were laboring until 10, 11, or 12 o'clock nearly every night printing material, contacting community groups, and speaking at meetings. Still attempts to delegate authority and work were unsuccessful. Dependability outside this circle of elites was low, and materials to be duplicated—for example, advertising meetings and publicizing activities—necessitated deadlines that only the core group was disciplined and responsible enough to meet. Transportation also was a problem for some students who were willing to work but lived on the edge of the city and had no convenient means of transportation so that they could meet centrally. School responsibilities presented an obvious problem, and the work was left to the few who were willing and able to make the necessary sacrifices.

The Process of Building a Large Following
Contains the Seed of Its Own Destruction

The core leaders' chronic inability to spread the work load, a problem for most temporary, low-resource organizations we suspect, not only caused discontent among the core group, but eventually resulted in charges that ASUO leadership was "ego tripping" and "power drunk." The leadership responded defensively that it had no help and that if the ASUO was to mobilize community opinion, then the tasks the core group was performing must be accomplished reliably and well. The rationale underlying both charge and defense is justified and, unhappily, the conditions giving rise to both tend to be mutually reinforcing. In any organization in which there is a great deal of work to do and only a handful are doing it, the natural tendency of the core is to self-righteousness, a feeling that is justified by their personal experience but becomes self-defeating in terms of the larger objective—building a cohesive movement. Cliques usually have a damaging effect upon group morale: they plant the seeds of internal dissent and strain the bonds between leaders and followers. Therefore, though the leadership is faced with the practical impossibility of effectively involving most followers, it still must at least give the appearance of making exhaustive attempts to share the tasks and decision-making authority.

But, like other organizations of this kind, the ASUO core leadership was too busy and spread too thin to see discontent emerging, so the problem was underestimated. In retrospect this insensitivity seems to have been a primary factor in the slow disintegration of the ASUO's mass following.

By early November 1968 the ASUO leadership had planned and set a target date of December 3, 1968, for a mass demonstration at the school board. The message was conveyed both to interested community groups and the Oakland Education Coalition (OEC). The OEC generally cooperated with the ASUO and, in fact, often seemed to look to students for direction. In conjunction with the demands we planned to present to the board, the OEC drafted 6 more, bringing the total to 14.

On November 11 the ASUO called an emergency session; trouble was brewing at Fremont High School. The president of the Oakland Federation of Teachers was present to tell the ASUO what had been occurring at the school. He also discussed a possible teacher walkout to protest the Board of Education's refusal to acknowledge a situation that had already degenerated to general violence. The school had sustained numerous and regular firebombings; militants were arming themselves; and racial tension was intense. It seemed only a matter of time before serious injury would occur. Teacher reaction to Fremont's trouble was divided; some wanted police to patrol the halls. Students and teachers at the ASUO meeting agreed that uniformed policemen would only add to the problem, perhaps leading to open gunfire in the halls ("Students Are Serious About Goals," 1968).

At this meeting the ASUO received its first significant news coverage from a small, liberal neighborhood newspaper, the *Montclarion.* A reporter for the *Montclarion* was present to report on the meeting; in subsequent weeks this *Montclarion* reporter was to play a major role by maintaining our existence to the liberal community. In fact, she was probably the most important figure outside the movement; she favorably and regularly publicized our aims and our encounters with the Board of Education. In order for a pressure-type organization to function at all effectively, publicity is crucial, and the *Montclarion,* although limited by size and status, performed this service for the student union.

On Friday, November 15, 1968, student violence erupted at Oakland Technical High School, forcing it to close. Conflicting newspaper accounts set the number of participants from 12 to 200 students. One hundred ten windows were broken, several small fires were set, furniture was overturned or thrown out of windows, fire alarms were set off, and fire extinguishers sprayed. Two students were beaten; one was knocked unconscious. A physiology teacher suffered a depressed fracture of the upper jaw after being struck three times while trying to halt a student who was attempting to break into the school treasurer's office. The demonstration was triggered when the police arrested 15 truant and loitering students across the street from the campus. Militant student leaders disrupted classes to inform students and to call for a boycott in protest. Shortly after 1:00 p.m. riot police arrived and dispersed the crowds. Later, a number of firearms, including several rifles, reportedly were found in a locker-to-locker search.

These events escalated ASUO activities, and the leadership moved to capitalize upon renewed interest and newspaper coverage of Oakland students.

However, these events correspondingly heightened administrative intimidation, making the leaders' task more difficult. As a relatively weak student group, with no official adult sponsors or advisors, the

ASUO was harassed by the school administrators, which markedly diminished its following. ASUO leaders were threatened with suspension and expulsion for their activities. Curiously, the administration seemed to be aware of planned activities and actions before they occurred. For example, students were contemplating the idea of a mass walkout, followed by a march with picket signs and leaflets, through downtown Oakland to the school board offices. It was cancelled after a few sympathetic teachers reported to us that school administrators were aware of the plan and were taking preventive measures. Later, someone who had been working closely with the ASUO as an unofficial advisor disclosed that she had discovered an informer in the organization.

On November 19, 1968, a huge mailing of the amended disciplinary codes was sent to the parents or guardians of each student in each of the six Oakland high schools. The amended code stated, in effect, that any student participating in any form of demonstration, loitering within the specified perimeter of school property, or leaving school under illegal conditions (walkouts, boycott, or strike) not only would be subject to expulsion or suspension, but arrest as well (letter to Oakland Board of Education from Superintendent Stuart S. Phillips, November 19, 1968; see new disciplinary codes).

In addition, reference to the ASUO was excluded from school newspapers and student government discussions; students were told that the ASUO had "nothing to do with student affairs." Journalism teachers reportedly were instructed by the assistant superintendent not to allow anything to be printed concerning the ASUO because the organization was "communist inspired." Principals had ordered teachers to report any student in possession of ASUO literature. The names of ASUO leaders were listed as student rebels in local and federal government files. Some even appeared on a number of drug abuse control "dope lists" that circulated among school administrative offices. The leaders of the student union were warned by a supportive Justice Department community relations worker that three task forces of college students had been established to spy for local and federal officials. The college students were to send names and descriptions of activities to Washington, D.C. Finally, ASUO activists were promised that college and scholarship recommendations—a necessity for aspiring low-income minority students—would be withheld or negatively cast because of political activism.

Another problem that the ASUO regularly faced was the rule prohibiting distribution of leaflets on campus. The regulation was circumvented by involving large numbers of students in the distribution process. One would take perhaps 500 leaflets and divide them among 10 people, who would in turn divide them among 10 more, and so on. It became obvious to the administrators that they could not take punitive action against so many. The leaflets seemed to materialize in the hands of the students. As a result, the ASUO appeared larger and more organized than it was.

From time to time, ASUO leaders were called to the school administrators' office to speak regarding the leaflets. Initially, there were attempts to communicate openly, but political and social circumstances seemed to mold exchanges between administratror and student in the shape of confrontations. Even if an administrator was sympathetic, he or she would feel the pressure from those above him or her, as well as from conservative public opinion. For many, it seemed that a principal's primary function was "to keep the lid on things" to prevent student unrest. In view of this apparent condition, the ASUO leaders firmly believed that if change in the form of constructive programs was not launched, destructive frustrations would explode on a much larger scale. The ASUO, moreover, had an image to preserve in order to maintain a following, and conversations that appeared too friendly might be construed to be fraternization. Hence ASUO leaders were the agitators and school administrators the establishment bureaucrats.

Low-resource activists must be fully and emotionally committed to their purpose; sympathizing with the political opposition is impractical and demoralizing. The situation must be simplified, the course resolute, and the battle lines clearly drawn. The appearance of uncertainty and indecision can destroy the effectiveness of the mass movement as a method of influencing policy.

In later chapters, the reader will see that the tactic of appearing confident and knowing in an uncertain context is generally useful for the short-term but becomes dysfunctional if pursued because it is a stance from which learning and, thus, adaptation are very difficult.

The Seeds Germinate

By the end of November, student leaders began finalizing plans for the December 3rd mass petition of the school board. It was at this time that the ASUO experienced an internal power struggle that threatened its existence. At the beginning of the academic year when one influential student leader, the Black Student Union chairman at Oakland Technical

High and a member of the Black Panther Party, was approached, he had declared that the ASUO was not militant enough in its demands, or its strategy, and that it included too many whites. He, therefore, would not participate in or endorse the organizing efforts. However, several months later, as the community coalition was nearly ready for its school board presentation, this student found another, more damaging forum for his accusations against the ASUO. At the last major strategy meeting, three days prior to the meeting with the Board of Education, approximately 25 student leaders from the six Oakland high schools were present, including the Black Student Union Chairman from Tech. The following is one student leader's personal account of that meeting:

> The student who normally chaired the meetings at the last moment could not attend, which resulted in me having to preside and to explain and submit the finalized strategic plans for approval. It was at this point that the Tech leader made his bid to influence and possibly take control over the general body. He proceeded to denounce the ASUO and the tactics that were to be employed. It was evident that he was challenging the leadership and the movement itself. It was also apparent that he had to be defeated verbally, or at least held in stalemate, in order to maintain the fragile coalition. The political ideology of the community support that the ASUO had accumulated over the past several months was liberal-moderate, and these supporters had an understanding that certain tactics which they had previously approved were to be implemented on December 3, 1968.[1] It was too late for radical changes in strategic plans. On numerous occasions, fearful community leaders accused ASUO leaders of not "leveling" with them regarding what had been planned. Naturally, most of the organizations were afraid of violent incidents, and a change in tactics might cause mass confusion and a breakdown of confidence in an already distrustful environment among the individuals and organizations participating in the presentation. Hence, since students were largely determining the direction and thrust for the supportive community, to lose control of the meeting was, in effect, to lose control of the entire movement.
>
> After a short period of heated debate, which was characterized by mutual accusations and ideological rhetoric, the Black Student Union leader from Tech stood up in disgust and called the BSU leaders to convene in another room. He had succeeded in splitting the meeting and potentially the movement by taking many of the influential black leaders with him. The majority of the leadership remained, however, and at least half of the leaders that did depart (it was later discovered) left, not to break the movement, but to hear what the Tech leader had to say. Nevertheless, the split, particularly at that moment, had an extremely demoralizing effect. Although it was reported that the Tech leader had no immediate plans, it

was feared and rumored that he would attempt to rally a few students to disrupt the presentation. And if trouble did erupt, there was a good chance that the public would attach the blame to the ASUO. For this reason, the ASUO leadership was ready to cancel the presentation until 12 hours before the meeting. However, the ASUO leadership was not altogether helpless; they were prepared to utilize a coercive channel created by previous events to "blow the whistle on the Tech student." That is, they knew he had been arrested during the violent incidents at Technical High on charges that included unlawful assembly, disturbing the peace, rioting, and insulting teachers, and that he was currently released on bail [see San Francisco *Chronicle, 1968*, on Harridon arrest]. The ASUO leadership was actually standing by to report him for planning further disruption, which could send him to jail and diminish his chance in court in the first charge.

The defensive action that the ASUO leaderhip was prepared to initiate was in a sense blackmail of sorts. Later one of the ASUO core group, posing as a black student leader, telephoned the Tech leader's house on the pretense that he was seeking the "scam" or lowdown on the ASUO and what was being planned. The "fake" phone call disclosed that nothing was being planned after all, except discouragement of students from participating, and the presentation was able to proceed on schedule.

The experience of the ASUO is indicative of the struggles among personalities, organizations, and pressure groups to cope with the often dimly perceived activities and purposes of one another. The ASUO is an example of low-resource pressure groups' common inability to be effective. Their force is lost in internal conflict over power and control. Such struggles repeatedly have occurred in programs in which money and status are at stake (as in the federally sponsored poverty programs), opening the door to corruption and personal exploitation. Strong-arm tactics in power disputes tend to permeate movements among low-resource activists and, indeed, the politics of the poor. In fact, you will see in the next chapter, which traces the reaction of the Oakland City Council to the Office of Economic Opportunity-sponsored Community Action Programs (CAP), that such internal disagreements apparently drained the CAPs of their effectiveness vis-à-vis the Council, which, for a time, had no way of controlling them.

In the final days before the presentation, a few last preparations were made, including printing and distributing an instructional leaflet and arranging and coordinating car-pool transportation to the school board from each campus. A student press conference on December 2nd also was being planned. But the student leaders from the various organizations who were asked to participate expressed doubt that they could legitimately represent their organizations to the press. At the last moment the conference was cancelled, and the local media were hastily notified of the action. In the confusion, one television station and one newspaper, the *Montclarion*, were accidentally overlooked, and both arrived at the designated location. After angry outbursts from an upset reporter and camera crew, apologies and an explanation were sent to repair and to maintain favorable press relations.

The days immediately prior to December 3rd were cold, rainy ones, and wet weather tends to dampen spirits as well as everything else, naturally, limiting participation. The morning of the third was clear, fears were dispelled and activities proceeded as planned. Approximately 300 students, teachers, and parents arrived to march on the picket line, jam the Board of Education meeting room, and fill an upstairs auditorium in which boardroom proceedings were piped in through loudspeakers. Public school security police were plentiful and on several occasions prevented people from entering the building. Student monitors were stationed outside to keep the picket line moving; the line had grown to more than 100 persons who snaked the length of the block.

After the ASUO leaders, addressing the Board, described the deteriorating condition of Oakland's educational system and the nature and intent of the ASUO demands, community speakers came forward, supported by an enthusiastic audience, to support the student effort. The speakers frequently pointed a condemning finger at the administrators in an attempt to raise public ire. The school superintendent issued an immediate response; he had prepared a 17-page report that explained why particular demands could not be met and defended programs already in operation. In rebuttal, the ASUO intended to offer some practical, well-founded alternatives to the apparent roadblocks preventing the implementation of alternative programs and to expose, from careful study of and long experience with, the system's inadequacies. In this way, the ASUO prevailed upon the Board, who was already pressured by an aroused community to schedule a series of "negotiation meetings" to discuss in an open public forum possible solutions to the Oakland School system's problems. This was a major victory for the ASUO; it could maintain its existence through publicity and continue to exert political pressure. Though the school board members had known for several weeks about the ASUO presentation in which large numbers were expected to take part, only four of seven school board members—barely a quorum—attended.

The Board was forced to consent to the meetings or face repeated verbal attacks and possible political repercussions for being overtly unresponsive to a responsible, broad-based segment of the Oakland community. In fact, a special Board of Education session was held the following morning to draft a written reply to the students and to examine the superintendent's 17-page report that the board members had not seen.

The presentation itself could be judged successful in terms of the action and interaction that occurred at the administration building. Though it was printed on the front page of the Oakland *Tribune* and described in all the major Bay Area newspapers, the ASUO presentation was overshadowed by events that could not have been foreseen and that literally cut in half the ASUO's impact on the citizenry: San Francisco State College, under the flamboyant leadership of Dr. S. I. Hayakawa, erupted in a violent "Third World strike."

That same day, December 3rd, the San Francisco police, augmented by a tactical squad, had stormed through the campus like shock troops—scores were injured, beaten, and arrested as the school entered a period of turmoil unlike any in the college's history. It is obvious that such a comparatively mundane occurrence as a peaceful protest in Oakland could not possibly compete for news coverage with clubs that were smashing flesh and bone. At that particular time, it is very likely that every television camera in the area was at San Francisco State, stationed on roof tops, behind barriers, or some other vantage point to record the drama of embattled administrators and demonstrating students.

The weeks that followed were somewhat anticlimactic. The series of meetings with the school board were frustrating at best and, based upon any criteria of immediate direct returns, virtually fruitless. Each session was a minor confrontation in itself in which the school board, save for one member, would not yield any ground or even admit that many of the system's troubles existed. In the meantime, the ASUO, and the coalition itself, was flagging. Instead of exerting public pressure upon this largely unresponsive and obstinate institutional body, it found itself slowly being talked and negotiated to death, sinking under the weight of verbal gymnastics and red tape.

In addition, leaders directed their efforts to politicizing the interested community, getting publicity when they could, and maintaining a watchdog stance on Board of Education policy and decision making. Operating out of newly acquired office space shared with other groups opposing war, racism, and poverty, the ASUO printed newsletters and bulletins, spoke at public meetings, and regularly addressed the Board on the condition of Oakland's educational system—problems about which most of Oakland's citizens were uninformed. These difficulties

included a high dropout rate, high illiteracy among high school gradu-
ates, questionable disciplinary procedures, and the school system's
reliance on outdated, so-called vocational education programs, preparing many students either for the army or unemployment lines.

It is difficult to calculate accurately the ASUO's long-range impact
on the Oakland Public Schools and the city. It was in part responsible
for launching a community effort through the 1968-1969 year that lead
indirectly to upgrading human relations programs, the further development of ethnic studies, the adoption of new, more relevant educational
materials, and the Board's hiring of a promising new superintendent.
Most important, the ASUO played a role in politicizing many students,
teachers, and citizens by exposing the failings of the school system on a
citywide basis. Its activities ranged from speaking before community
groups to participating in election campaigns. The increased student
involvement and awareness set some precedents, and as a result, in
subsequent months students were regularly included as consultants to
the school board and as participants in any decision-making or policymaking procedure that was to involve the community. Moreover,
student government, hitherto virtually a useless ceremonial structure,
began taking itself seriously and demanding changes for a system replete
with academic, political, and social problems.

PART TWO

At this point, it may be instructive to shift focus somewhat from the
Associated Students Union of Oakland to the problems inherent in a
low-resource organization.

In the 1960s a number of community-based pressure groups rose
rapidly to prominence in Oakland, flourished momentarily, and then
died. For the poor, blacks, and other minorities, who have by far
constituted the most vociferous and active organizations in Oakland,
change has not come easily or without cost. These disenfranchised
groups are powerless in the conventional sense because they have no
effective access into the political system; they are compelled to generate
their own political resources, employing tactics such as sit-ins, boycotts,
and other demonstrations (violent and nonviolent) in order to make a
difference.

The short life expectancies of issue-oriented, low-resource groups
attest that organizing under such conditions is an extremely difficult,

uphill battle. In addition to external obstacles like intimidation and harassment from established authority, no funding, or "friendly" major newspapers, these groups face internal problems: There is skirmishing within and between groups that can reduce newly organized segments of the discontented to a morass of disorganized citizens. This section will deal with some of the uncertainties of leadership, leader-follower relationships, and the tactics that are employed by low-resource pressure groups.

As we implied in the previous section, one explanation for the absence of cohesiveness among dissatisfied urban residents is that they distrust their own leaders. Distrust is sometimes initiated by power struggles for leadership based more upon personality, money, and political tactics than ideology. Even if such fratricidal breaks between rival personalities do not actually occur—that is, if leaders recognize that they must make concessions with one another if there is to be the essential minimal agreement within coalitions—the conflicting tensions are there and have a tendency to surface, transforming precious follower enthusiasm and fervor into cynicism and apathy. This was particularly true for federally subsidized agencies like the Community Action Agency supported by OEO. (See article on OEDCI conflicts 1969-1971, that is, *Tribune,* September 20, 1969; *Tribune,* November 26, 1969, "Aide Quits Poverty Council—Black Caucus Takeover.") One West Oakland resident bitterly regarded some of the CAA leadership as "poverty-pimp Negroes, just out to get their graft"; they were seen as opportunists "fighting each other for the scraps thrown off the Man's table."

Distrust of leadership occurs among the leaders of various organizations as well as among the community and organizational heads. The ASUO leadership was constantly watching out for itself and the organization so that they would not be unknowingly used or taken over by other groups seeking to fulfill their own aims at the expense of the students. Although it necessarily entered into coalitions, the ASUO maintained a rigidly autonomous stance. An organization's status and ranking in the community can be a very important source of support for leaders attempting to project their political ideology to a great many citizens. This is crucial for an organization's internal cohesion and for the stability of any coalition it might enter. The *reputation* of being either conservative or radical, politically experienced with well-known leaders or amateurish, is a primary factor in attracting followers, especially those who have watched pressure groups come and go and have become cynical and disillusioned. For this reason, it is imperative that pressure group leaders project upon the community the *impression* that their organization is and has been both active and successful. Onlookers will support only an organization that they feel is "doing something" and that appears to have the potential to become widely known, prominent, and reasonably powerful. Usually this is accomplished by attracting broad and repeated coverage from the media; to be ignored by the news media is not merely to suffer a loss of status but to cease to exist, to suffer a political death. The question of media will be raised again and discussed more fully later in this chapter.

A pressure group's composition is also an important factor. Many black students at one Oakland high school refused to support the ASUO on the grounds that the organization was too "honkyfied," although few of its members were white. The predominantly white upper-middle-class students residing in the hill areas of Oakland unwittingly had the power to destroy the ASUO simply by attending the meetings. They were easily the most enthusiastic members, and also the most naive; their white missionary attitude often offended and alienated the most tolerant minority students. ASUO leaders consequently found themselves in the position of actually having to discourage these students because they "turned off" other important student leaders and reduced the organization's status among the student population.

If any movement does reach the stage of a pressure organization, their encounters with established authority are critical. Often, when a group begins to exert pressure on local government, officials will co-opt it, diminishing its strength and cohesion by granting minor or secondary concessions. Acceptance of such enticements, depending on the militancy of the followers, interested citizens, and supportive organizations, might be regarded as an easy "sellout" to the target institution.

Before any pressure group can be effective, its followers, both active and potential, must undergo a politicization process. Sometimes this process results from personal experiences and predates involvement in a particular movement. However, this appears to be the exception more than the rule. The politicization process, engineered by the leadership to prepare their constituency for a unified effort, begins with every new movement. Mass meetings and mass rallies are the most common and effective methods of gathering supporters together. In this setting, rhetoric—sometimes revolutionary in tone—slogans, and propagandist literature have their most important and essential uses. Such artifacts usually have little value in terms of tangible, practical goals; they are deliberate misrepresentations of reality but are invaluable tools for building enthusiasm and support that adds to the cohesiveness of the general movement. Although slogans and terms such as "power to the people" or "we must have community control" would be difficult, if not impossible, to implement, they are easily, although superficially, understood. They appeal to emotion, which is the basic common denominator capable of transforming individual impulse into group action. The unifying property of emotional fervor is an essential prerequisite for the commitment of an individual to the group and is consequently paramount for the effectiveness of any protest endeavor. One finds, therefore, that most adherents to mass movements are necessarily and consistently misled through myth and rhetoric.

Thus there exists a disparity between thought and action. Although the political naivete of the followers enables them to become emotionally involved and "swept up" by the rhetoric that produces fervent enthusiasm, it is often only a momentary sensation that rapidly subsides as the planned confrontation or demonstration approaches. Between the time of the rally and the confrontation itself there is usually an interim period that gives the follower an opportunity to contemplate what was said and the action that he or she is about to undertake. In this light, the slogans that were so faithfully shouted may slowly begin to lose their importance as the ideological rhetoric increasingly must be compared to reality. The animal instinct for survival and preservation is strong indeed, but to the inexperienced follower its power is perceived only after the cheers and shouts have died and the moment arrives when a person must "lay himself or herself on the line." When a movement is removed from the simplified abstractions of rhetoric, slogan, and ideology, then the concrete realities of "how much one is willing to lose" and "how far one is willing to go" surface. The obvious, but not readily perceived, fact is that it takes great courage to risk severe self-sacrifice, physical or otherwise.

It is possible that some mass-based, protest movements are composed of highly politicized and experienced followers who realize what course of action their organization must take and who understand the consequences. We suspect it is more common that skilled leaders maintain the essential emotional involvement and conviction of the followers from the point of the rally to the point of actual confrontation through the use of rhetoric, slogans, and other forms of propaganda. One or both must be possible or movements such as the civil rights marches by Martin Luther King or the various activities of the Black Panther Party could not have happened. Their success, like that of all movements, rested on leader-follower sacrifice and suffering, two concepts that are very real indeed.

We have been leading to an important.point concerning organization and action. A talented speaker can excite and arouse an audience, at least for the duration of a rally, but an experienced leader does more than excite; he or she is able to initiate organizational commitment and action. The two points are not always synonymous; audience arousal certainly does not ensure its transformation into group action, especially when followers perceive great risk. When dealing with masses, a leader must possess the ability to sense what his or her followers are capable of and what they are prepared to do at each level of involvement and politicization.

To reiterate, ideological rhetoric and propaganda are absolutely essential for organizing and politicizing the followers. More important, rhetoric and slogans, properly employed, result in very emotional responses that bolster courage and draw attention away from or reduce the feeling of uncertainty over the potentially dangerous consequences of confrontation. Although the leadership must manipulate the followers through the use of such rhetoric, they themselves must be able to distinguish it from reality. For the leadership to be caught up unconsciously in blind emotion can be fatal to a movement. Again, leaders must have the capacity to sense what their followers are willing to do at a particular moment. They must not fool themselves and overrate their abilities because of the fervent but temporary enthusiasm generated in an emotional atmosphere by their own oratorical ability.

The success or failure of low-resource protest groups rests with the leadership. They must make clear, level-headed, systematic decisions and judgments based on what they perceive to be the reality of the situation in order to move effectively their organization while suffering the least reprisal possible. Hence, although the powerless pressure group leader must repeatedly be a dogmatist in public speech and manner, the political and sociological nature of his or her following demands that he possess deftness and versatility in those private decision-making processes that control the destiny of the organization.

On the one hand, public dogmatism reduces the participants' sense of uncertainty about the nature of a situation as well as minimizing their anxiety about the personal risks associated with activities required of them. On the other hand, the low-resource pressure group leader's stock in trade is manipulating established authorities uncertainty vis-à-vis the potential of his or her following. In short, the leaders negotiating for the group do not act to reduce uncertainties dogmatically but instead, use ambiguity as a tactical weapon as they construct a convincing bluff.

If the established authorities overreact to the pressure group leader's flamboyant public oratory and initiate reprisals against particular leaders or the general membership, they promote cohesion and increase the common resolve among the group or groups affected by the rancorous actions. Martyrdom brings protest from the level of ideological abstraction to immediate, tangible occurrences that, by vicarious participation, draw protest supporters into a collective brotherhood of the victimized. A good example of this identification with the victims of violence can be seen in a major community protest in May 1969, resulting from the school board's decision to hire a new school superintendent. However, to grasp the situation and the emotion it fired, a short review is in order.

When the superintendent resigned, the school board, under pressure from the liberal community, established procedures to provide for community participation and a blue ribbon screening committee to take part in the selection of a new administrator. Apparently the new procedures and the committee were ignored or circumvented; earlier in that same week, the newspapers surprised nearly everyone by reporting that the selection already had been completed. The following day it was disclosed that the board's choice for superintendent had been involved in a million-dollar financial scandal, a conflict of interest case involving a textbook company of which he was a director. The liberal community was outraged, not only about the man, but, more important, over the arrogant manner in which he had been chosen. Community control, public participation, and institutional responsiveness are issues that are always working near the surface. At that time, the public school issue was so sensitive that the blatant disregard of the public's express wish to play a part in the appointment further alienated a relatively large segment of the city.

A sit-in at the Board of Education followed, the police were called, a violent confrontation ensued, and several people were arrested. During the melee, metal objects were thrown, chairs overturned, and chemical mace sprayed. The executive director of the poverty program, the director of the Oakland Black Caucus, the president of the Oakland Federation of Teachers, and an ASUO student leader and president of Oakland Tech High were among those clubbed or otherwise abused. A mass rally occurred the following evening, and the president of the Oakland Federation of Teachers was asked to address the large crowd. Like many before him, he spoke of the issues and the brutalities that he had experienced personally. His words had a dramatic effect as he described his battered ribs, badly bruised body, and how he had urinated blood, a condition apparently caused by being repeatedly beaten about the kidneys by police and school security guards. Several times during his halting delivery, he appeared to break down emotionally, evidently overcome by the traumatic experiences that he had suffered. Many in the audience also were emotionally moved and identified with him. Such sacrificial leadership brought hard realities into focus; the issue no longer involved just the superintendent but also the martyrs and, in effect, those in the audience who must be vindicated.

Despite common outrage over martyred leaders, vigorous tactical disagreements and power-diminishing splits developed among the protesters. One of the primary sources of conflict was the failure of the "radicals" to separate and determine the underlying differences— beyond tactics and ideology—between a radical movement and a liberal one. Too often the more revolutionary battle verbally with the more moderate membership within the low-resource pressure group, urging support of radical tactics, while, at the same time, calling for mass action. However, it may not be possible, at least in twentieth-century America, for an organization to embrace the characteristics both of revolutionary and liberal groups, that is, radical tactics in the context of a collective effort with the broad appeal of a pressure-type movement. This depends, of course, on the political and social environment; in a discontented, unstable atmosphere, mass radical action certainly is possible.

In general, however, the concept of a radical mass movement is a contradictory one. Rather, there are two distinct groups. One is the radical vanguard, a small faction working outside of the established order, perceiving great risk and perhaps facing possible imprisonment, injury, or death. Then there are the more moderate organizations that are to be classified among pressure groups (both powerless and powerful), working more or less within established boundaries and using public sentiment as their primary weapon. It is true that revolutionary organizations may provoke the sympathy and tacit approval of many, but they do not generally enjoy active participation from the general citizenry. "Picking up the gun" is a tactic adopted by few. Hence there is either the liberal mass movement or the radical vanguard; the leader cannot employ the tactics of one and enjoy the following of the other.

It has been demonstrated that violent actions and confrontations can initiate badly needed reforms in urban America. However, such strategies are equally likely to result in a backlash in which little or nothing is achieved. Regardless, the employment of revolutionary tactics to attain nonrevolutionary goals will surely lead ultimately to a group's destruction, leaving no chance for it to fulfill the moderate purpose of acquiring power in the existing governmental structures. Jesse Jackson, then a spokesman for Operation Breadbasket, economic arm of the Southern Christian Leadership Conference, argued a strong, pragmatic case for nonviolent tactics in order to maintain and retain his organization. It is naturally an ideology that is supportive of a program that is immediate, tangible, and practical.

> We do not have the military resources to deal with the American power structure. There's no sense in facing tanks with a .22 pistol. Our circumstances and terrain would not give us the freedom to use a violent strategy. The ghettos are built like a military stockade. America never needs to actually come in. The lights can be turned off, the water shut off and the food supply stopped. We could be eliminated in the ghetto without anyone even crossing the railroad tracks to get us. [*Playboy*, 1969].

Simple survival thus becomes a primary task for issue-oriented organizations; if leaders fail to draw the important distinctions between liberal and radical roles, internal disputes will develop that such groups can ill afford.

At this point, we turn to the problem of devising a specific tactical strategy to cope with the difficulties of survival and effectiveness. The problem is clear-cut: How do particular individuals legitimately acquire authority in a powerless situation? Part of the answer lies in a rather limited number of avenues and methods available to low-resource organizations. It is the subject of the following section.

Tactics: Making the Most of the Resources at Hand

In the interest of understanding the predicament of the powerless, Gresham Sykes's study of a maximum-security prison may be helpful for drawing a meaningful analogy between the circumstance of the prisoner and that of the pressure group with few resources. Sykes points out that although the prison is surrounded by four walls, its inhabitants are not altogether cut off from free society. There are ways in which the prisoners can communicate and project their grievances to the public and expose some of the ills hidden within the prison itself.

> At certain times as in the case of riots, the inmates can capture the attention of the public; and indeed disturbances within the walls must

often be viewed as highly dramatic efforts to communicate with the outside world, efforts in which confined criminals pass over the heads of their captors to appeal to a new audience. At other times, the flow of communications is reversed and the prison authorities find themselves receiving demands raised by a variety of business, political, religious, ethnic, and welfare interest groups [Sykes, 1958: 8].

Like the prisoner, low-resource pressure groups are in a difficult position. They too are cut off from the political arena and the public, not by walls, but by lack of reliable support, finances, and vehicles for carrying their message to the community. In fact, so isolated are they that, akin to prison inmates, they cease to exist in the public consciousness if they do not reach the news media. For them, there is no controversy unless controversy is created.

Since few pressure groups possess an independent ability to put their case before the citizenry, they must manufacture their own resources, using established news media to gain support for their activities in the hopes of exerting pressure on the target. One finds that the strategy of the powerless is always directed to the news media because the use of publicity is probably the pressure group's primary tool and weapon. But resource-poor organizations, like the members of a captive society, are invariably forced to perform acts, release statements, or capitalize upon that which is spectacular, inflammatory, or "newsworthy" to call attention to themselves. This is commonly achieved by demonstrations, mass meetings, picketing, and so forth, in which a great deal of angry rhetoric attempts to induce the media to cover the extraordinary, thus building an aroused, more politically aware community and bringing pressure to bear on the institutional target.

Organizational leaders verbally attack individual officials in public, blaming all the ills of a system on that individual and criticizing the political body as a whole at the same time. This tactic may serve three purposes:

(1) It attracts publicity.
(2) It provides supporters of a cause with a tangible scapegoat or "enemy," helping them concretely to focus their enthusiasm and interest on an easily identified object rather than upon abstract principles and ideology. Through skillful use of rhetoric and propaganda the situation is simplistically reduced to one of the "good guys" (us) versus the "bad guys" (them).
(3) It often gives the impression or appearance of success, which is essential to the organization's morale and political status in the community.

A public, "vicious" attack simplifies and concretizes the issues for the followers while, at the same time, throwing the established authority somewhat off balance by raising questions for them about their own policies and the capabilities of their antagonists.

City officials who are minorities were particularly susceptible to criticism and attack from irate groups representing minority interests and militant groups in the city. During a meeting concerning the school superintendent crisis on May 8, 1969, the director of the Oakland Economic Development Council, Inc., made comments to the school board in a tone of controlled rage and inferred that two black board members had "sold out." Through the summer of 1969, criticism construed to have racial overtones became increasingly intensified. For example, when the president of the Oakland Teachers Federation spoke against a $75,000 program that would send "human relations" counselors to Oakland's six high schools and questioned the board's capacity to administer the program, a black board member lashed out angrily:

> I'm tired of you white Jesuses telling me how to run my life.
> I'm tired of being chastized as the nigger on the Board.
> I'm nobody's nigger. I've been black for 58 years and I was suffering before you grew your beard [*San Francisco Chronicle*, 1969].

Such statements, regardless of particular racial demarcations, may be precisely the kinds of responses pressure group leaders want to draw out because they attract publicity. Even if the words that threaten and the accusations that antagonize do not provoke public outbursts from city officials, they still may be printed.

But the use of the news media as a resource is limited. Pressure groups must rely on publicity; it is their most effective political tool. However, it is difficult to pursue a regular, goal-oriented program as it is the nature of publicity to be irregular. That is, media coverage is obviously not a constant force that can be tapped at will. In order to be newsworthy, interest groups often must abandon original goals, sacrifice or defer their master plans, and capitalize, instead, on crisis situations, taking advantage of newsworthy institutional ills, social conditions, or administrative blunders.

When a pressure group has established itself and its position with the media, the question is how to use this new resource. The two most common tactics are the bluff or "anticipated" citizen support, which are employed to encourage and enter bargaining positions vis-à-vis institutional authority. Bluff or anticipated support can be employed to threaten, coerce, or pressure officials to respond to the dissenting group. In effect, the bluff raises the uncertainty level of the established authorities vis-à-vis that of the pressure group leaders.

Once an organization has regularly been covered by the media, it is difficult, if not impossible, for observers to determine precisely the size of its constituency or whom it represents. This ambiguity provides an opportunity for bluff. The pressure group may give the *impression* that it is highly organized and highly representative, a powerful group that can exercise coercive strength at will. The pressure group therefore can use others' uncertainty about its true strength to threaten or force established institutions into open confrontation. As an example, an organization may be able to build a temporary coalition or muster momentary support on an issue and organize a demonstration, confrontation, or mass meeting. If the turnout is large enough, it can say with a credibility established by the media that it represents "the community," "the people," or "the students." In truth, however, the turnout is not necessarily representative of the whole community and the persons in question are not likely to be regular and reliable members of the pressure group. Remember that large-scale support is generally quite temporary, and group leadership is fortunate indeed if it can sustain active follower enthusiasm for more than a week. Nevertheless, the appearance of mass support provides greater bargaining strength. When the interest group is organized, at least among its own vociferous leadership, it is able to employ the rhetoric of group representation even after its support has died away. If its demands are not taken seriously, further escalating action can be threatened with an imaginary, "reliable" following.

Of course, wise leaders do not make threats that are absolute, overextravagant, or ones that, if a bluff were called, would leave them exposed as powerless, immobile, or without support. The low-resource pressure group is attempting not only to fool institutional authorities about its size and strength but is also attempting to convince the citizenry. If a threat that is both unretractable and empty is challenged valuable status as an organization is lost. This means that if the pressure group leadership cannot deliver on a threat, they should have an escape. If the leadership understands that realistically it cannot make good a threat such as shutting down a school system with a boycott or a citywide labor strike, then it may still threaten such an action, but it must be stated in such a way that a strike or boycott is implied or inferred as a fair possibility, not an absolute certainty.

Within this game of bluffing, it is not always essential that opposition leaders be fooled before they are forced to respond to group demands. If a large portion of the interested community is convinced, the established authority may not wish to chance giving the pressure group an increased following and legitimacy by ignoring them, thus inviting the ire of the interested, partisan members of the community. For example, the Board of Education may have known that the ASUO had quite limited power and that its representation could hardly be said to extend to the entire student body of Oakland's six high schools. Actually, no group or individual in or out of the ASUO truly represented any cohesive faction, let alone the entire student population. Yet on December 3rd, 1968, the ASUO was able to gather relatively large student support from the six high schools to support its petitions. Building community backing for its position, the ASUO leadership pled its case before several community groups, carefully using rhetorical phrases such as "*the students* are organizing for better education," implying that the ASUO spoke for all the students of Oakland. So long as the public was presented with this image, conveyed mostly through speaking engagements and the press, the Board of Education, regardless of how large or strong they perceived the ASUO to be, was compelled to deal with the organization or face being accused by the citizenry of being blatantly unresponsive to students and the "broad-based community."

Anticipated citizen support, a variation of the outright bluff, is also an important tactic. The leaders can make demands or protest particular issues, expecting or anticipating large community backing if their grievances and programs are not received favorably, a support that they do not immediately have at hand. Implementation of such a threat is made possible by the media because repeated coverage literally gives the pressure group an existence by informing the community of its activities and gives it status and the reputation of being *the* leading organization of its kind. The leadership may exploit these conditions and threaten to incite large community protests, at times carrying through on such a threat.

In order to maintain the resources provided by publicity and status, the leadership must project the appearance of a united effort; low-resource political actors cannot afford to appear disorganized, quarrelsome, and divided. An organizer must either appeal to existing organizational leadership for support or at least neutralize other groups that reside in the same political quadrant to safeguard himself or herself from attacks that cause power splits.

CONCLUSIONS: THOSE SQUEEZED BETWEEN HIGH STAKES AND THE DIFFICULTY OF KNOWING CAN USE OTHERS' UNCERTAINTY TO IMPROVE RELATIVE ADVANTAGE

This insider's view of Oakland high school students' attempts to organize and to alter school board policies offers valuable lessons for others who cannot withdraw or would otherwise avoid highly uncertain situations. Chapter 2 depicted citizens who, for the most part, were adapting passively to their environment, whereas this chapter has portrayed persons unwilling any longer to suffer quietly an institutional climate they feel is not good for them and so set out actively to modify it. One quickly finds, however, that deciding to act is of lesser magnitude than achieving meaningful action, particularly if the resources commonly associated with potential authority—for example, money, status, knowledge, information, institutional positions, and so on—are not at hand.

Typically, those who do not have these "more easily negotiable" resources fall back on large numbers, which are a potential resource for anyone regardless of personal circumstance. The students in Oakland quickly found that even this asset cannot be exploited without concentrated, hard work. It requires tireless, continuous effort to organize, activate, or pretend to possess a large following.

The students' experience also suggests that mobilizing a large number of potential followers is not always sufficient for making a noticeable, lasting impact on policy outcomes. The few organizers, leaders and spokespeople must be prepared. Providing they can bluff with numbers and well enough to lever themselves into a position of prominence and importance to the institutional decision makers, if they are to be effective, they still must be fully informed regarding their proposals, including cost, implementation, likely objections, alternatives, and personal characteristics of relevant policymakers. Being informed, like organizing, requires considerable personal investment; it, too, is time-consuming, hard work.

The students' experience also indicates, however, that the hard work does pay off and, as you would expect, that effectiveness increases as experience is acquired. In different words, one might think of this as the power of staying power. The longer leaders can hold a following, hold media attention on their activities, and continue as spokespeople, the greater is established authorities' uncertainty regarding their potential and the more likely they are to effect noticeable changes.

In retrospect, did mobilizing a great many citizens and subsequently achieving access make any difference in school board policies? In the very short time span covered in this chapter, it does not seem that the students achieved their objectives. Rather, they encountered coping tactics from the school board and other community notables who were at root conservative (trying to change slowly), and the tactics of the established community outlasted the ASUO, whose leadership and membership were intrinsically less stable than that of the older, entrenched interests. If the students had more staying power, the evidence suggests that some accommodation would have been reached and the students would have, in some measure, altered school board policy in Oakland. Until this point, we have been thinking of the ASUO as a subset of citizens with a high stake in particular public policies. Those things that are important to us stimulate learning, investment, and action. But the case of the ASUO students further indicates that the perception of great risk makes action more difficult and less likely. Intimidation, however, reduces the perceived risk in action. It might be fruitful, then, to think of the interaction between ASUO leaders, their membership, and the established interests in the community as one of uncertainty management. In this context, uncertainty becomes a tool that can be employed to improve relative advantage.

Most of us feel that we are better off at lower positions on the uncertainty continuum described in Chapter 1. In a competitive or adversative setting, the students' actions suggest that we tend to operationalize this often vague, ill-formed feeling in such a way that those who appear most sure have the advantage.

This reaction offers at least two types of strategies for the intelligent adversary. First, of course, one attempts to reduce his or her own level of uncertainty: Amassing resources, acquiring information, and careful preparation are some methods for doing that. A second, perhaps more interesting and sophisticated set of strategies may be employed to increase others' uncertainty. This second kind often is used to confuse and delay an opponent, providing more time for organizing, becoming known, and acquiring adequate information. Remember, increasing perceived risk reduces likelihood of action. In the case of the Oakland high school students, it might be argued that their attempts to organize a pressure group increased the school administrators' and board members' uncertainty regarding how the ASUO could and would affect their professional lives.

Organizing, then, may be one way of producing confusion, especially for those who are established, that is, those who occupy legitimate positions as policymakers or decision makers. Of course other tactics include engaging in unexpected, threatening, unpredictable, or misleading activities. Such interactions can become quite sophisticated and complex to the point that most of the individual participants are but dimly aware of what is going on and act increasingly on intuition or "feel." We suspect that strategic uncertainty management is very like a good poker game involving several players. If an outside observer were to analyze fully the actions of each player at each step of the game, it would be a lengthy, abstract, and sophisticated exposition of the laws of probability. The point is that if each of the players then reviewed the analysis, it is not likely that any would recognize many of his or her specific actions or the overall progression of the game. Rather, they would have been playing with their active intellects largely informed by an intuitive sense of the game. But possibilities and questions are developing to the point that the material in these first two chapters cannot inform them. Let us hold this embryonic conception of uncertainty management and seek to develop it by turning to a problem of coping in the public arena from the point of view of established policymakers under stress.

We turn now to a detailed study of the Oakland City Council's behavior when confronted by the community action antipoverty programs sponsored by the Office of Economic Opportunity. These programs presented the Council with problems very much like those the school board faced by the ASUO. The Council is the city's established policymaking board while the antipoverty spokespeople—relying heavily, though not entirely, on the resource of "potential" numbers—demand policy changes to improve the lot of Oakland's poor. The antipoverty organization was somewhat more stable than the ASUO, though it did not have the staying power of the Council. It had more financial and informational resources that the ASUO, but these were slight compared to those available to the Council. The Council was then forced to engage a low-resource pressure group that was somewhat more formidable than the ASUO.

In the next chapter, we will ask, What are coping tactics like on the established, relatively advantaged side of the coin? Are they entirely different from those of the resource-poor organizations or do they appear very much the same? And finally, what can the Council's experience tell us about coping with uncertainty in a public forum?

NOTE

1. Among those groups the ASUO addressed, ethnic community organizations notably were often the most conservative. See Silberman (1964: 334) on the reluctance of the poor to act.

4 ON THE OTHER SIDE OF THE LOOKING GLASS
The City Council

IN THIS CHAPTER, we look closely at the coping technique employed by formal organizations that have been present only as shadows thus far in the analysis. Tradition, standard operating procedure, screens or buffers, and policymaking by veto all are widely recognized characteristics of formal, bureaucratic organization. Although such a collection of procedural cornerstones may be seen as having many different purposes—even pathological ones—at root they are methods for coping with changing conditions, conflicting demands, amorphous problems, and the like. From this point to the end of the analysis, as we look at very different administrative settings and conditions, we will find that familiar coping mechanisms surface again and again. Sometimes they are helpful; some can be used as tools for manipulating relative uncertainty levels; often they aggravate the very condition they were intended to ease, but always they are natural.

The common explanation would be that such varying consequences result largely from different substantive conditions, personalities, or any number of other situation specific factors. The following several studies of uncertainty management in the political and administrative context, however, indicate that this explanation is not particularly illuminating. Our alternative hypothesis is that no one is trained to view policymaking and administrative decision making as a process that can create and use ambiguity to advantage; in fact, formal and informal management training stresses precisely the opposite ethic: reduce and avoid uncertainty. Thus, in essence, we find that the procedures employed in a context of high uncertainty are those developed to constrain it, and so are not always the best for coping with and adapting to it. Nevertheless, this research suggests that most individuals have an instinct for coping rather effectively under conditions of high uncertainty. We will return to an extended discussion of this theme in the final chapter but now we begin an examination of response to high uncertainty in formal policy-making organizations.

One of the credos of our culture is that elected officials represent the citizenry and decide on matters of policy for them. Elected officials then are logical targets for those who wish to affect a decision on a policy matter. Our legislatures, executive departments, city councils and commissions, and special district governing boards do receive many, many demands. The City Council in Oakland is no exception; its agenda is crowded by personal entreaties, proposals initiated by the city departments, and questions that arise in the day-to-day activities of a large city government. Although the Council may appear to command many resources when compared to a struggling community group like the ASUO, its capacity is rather limited relative to the demands on its membership.

The Council attempts to restrict most of its activity to pro forma approval of routine requests. But what about those appeals that are not usual, familiar, or readily understood? In other words, how does the Council respond when faced with a group that wants something it either is not prepared to give or does not understand? If the Council members reject the request, they have to consider the possible consequences if the petitioners are powerful. If they do not understand the appeal or, more correctly, if they do not have confidence in their ability to judge the result of a positive or negative response, they are in an unhappy situation indeed, particularly if the request comes from a seemingly powerful or important person.

The point is that from time to time any body of elected officials is confronted by unfamiliar problems, and they have little choice but to cope as best they can. The history of the community action antipoverty programs in Oakland provides an excellent example of one such body of elected officials, the City Council, grappling with the leaders of these programs. How did the Council respond to the difficulties and ambiguities raised by these uncommon policies?[1] Perhaps we can best understand the Council's behavior if we begin with a more complete understanding of the City Council, the development of the Community Action Programs, and the implementation of these policies in Oakland.

A CHARACTERIZATION OF THE COUNCIL

The majority of our local governmental bodies are, if fact, rather simple political organizations. Elected officials are few in number, part-time, ill-paid, and understaffed. However, few towns or cities today, including Oakland, are either small or simple. They face increasing requirements for services in the face of decreasing revenues. The concomitants are urban blight and an increasing proportion of the population below the poverty line. Of course, these circumstances serve to increase tax rates. The history of these problems in our cities clearly indicates that they are not quickly or easily controlled. Thus, most town councils are so burdened with maintenance legislation that opportunity for acquiring expertise is minimal during the few hours each week that can be spared for public business.[2] Any expertise a councilman may exhibit must come from long incumbency and/or transfer from previous public or private experience.

Oakland's Council is no exception. It is composed of nine men. The Mayor has a staff consisting of one assistant, two secretaries, and a receptionist. The remaining eight councilmen must share a single office and one secretary. Oakland's Councilmen receive $3,600 per year in salary. Thus, they are rarely able to invest more than a few hours a week in their public office. They meet in formal session twice a week normally for about thirty minutes.[3]

Internal specialization consists of two standing committees. One is Ways & Means that considers questions about city revenues and expenditures—in short, the budget. Oakland, as one observer said, "does not have a Wilber D. Mills (at his best) on its council" (Meltsner, 1971: 60). He does go on to say that Oakland's Councilmen are fairly knowledgeable about the city's fiscal situation and that they are reasonably responsible guardians of the city's purse (Meltsner, 1971: 60-71). The other committee is Civic Action. It is charged with any studies or problem resolutions that involve community participants, including nonfiscal complaints, problems, or questions relating to immediate or proposed agenda items brought to the council by community members. The Civic Action Committee does not function to highlight issues and conflicts in public hearings. Rather, it acts to buffer the Council from community-based harassment during formal council meetings. Actually both committees function to buffer or insulate the Council as a whole. I suspect that most, if not all, political organizations consciously employ their more specialized suborganizations for buffer *as well as* employing them for the admittedly necessary purposes of more focused, more informed, more probing evaluation. These two committees normally meet twice a week in the afternoon prior to the evening Council meeting.

If neither committee has reason to meet, or if the Council is faced with an issue that seems to the mayor and/or Council members as more usefully treated by the full Council, the mayor schedules a work session. A work session normally meets just prior to a formal Council meeting. It is open to the public but not advertised, not held in the Council chambers, no minutes are recorded, and votes taken are not official. The Council finds this a useful device for focusing its attention for an extended period on one issue area. The only other time during the week that the Council members meet together is at dinner after work sessions or committee meetings.

One author has described complex social organizations as a function of the number of components, differentiation among components, and interdependence of these components (see LaPorte, 1969). According to these criteria a Council—such as that in Oakland—composed of few, part-time elected officials, who hold few, short meetings, have minimal personal staff, and little or no functional specialization or differentiation seems relatively uncomplicated. In contrast, the California Assembly, for example, with many different specialized committees, is a complex organization. Another salient characteristic of many city councils, ostensibly responsible for policy formulation and alteration, is that they are overpowered by the administrative staff, which theoretically is charged only with program maintenance.[4] Oakland is not unusual in this regard. Common sense tells us that a small, occasional Council like Oakland's is not likely to impose its will on a large, well-paid administrative arm directed by full-time, career professionals.[5] The Oakland Council simply does not have the information, expertise, or person hours required to evaluate and oversee administrative activities. The perennial argument that the Congress needs more staff to enable it to perform responsibly indicates that this kind of problem is by no means limited to part-time legislative bodies such as that of Oakland. In Oakland this inherent difficulty was aggravated by a city manager who believed that a part-time Council "should give part-time advice and not be active in administration" (Meltsner, 1971, p. 58). Similarly, another observer has written, "armed with his considerable advantages, the City Manager defines 'policy' and 'administration' (so that) 'administration' is very large and 'policy' is very small" (Pressman, 1971).

Thus the Oakland Council rarely intervenes in either shaping or operating city programs. In a very real sense this Council, and I suspect others as well, increasingly finds itself fundamentally cross-pressured in its public roles. It does not possess the capability for active formulation or oversight, but it is clearly influenced by our traditions regarding popularly elected officials and legislating functions. The Council, in formal meetings, repeatedly demonstrates that members feel an obligation to respond to requests from citizens. Although they may not want to endure lengthy debate about conflict-laden issues—leash laws, rare pet permits, awarding cable television contracts, or oil pipeline routings—the Council does ensure that such issues are heard.

The Council has a demonstrated aversion to conflict. Conflict absorbs time and energies, and can be psychologically punishing. Such issues are, therefore, likely to be aired in committee, at a work session, by a mayor-appointed commission, or by a relevant agency in the city manager's office. Several of those issues listed above have been the subject more than once of debate by several such "suborganizations." An issue would repeatedly be routed away from the Council chamber until the problems it presented were largely worked out and agreement assured. The record indicates that, although the Council may not want to become actively involved with controversial issues and programs, it does want to exercise its prerogative of final decision regarding citywide programs. Of new programs of the kind that have poured into our larger cities since 1960, the Oakland Council has not willfully released one to community control or to other governmental units; among others Redevelopment, Model Cities, Manpower, and New Careers programs remained ultimately answerable to the Council.[6]

In view of our tradition of responsibility, it is understandable that a relatively constrained organization such as the Oakland Council has evolved a set of institutional processes and procedures that enable it to retain a veto power without requiring immersion in a particular program or issue area. The Council has developed extensive and largely implicit coping aids that buffer it from those constituencies affected by a program. In Oakland, programs are operated and most problems are resolved by departments in the city manager's office.[7] The decision process is guided by the manager together with citizen advisory committees or commissions. The Council's role is largely one of perfunctory acknowledgment and approval. A proposed alteration in the Municipal Code, an expansion or reduction of park and recreation facilities, or a proposal to construct a new city-owned and operated off-street parking garage are instances of policy developed, debated, and decided upon largely at the department/commission level. The "finished product" is forwarded through the city manager who further screens it. It then proceeds to the Council for final approval. Alterations, regardless of their scope or importance, are nearly always routinely approved by the Council without comment. If a question is raised by a constituent, the Council members listen politely and ignore the point or immediately return the proposal in question to the city manager for resolution. On occasion, a considerable, well-argued opposition remains after a proposal has been routed or rerouted to the manager. The Council, however, almost never reverses or denies the action recommended by the manager's office.

Table 4.1 displays three issue or problem areas that frequently confront the Council. It demonstrates that the Council rarely acts in other than routine ways. The administrative recommendation was reversed only three times in nine years across these three issue areas. Each reversed, deferred, or nonroutine decision action resulted from an appellant citizen or group of citizens that had not been "screened out."[8] It is not surprising that the record indicates those who did penetrate the Council's screens were relatively affluent, business people who had a considerable stake in the decision's outcome and a relatively sympathetic ear from a socially similar Council membership. In short, they had resources and were using them for something that was important to them.

The membership of the Oakland Council traditionally has been selected from the city's business or professional population. During the past ten years, blacks, browns, and orientals have become the majority on the nine-man Council.[9] Still, almost 90% of Oakland's Council members since 1960 have been businessmen or business-oriented professionals like accountants or lawyers.[10]

The Council in Oakland is not a step on the ladder to higher elected or appointed office. In fact, though there are a few exceptions, city politics in contemporary America seems to act more as a barrier than a stepping stone to high public office.[11]

The persons who have served on this council, at least in the past ten years, have not been the more prominent, more affluent business or professional leaders in the community. Most citizens in Oakland do not even know the Councilmen by name; Council members' social activities are rarely noted on the society pages and their official functions, if reported at all, are usually lost in the paper's obscure regions.

However, councilmen are invited to many civic events and to official functions in other cities. They are asked to speak or to officiate at civic

TABLE 4.1   The Council Is Effectively Screened from Any But Routine
            Decision Requirements

	Treated Routinely	Treated Nonroutinely*	Totals
	Cabaret Licensing Decision January 1962 – November 1970		
Upheld	14	1	
Overturned	0	1	
Deferred	0	0	16
	Municipal Code Decision October 1963 – June 1971**		
Upheld	19	1	
Overturned	0	0	
Deferred	4	0	24
	Street and Engineering Decision June 1962 – June 1972**		
Upheld	102	2	
Overturned	2	0	
Deferred	2	3	111

SOURCE: City of Oakland, Council minutes.
*Nonroutine treatment is defined as any discussion, debate, or dissension by the Council surrounding a proposal being considered.
**Slight difference in time periods due to limited availability of records.

occasions and in clubs throughout the city. They meet those in the city who are business or professional leaders, active in civic affairs, and socially prominent. The councilmen come in contact with and are treated as prominent citizens by officials who come to Oakland and by those in other cities or countries. A councilman may visit as an official representative of the city. Most seem to be serving for the added community status and these few perquisites.

In summary, most of Oakland's councilmen have not aspired to higher public office excepting, perhaps, that of Mayor. Oakland's council seats have been filled by men who, like most of us, do not have more then a momentary ambition to shape public events. But, it is possible that those of us who do not share such ambitions find it more difficult to act decisively when confronted with nonroutine, unsettling situations.

Oakland's Council, because they are primarily businessmen, has been and remains more attuned to and in sympathy with Oakland's business community. Thus, the councilmen are more concerned about such governmental problems as costs, revenues, administrative efficiency, and operating rules that are clearly related to their vocational experience. One councilman stated the prevailing attitude very succinctly when he said,

> We are like a board of directors—the mayor is essentially a president of a corporation, a large corporation, and we meet with him and settle things like a board of directors.[12]

When asked which groups, if any, were active in problem areas of concern to the Council and appeared before the Council in formal session: Six of seven councilmen interviewed named at least one business association and two of seven named only business associations; three of seven also listed prominent service clubs like Rotary, Kiwanis, and the like, and one of seven listed a neighborhood improvement association in addition to business and service groups. Of the seven, one named only a neighborhood improvement association.[13]

When asked to name persons whose opinions, in general, are important in Council decisions, the responses were similar: Two of seven named people from the business sector in their first three choices; four of seven named two people from the business sector in their first three choices, and one of the seven replied that no one was influential.[14]

Tax rates and the manager's budget are the Council's foremost considerations. After these, the local economy and the physical development/redevelopment of the city are continuing problems that have been important to recent councils. They are also interested in reducing unemployment and stimulating business activity, particularly in the downtown area. In the councilmen's minds, these problems are inextricably intertwined. Thus, they are usually receptive to proposals that are intended to make Oakland more attractive to new business and/or will stimulate the existing business community.

The Council is also more than usually attentive to the taxpaying property owner. In short, the council members' experience, perspectives, and acquaintance networks make it likely that certain persons and/or types of proposals will get a sympathetic hearing and will stimulate action more quickly than others. It seems that the Council tends to look on the problems of government as similar to and quite often a part of the problems of the city's business community.

The cabaret licensing controversies that reached the Council were among the more actively contested issues in the period covered by Table 4.1. Each occurrence brought unusual numbers of partisans, property owners, and businessmen of the Council Chamber. Several divergent points of view were widely and vociferously represented by advocates of a neighborhood's business community, those who advocate a quiet neighborhood free from noisy bars, those who fear increased risk of crime and diminishing property values, and those who anticipate increased property value.

The questions that reached the Council concerning the Streets and Engineering Department functions, though usually treated routinely, should not be quickly cast aside as trivial. The appeals that required Council approval largely concerned physical alteration that affected groups of people: A street is widened, and a once quiet neighborhood will be inundated with volumes of traffic, and a once thriving business area will be slowly starved. Winter rains have washed out a major access street, and some people can no longer drive to their homes. Sewer service is extended or improved, and a sewer service charge is levied on the neighborhood residents who are mostly elderly, retired persons on fixed incomes. Obviously city actions on such matters will not appear trivial to those affected. Fully 20% of the Streets and Engineering proposals treated by the Council in the period covered by Table 4.1 were accompanied by comments from people on the chamber floor and usually affected property owners and neighborhood businessmen.

In contrast, proposed changes in the Municipal Code that might reasonably be expected to stimulate considerable community interest, participation, and comment have not done so. The 24 proposed amendments that reached the Council from October 1963 through June 1971 were neither supported nor repudiated by any residents, and only one Council discussion occurred in the Council chamber; 4 were deferred at the request of the city manager. It is not completely clear why questions regarding the granting of cabaret permits or altering streets activate pockets of sentiment whereas changes in the Code, such as prohibiting automobile washing, repairing, and storage on city streets, do not. Perhaps it is the less neighborhood specific, more citywide, flavor of proposed alterations in the Code that discourage activity. However, the foregoing example suggests that code changes often affect certain specific populations more than others. Still the record indicates that proposed alterations in the Municipal Code, at least in the 1960s, did not stimulate citizen activity.

In view of the limitations on Oakland's Council suggested above, institutional screening processes that admit only refined, essential questions and minimum controversy are sensible, perhaps essential. But such insulated institutional arrangements and decision patterns have become largely accepted by councilmen, administrative staff, and citizenry as the only proper approach to local governance and subsequent provision of public services.

Operating primarily as approving bodies, several stages removed from active intervention in shaping or guiding city programs, many cities' councils have been quietly stable and largely invisible to their respective communities. Again, Oakland's Council is no exception; in the 1960s, 9 of the 17 first-term councilmen were appointed to office; 29 of 34 election winners were incumbents, 12 of them ran unopposed (Pressman, 1971). Such a record indicates stability and low visibility. According to a one-month study, little news coverage—about 1.6% of its total news space—is given community institutions by Oakland's major newspaper and turnout for local election is traditionally less than 40% of the registered voters (Silva, 1960: 4). Registered voters compose about 60% of the population. Thus only 25% of Oakland's population even participates in the voting act, not to mention the more active political life of city hall.[15]

It seems that in several respects the Oakland Council is like formal political organizations in American towns and cities.[16] The Council is uncomplicated and fundamentally overtaxed. It is not equipped to treat, and in the past it has not often had to deal with, unfamiliar, nonroutine legislative requirements. The Council must lean heavily on the manager and his professional staff for program definition, alternative formulation, analysis, and operation. Moreover, it is obvious that they must rely even more on the staff when confronted with major changes in existing policies.

It is important to understand that Oakland's Council expects that it should be allowed to deliberate quietly without being bothered by confrontation with members of the community who do not agree with council opinions and/or decisions. In the Council's view, conflict causes delay and is unpleasant, but confrontation is wrong. Confrontation is simply not legitimate in the decision process. Oakland's small weekly newspaper, the *Montclarion,* writes of the Council that "open debate or requests for citizens' views [on issues is] rare." The *Montclarion* reports that the Council contends that this quiet, in-the-shadows style permits "professional problem-solving in a calm atmosphere, untroubled by the passionate claims of litigants." The *Montclarion* (June 10, 1970) concludes that this legislative style "probably could not stand in time of crisis."

The Council does seem to have difficulty when it is forced to deal with passionate litigants. One evening, for example, an unusually large number of residents came to oppose a request that a section of their neighborhood be rezoned from residential to commercial. At the beginning the council was clear among themselves that they supported the request. They did not want to hear the neighborhood speakers opposed to the decision. The Council attempted to suspend their rules enabling citizens to speak. The attempt died in confusion. Many councilmen were obviously becoming increasingly confused as many neighborhood residents spoke in opposition. After considerable "water-muddying" from all participants, the time for voting approached. As the vote was taken, the councilmen were so confused that they voted only 5-4 to approve the rezoning request that had come through the manager's office. Then one particularly confused councilman immediately offered a "compromise" motion, which in effect completely reversed the previous vote. This motion was then voted on immediately and missed passage by one vote.[17] The point is that Oakland's Council does not function comfortably or smoothly when confronted with the unexpected.[18]

Oakland's legislative body is constrained by its structure, the demands placed on it, and the ideological and the cultural preferences of its membership. These constraints reduce its function largely to legitimating or approving routine requests emanating from the city manager and/or his professional staff.[19]

COMMUNITY ACTION ANTIPOVERTY
PROGRAMS IN OAKLAND

Beginning in the early 1960s, this rather stable, complacent political setting was quietly infested by a most unusual kind of federal program. New antipoverty programs that encouraged community participation in the planning and policymaking processes entered Oakland with all the force and drama of a small brook. As the seasons progressed, however, this brook was augmented by frequent, heavy rains generated by an eastern high pressure area and began to swell until, at times, it seemed as though it would inundate the city.

The first community action antipoverty program to enter Oakland, in 1961, was one of the Ford Foundation's "Grey Areas" projects. These projects were conceived by individuals at the Ford Foundation as attempts to reduce urban poverty by direct community action rather than by older, more common physical redevelopment approaches (Marris and Rein, 1967). Ford granted Oakland two million dollars in 1961 for such a program.

President Kennedy decided in 1963 to make an antipoverty program a major part of his request to the Congress in 1964, but by the time the proposal emerged from its gestation in the Budget Bureau, Lyndon Johnson had become President. The Budget director, supported by CEA economist Walter Heller, sold this proposal to President Johnson (Sundquist, 1968: 138). This new idea of community was never fully grasped by President Johnson or his advisors. The Budget Bureau had left the impression that the agencies would be set up by the local governments. This would increase local executives' stake in the program, thus, garnering their support.[20] Similarly, when this proposal—which was incorporated into Title II of the Economic Opportunity Act— passed Congress in 1964, the congressmen did not comprehend the ideas or implications of community action. They completely ignored the "maximum feasible participation" clause because the provision that community action plans must be developed and conducted with the maximum feasible participation of the residents and members of groups affected by the program generated congressional confusion and ill-feeling (Moynihan, 1970: ch. 5).

This community action program (CAP), administered by the Office of Economic Opportunity (OEO), was not the only large, federally engendered poverty program to find its way to Oakland. On the heels of the Ford Project came the concentrated employment program (CEP) administered by the Department of Labor.[21] Regional offices of the Labor Department were assigned formal responsibility for local CEP funds, but federal policy favored designation of the local community action agencies as "prime contractors" for CEP funds. In other words, the local CAP agency was the de facto administrator of these funds. The concentrated employment funds added considerably to the financial and overall strength of the community action program (CAP) in Oakland. The Office of Economic Opportunity granted Oakland's community action agency approximately two million dollars per year; the CEP funds raised this total to approximately 10 million dollars per year. Thus, a substantial amount of money was entering Oakland for which expenditure decisions were to be made with the maximum feasible participation of the poor.[22] These federally designed and funded programs, Concentrated Employment and Community Action, were unusual approaches to the solution of urban problems. The following analysis of the Oakland City Council will focus on the Council's adaptation to this externally generated program set.[23] The fact that unresolved confusion existed regarding this kind of antipoverty program indicates that the recipient municipalities would be particularly likely to suffer from varying and oft-changed federal, state, and regional interpretations of the program's purpose, intentions, and basic guidelines. Obviously, local administration of such a program would be fraught with frustration and uncertainty. Thus, this particular municipal experience offered an unusual opportunity to observe elected representatives reacting and adapting to a nonroutine predicament that persisted over a period of many years, generated serious ideological conflict, involved a considerable amount of money, and affected many people in the community.

INITIAL COUNCIL RESPONSE TO
A NEW ANTIPOVERTY PROGRAM

December 1961 the Council created, at the request of City Manager Wayne Thompson, the Interagency Community Projects Division (*Montclarion*, June 10, 1970).[24] This new agency was to be a staff agency under the Manager; its central purpose was to receive and disburse the Ford Foundation Grey Areas funds. The agency's staff was funded entirely by the Ford grants, and their offices were located away from city hall. The agency staff was supported by a 15-member citizens *advisory* committee.

Although no measurable city resources were invested in the Interagency Division, the Council retained approval power over all its requests. They were submitted to the city manager before they were passed on to the Council. At this point the community action program in Oakland was new, small, controlled from city hall, and it served an apathetic ghetto population. Despite this program's unusual promise of direct services to poor residents, the first wave of community action programs was hardly noticed by the Council. The Grey Areas program was quickly integrated into the manager/council supervisorial and decision-making routines common to other city programs. In other words, this program set progressed smoothly and quietly through its first two or three years in Oakland.

However, less than three years after the Ford grants to Oakland, growing numbers of federally sponsored development or antipoverty programs in the community were causing concern among the city's elected officials. In late 1964, Mayor John Houlihan had become worried enough about the city's ability to supervise these programs that he proposed drawing these programs together into an *Industrial* Development Commission.[25] Houlihan declared during a public council meeting that he was afraid of confusion and disorganization with many different poverty programs from many different sources: DOL, HUD, OEO, and EDA all sponsored programs in Oakland.

Houlihan was quite clear that the Council must not lose its ultimate control over these programs, despite the growing burden these programs were placing on it. The records indicate that the other councilmen shared the mayor's concern about the growing complexity of the federally funded antipoverty program set in Oakland.

Table 4.2 compares the items reaching the Council regarding the community action antipoverty program to those related to a more typical important program area, streets and engineering. This comparison demonstrates that though the Council workloads generated by these two program areas in 1963-1964 were approximately equivalent—S&E = 11, A/P = 10—three years later, in 1966-1967, workloads generated by streets and engineering had remained essentially stable though decreasing a little, whereas the community action program was requiring exponentially greater Council attention.

Table 4.2 clearly suggests that the Council's increased anxiety regarding complexity and control was not entirely misplaced. It was beginning to look as though they had good reason for concern.

Mayor Houlihan's proposal, enthusiastically supported by the Council, that Oakland's antipoverty program—presumably encouraging maximum feasible participation by the poor—should be cast in terms of *industrial* development suggests that Oakland's approach to the eradication of urban poverty was ideologically not the same as those who developed and guided the idea of community action at the federal level. The Council's growing organizational concerns notwithstanding, part of the reason for establishing an Industrial Development Board was to enable Oakland to qualify for, receive, and disburse approximately 1.8 million dollars per year Title II, OEO community action grants.[26] Ironically, the proposed Industrial Development Commission, though

TABLE 4.2   Council Workload Comparisons[a]

Year	Poverty Program Items/Meetings	% >	Streets/Engineering Items/Meetings	% >
1964-1965	55 / 33	400+	7 / 7	40
1965-1966	106 / 55	90+	7 / 7	-0-
1966-1967	108 / 58	-0-	5 / 5	-30
1968 ---------------- OEDC Becomes Independent --------------------				

a. Average meetings/year = 85 in this time period.

enthusiastically received, was to develop slowly and never to serve as a conduit for Title II grants. Rather, the Interagency Projects Division and its citizens advisory committee had been quietly planning and working to become the OEO conduit. Before the Economic Opportunity Act had passed Congress, the city manager had requested the Interagency Division Director and his staff prepare a "Community action" proposal.[27] In the process of designing this proposal, the Interagency's Projects staff consulted with leaders of several black and Chicano organizations as well as the 15-member citizens' advisory committee. The resultant community action proposal was approved by the city manager, the mayor, and the Council, and submitted to Washington where it was approved in late 1964. Thus, Oakland became one of the first cities to receive grants under the new Economic Opportunity Act. But the city did not seem quite prepared for such ready approval; its proposed Industrial Development Board was not sufficiently developed to qualify for receipt of these funds.

It was apparent that existing organizations would have to be used, in modified form, in order to qualify for the OEO grants. The 15-member citizens' advisory committee to the Interagency Projects Division was the only existing body that qualified as an organization that encouraged community participation in the administration of antipoverty programs. The mayor with Council approval appointed additional minority representatives, and this expanded committee became the 29-member Oakland Economic Development Council (OEDC).

At the same time, the city manager expanded the Division staff, and Dr. Norvel Smith, director of the Division, was appointed to direct the "new" Human Resources Department (DHR). The first meeting to the newly organized OEDC was called, in December 1964, by the Mayor acting as President Pro-tem. The character of the first meeting foreshadowed the later difficulties that the Council and the "representatives of the poor" would have with one another. Questions regarding who was to have authority over program and/or budgeting decisions were of central concern (Kramer, 1969: 110). The functions and authorities of the respective bodies were not clear to the participants, because OEO guidelines were sparse, too general, and unclear.

When the OEO sponsored community action program began in Oakland, the Council clearly did not intend or suspect that "community participation" would affect its traditional relationship vis-à-vis city programs, in short, its prerogatives to approve program form, substance, and/or funding priorities. In the beginning, the Council's interactions with the new OEO and Labor programs did not deviate from their previous interaction patterns with the Ford Foundation supported Grey Areas Projects. In fact, the records indicate that the Council, led by Mayor Houlihan, regarded these new federally supported antipoverty programs simply as expansions of the Ford Program. The OEDC membership, like that of its parent citizens' advisory committee, was a composite of leaders from well-known minority organizations such as the NAACP and prominent professional citizens in the community who happened to belong to an ethnic minority. So, too, the staff of the "new" HRD were, for the most part, well acquainted with the routines and preferences of the city manager and the Council.

True, a considerable amount of ambiguity existed, ambiguity magnified to an unusual degree by that confusing phrase in the OEO Legislation stating there shall be maximum feasible participation of the residents of the areas and members of groups. Still, in the first months of the OEO community action program's life, it is apparent that the Council did not anticipate the difficulties that could be raised for local officials by this community participation mandate. On the contrary, this early period was a congenial one in part because the OEO had not yet disseminated guidelines to ensure participation of the poor in the decision process.

In April, 1965, OEO's regional office in San Francisco declared that one representative from each designated target area should be included on the OEDC. Just before this pronouncement, the DHR staff had been attempting to convene meetings in target area neighborhoods so as to facilitate consultation with small advisory groups in each target neighborhood by the OEDC (Kramer, 1969: 111). Until the April OEO directive, however, there was little indication that the OEDC membership intended to invite representatives from the target areas to join them as *voting members.*

When the OEDC received OEO's directive concerning community representation, Superior Court Judge Lionel Wilson had replaced Mayor Houlihan as president of the OEDC. Judge Wilson, responding to this pressure, accepted a Human Resources Department recommendation that the newly forming target area advisory committees choose and screen two more certified poor from each target neighborhood for inclusion on the OEDC.

The formation of neighborhood advisory committees coincided with a change in relationships among participants in this program from one of passive congeniality to one of strain. This change was to have considerable impact on the Council but, at this point in the Summer of 1965, OEDC/DHR and the target area committees were essentially the only program participants affected. It was some time before the Council's routines were disrupted by divisive issues, questions, and proposals.

COMMUNITY ACTION DISRUPTS THE
COUNCIL'S SCREENING PROCESSES

Most target-area advisory committees had difficulty simply finding enough interested neighborhood residents to fill out the 25- to 30-member committees. Moreover, there did not seem to be a clear pattern of expectations among those who were "elected" to these committees.[28] It seems likely that the full panoply of familiar self-interested or altruistic, and ideological reasons for joining existed among the target committees' membership (Kramer, 1969: 115-116). It is clear, however, that they had from the first an activist orientation toward their role in the OEDC and its programs. The leadership of the OEDC and the director of the DHR had intended an advisory role for these committees and did not welcome this activist perspective. As a result, the relationships between OEDC/DHR and the target-area committees were strained from the first.

The target-area committees felt that maximum feasible participation meant that they should have control over the OEO community action funds in Oakland and should make decisions about who should get what for what purpose. The OEDC, at this time in 1965, believed its role to be that of recommending needed services that could be established or improved in the target neighborhoods with community action funds. It was understood that the final responsibility for decision rested with the Council and administrative oversight with the city manager and his DHR staff. The OEDC's role fit perfectly with the Council's traditional function in the city's policymaking administrative processes; that desired by the target-area committees did not. No Council is likely to be comfortable yielding its authority over a public program to another group in the community. Nevertheless, the OEDC and the DHR moved a considerable distance to accommodate the target-area committees.[29]

After the OEO directive regarding neighborhood representation, the target-area action committees (TAAC) were allowed to select delegates to sit as voting members on the OEDC. A short time later the OEDC Executive Committee reluctantly expanded to include one representative from each TAAC.[30] But these accommodations by the OEDC/DHR resulted in increased rather than decreased tensions between the TAACs and the OEDC/DHR.

After they had established some intercommunications via their representatives on the antipoverty board, the TAACs met together and agreed that TAAC members should

(1) constitute 50% of the OEDC and of the Executive Committee;
(2) review and *approve* all OEDC programs;
(3) review and *approve* each request for services;
(4) *approve* all reports forwarded to OEO;
(5) be granted advise and consent privilege regarding DHR staff employment; and
(6) have final authority over the DHR staff.[31]

The position statement that outlined these demands clearly indicates that the TAACs who had changed their names from advisory to action committees wanted considerably more power at the expense of OEDC and the DHR. Increasingly the target-area revisionists viewed the OEDC and DHR as "city hall," clearly felt that "city hall" had no feeling for the problems of the poor, and would be unlikely to allocate poverty funds in the best interest of "the poor."

On the other side Kramer reports that the DHR/OEDC were cynical regarding the TAAC members' altruistic motives. Many of them regarded the TAAC as *unrepresentative* (Kramer, 1969: ch. 4). For example, one target neighborhood that was known to have a substantial Spanish surname population did not have a single such representative on its TAAC.

The Council, by this time, was beginning to receive some indications that the federally sponsored, community action programs were becoming more than simply routine, city-administered services. First, Table 4.2 above indicates, by late 1965, the Council was receiving rapidly increasing numbers of items generated by this program set. The requirements and/or requests from it were becoming the most frequently recurring item on the Council agenda.

Second, in December 1965 the first disruptive request from the poverty agencies penetrated the Council's screening system. The Human Resources Department, supported by the OECD, had forwarded a request that the Council authorize an expenditure of $1,500 to enable the DHR to publish a news bulletin that would publicize DHR services and views.[32] This was the first instance of an unusual or unexpected request, initiated by the community action antipoverty agencies, appearing on the Council's agenda. The Council's first response was surprise, suspicion, and *no*! However, before a final vote was counted, the DHR director persuaded the mayor that the Council should wait for a more complete report before voting. The question was rescheduled for the following week. At this next meeting, the Council was still not sure about supporting the idea despite a soothing, calming description of the intended style and purpose of the newssheet. The vote was delayed again. At the following meeting the DHR director, Norvel Smith, succeeding in calming council fears sufficiently that the enabling authorization for $1,500 was approved.

The Council's first response was produced by their belief that the proposed plan was to publish, with public funds, an editorializing newspaper. They did not view the purpose of the antipoverty program to be one of providing social and political "education" so they rejected the proposal. The DHR director argued that the DHR did not intend to editorialize but that they proposed simply to more broadly publicize their services and to educate target-area residents about them. The Council wavered after the director's plea but they were still wary of the "educative" aspect of the bulletin, so they delayed the question. The Director continued to press and, several weeks later, the Council reluctantly acquiesced. But the OEDC was perturbed that the Council had, for the first time, nearly rejected a proposal that was, from their point of view, needed, inexpensive, and legitimate. When tested, it seems that the OEDC position was not so divergent from that of the TAAC's in that they were beginning to question the Council's right to reject their "legitimate" requests.

This episode over the OEDC's news bulletin also marked the beginning of a visible change in the Council's attitude toward and treatment of the community action antipoverty program in Oakland. Just a few weeks after the news sheet question, the mayor spoke at length during a Council meeting, warning of militancy emerging in target-area neighborhoods and of the increasing attempts to "bypass city hall."[33] Moreover, the Council was beginning to question other DHR/OEDC requests rather than wordlessly approving all their recommendations as they had in the past. It also started requiring the Human Resources Department to issue a quarterly report indicating how much industry was being attracted to Oakland by the antipoverty funds. The Council held on to its conviction that unemployment can be reduced only by attracting industry.[34]

In the Spring of 1966, the Council was again disquieted by the activities of the antipoverty board when they began to hear there was a growing movement prompted by some TAAC activists to attract radical poverty organizer Saul Alinsky to Oakland. The Council membership associated Alinsky with militant activism, increasing strife, and risk of confrontation. Newly appointed Mayor John Reading in his first mayoral address appealed to activists not to create more "hate and anger and divisiveness" by bringing Alinsky to Oakland.[35]

The growing conflict between the Council and OEDC culminated in the fight over a community-proposed, OEDC-supported citizens' police review board—the most important factor contributing to the dissolution of the former traditional, passive, and buffered relationship between the Council and the community action agencies. The OEDC proposed to the Council, in the form of a request to the Ford Foundation for the necessary funding, that the OEDC supervise the establishment of a community-based police review board. The Council's, the manager's, and the Police Department's immediate reaction was very negative. In the ensuing months they became unalterably opposed to the idea of such a board, whereas OEDC seemed equally determined to establish it.[36] It is not surprising that as the strain between the OEDC and the Council increased, antagonisms between the OEDC/DHR and the TAACs diminished markedly.

Reading, the new mayor, attempted to smooth and restore the deteriorating relationship. He proposed that a committee be established that would be composed of representatives from the Council, the Police Department, and the OEDC. The committee was to find a compromise to the review board proposal acceptable to all parties. Both the Council and the OEDC agreed to the idea of a compromise. But, before the OEDC would agree to negotiate, they stipulated that the Council must pass a resolution that admitted the need for some action regarding law enforcement in Oakland. The Council was most reluctant to meet the OEDC's stipulation, but after several false starts that resulted in considerable delay, the Council, under sustained mayoral pressure, passed a resolution that was acceptable to the OEDC (Kramer, 1969: 136-142).

While a negotiating committee was forming, the OEDC submitted— to Ford directly without getting Council approval—the application requesting funding for a citizens' review board. Of course the city manager, who did not know that OEDC had submitted it to Ford, was holding OEDC's request for city ratification on his desk. He knew that the Council did not want to see it, and was, therefore, simply performing his normal screening function. Somehow the Council learned the OEDC had submitted the request and they were outraged.[37]

At this point the attempts to form a compromise committee were nearly abandoned. The Council declared publicly that it would veto any grant from the Ford Foundation whose purpose was to establish a "private review board."[38] Still, the Ford Foundation granted the OEDC the requisite funds. The Council, however, would not allow release of the Ford funds to the OEDC. The OEDC maintained, supported by a legal opinion prepared by the Legal Aid Society, that the Council had no power to withhold these funds. The Council relied on the opinion of the city attorney that the Council was trustee for all funds intended for the OEDC (Kramer, 1969: ch. 4). The OEDC and Council remained stalemated over this issue through 1966 and 1967, growing generally more antagonistic toward one another. In 1967 the OEDC began exploring the possibility of becoming an independent, nonprofit corporation in order to remove itself from the Council's veto power.

THE COUNCIL'S BUFFERING ROUTINES
BREAK DOWN

After the police review board controversy began, the Council became increasingly hostile, ambivalent, and confused in its interaction with the Office of Economic Opportunity and OEO supported agencies in Oakland. Vituperative confrontations occurred between antipoverty leaders and spokesmen both in Council chambers and out. The Council was provoked by OEO representatives and certain minority community leaders who, under the rubric of community participation, encouraged and abetted OEDC activities that did not have Council approval. By 1967 it is apparent that the Council's comfortable, routinized, noncontroversial relationships with target-area representatives had been severely crippled. In one Council meeting, a dissident spokesman berated the Council for not actively encouraging greater minority participation in these antipoverty programs, and Mayor Reading heatedly retorted that although there was a *small* group in Oakland that could not be satisfied, many people of "good will" were contributing time, money, and effort to "cure the evils of poverty."[39]

The Council increasingly tended to adhere to a conspiracy theory during this period of strain and controversy between itself and an increasingly active, informed, and vocal sector of Oakland's economically deprived minority population. The mayor often remarked about the "second government in Oakland" supported by federal monies.[40] When the Council began to suspect that there was a second government forming in Oakland, a government that intended to thwart council prerogatives, it is clear that for them the community action, antipoverty programs were no longer distant activities, providing services in ways that met council expectations and thus, requiring little or no Council attention to the details of program administration.

The Council, increasingly suspicious of OEDC activities in general, was particularly concerned about the influence and activities of the neighborhood TAACs. Responding to these growing misgivings, the Council took clear steps to increase its immediate information about and control over OEDC/DHR activities. For a first step, the Council removed the community action programs research and evaluation activities from the Department of Human Resources to the city manager's immediate staff. For another, because the regional OEO representatives were suspected of conspiring with the OEDC/DHR to deceive and thwart the Council, the mayor wrote to OEO in Washington requesting the OEO channel *all* administrative information through the city manager.[41] Finally, the Council in calendar 1967 devoted three long work sessions to the community action antipoverty programs in Oakland. There had been no such meetings devoted solely to the community action antipoverty programs before 1967. Moreover, it is difficult to imagine, given the usual councilmanic behavior in Oakland up to this time, that the fact of a rapidly expanding program set alone could account for such uncommon intrusion into a program's operation. Rather, such actions suggest that the Council's usual screened, routinized interaction patterns had been seriously disrupted by a few target-area residents claiming a large potential "poor" following, federal government authority, and attempting to expand "participation" to include control over the distribution of community action funds.

Further indication of the Council's altered decision style vis-à-vis the OEDC/DHR is provided in Table 4.3. This table includes only those items that required an approving or disapproving vote by the Council. It does not include position statements or general business regarding "what should be done" not put in the form of a specific request before the Council. The columns labeled Routine and Nonroutine represent the author's judgment about the type of issue before the Council. Quite simply, those issues that commonly appeared on the Council agenda, and/or issues that were clearly implied by a prior decision are listed in the Routine column. The majority of the items requiring routine action were lease agreements/extensions, contract renewals, shifting funds internally from one account to another and so on.

The Nonroutine column label includes expenditure of city rather than federal or foundation monies for antipoverty projects, establishing or accepting new programs, setting new directions in an existing program, approving civil service exemptions, and so on.

The rows labeled "Routinely" and "Nonroutinely" represent the Council's behavior toward a request. If there was discussion beyond one or two innocuous comments, if there was discussion from the floor, if there were dissenting votes, or if the Council delayed vote, the decision was considered to have been handled Nonroutinely. Despite this rather permissive definition of nonroutine behavior, Table 4.3 indicates that the majority of the Council's formal actions regarding the antipoverty program were treated routinely. This is not surprising given the characterization of the Council outlined above. The Council simply does not want its formal, public meetings lengthened, confused, and made painful by the presence of serious controversies. Thus, the Council employs most of its resources available for screening to enable it to decide issues before Council meeting. Even the turbulence surrounding the community action antipoverty programs in 1966 and 1967 could not completely break this pattern.

The council becomes ambivalent. As the OEDC/DHR and the TAACs grew more cohesive and more vociferously anti-city hall, the Council grew increasingly concerned about the community action

TABLE 4.3 Nonroutine Decision Behavior Regarding Community Action
Programs Substantially Increases as Council's Traditional
Coping Mechanisms Begin to Break Down

	R	NR	Total
January 1962 – December 1963			
Rly	8	2	10
NRly	0	0	0
Total	8	2	10
January 1964 – December 1965*			
Rly	42	13	55
NRly	0	2	2
Total	42	15	57
January 1966 – December 1967			
Period of Maximum Council Involvement and Greatest Strain			
Rly	109	7	116
NRly	8	9	17
Total	117	16	133
January 1968 – December 1969**			
Rly	24	3	27
NRly	1	3	4
Total	25	6	31
January 1970 – December 1971			
Rly	17	10	27
NRly	1	6	7
Total	18	16	34

*OEO supported community action programs begin in this period.
**OEDC separates from the city in this period.
NR = Nonroutine. These are unusual expenditures of city funds, establishing of city funds, establishing or accepting new programs, setting new directions in existing programs, first-time Civil Service exemptions (but not exemption extensions and the like).
R = Routine. These are common decisions such as shifting funds, approving standard contracts and contract renewals, common staff appointments, lease agreements, and so on. Several such decisions might follow a single nonroutine decision.

Row Labels – Council Response

Rly = Routinely. These are requests and/or proposals passed without comment or apparent hesitation. It must be noted that these are conservative figures because much of the Council's decision behavior does not occur in their formal meetings and, therefore, the public record.
NRly = Nonroutinely. Conflictual, divisive, and/or dissenting discussion among Council members and/or between Council and floor. Any less than unanimous vote.

antipoverty programs. On one hand they wanted the federal money and they did not want Oakland to be riddled by open guerilla warfare as other cities such as Detroit and Los Angeles had been. Moreover, the Council did not want to yield its jealously protected veto-power over the programs.

On the other hand, the community action programs were becoming increasingly disruptive to their public lives; it was becoming painfully difficult for the Council to control the obstreperous OEO-supported, antipoverty organizations. Thus they also were inclined to let the programs go in order to relieve themselves of a difficult and painful problem. The Council seemed nearly balanced in its contradictory desires to retain authority over the community action programs and to get rid of the entire nest of problems. The Council wavered in this ambivalent state for many months, taking no action to resolve their predicament.

Actually, the Council seemed unable to invent alternatives that might generate palatable results. A workable compromise like the "dual green light" system developed by the model cities citizens' board was apparently never considered.[42] They became uncertain of any action and, consequently, they delayed. As the Council postponed action, their sense of uncertainty about the consequences of action increased and reinforced reluctance to act.

We might surmise that a council could have actively encouraged participation, neighborhood organization, in short, involvement in all phases of the programs' evolution in the community. Such a council might have regarded these federally supported programs as unprecedented opportunities to build active neighborhood organizations that could help dispense public goods and services that always seem to be undersupplied in our urban centers. This program could also be welcomed because it would be an opportunity to increase awareness and understanding of the community's public institutions, their limitations and possibilities among a segment of the population most needful of such an education. In other words, a council could have encouraged the development of politically under-educated citizens into more effective and committed advocates. Moreover, this kind of a council would be likely to support the idea of a police review board in the belief that shared power increases insight, understanding, and a sense of responsibility. They would not struggle to avoid conflict but would accept the storm in the hope that the seeds of a more aware, more cohesive, more responsible community could be planted.

But, though it can be helpful to outline such fanciful alternatives, the fact is we know of no city that received funds for the community action program and encountered community participation on a broad scale that was judged successful by the federal government, the city's government, or the target-area residents. The problems generated by the programs were not simple or easily avoided; values were not shared and each faction was hostile toward the others. We cannot reasonably expect that those sitting in city hall could have evaded difficulties that simply were not foreseen by the architects of the program, the Congress, or the President's office.

The OEDC moves to resolve the stalemate. The OEDC, after several months of frustration engendered by an ambivalent but hostile Council, voted unanimously to sever its relationship with the city. They resolved to become an independent, nonprofit corporation. The Council publicly declared that it opposed such a move.[43] Nevertheless, the Council began behaving as though the OEDC resolution had been the last word on the subject, and they had no part in determining whether the OEDC, as an independent organization, could become the authorized recipient of the OEO/CEP antipoverty grants.[44] This is not to say that the Council's ambivalence was immediately dissipated by the OEDC decision. Rather, they hedged, bucked, and delayed the final severance for several months.[45] In retrospect, it is clear that the Council took the path of least resistance. That is, being forced to choose, the Council's decision reflected that they preferred withdrawing from a painful situation to retaining authority.

Until the last possible moment, the Council acted as if its wishes were irrelevant because the OEDC and OEO could design an antipoverty program for Oakland that was not subject to its approval.[46] This simply was not true; when the separation was at last officially complete, in May 1968, the Council was required to formally resolve and officially notify the OEO that the OEDC (now the Oakland Economic Development Council Incorporated; OEDCI) had been designated Oakland's Community Action Agency by the Council. The Council did so resolve at a Council meeting on May 28, 1968. They also officially notified the OEO by filing a CAP (Community Action Program) Form #74 requesting that the OEO accept the OEDCI as a qualified recipient organization for community action grants.

Although these problems of separation were being slowly and painfully worked out by the actors involved, the Council sometimes vented its frustration by being less than cooperative about questions, requests, or individuals associated with the community action programs. For example, on November 2, 1967, a purely routine request for approval of an OEDC lease renewal was on the Council's agenda. The Council had wordlessly, routinely approved this kind of request literally dozens of times before, yet the members needlessly deferred voting on it for two weeks. The following is the essence of their response:

Councilman A: OEDC?

Councilman B: Does that (request) come under OEDC?

Councilman C: ... is there any reason this had to be voted on today? I don't like to have to vote on these things when I look at them for the first time.

City Manager: The existing lease expired yesterday.

Councilman B: I move that it be postponed for two weeks ...

Councilman A: Second.

Councilman B: I don't like these things coming up at the last minute ...

Councilman D: I don't think it is necessary to postpone it for two weeks.

Councilman A: Make it three.

Councilman D: One week would be plenty.

Councilman B: I change that to four (weeks) ...

Councilman C: I'll second the four weeks.

Councilman D: This is right in line with our other leases.

Councilman C: My feeling is that the matter could be continued at the next regular meeting of the Council. . . . There is a motion to continue this matter for one week.

Councilman B: That was not the motion ...

Councilman C: The only motion that was seconded was one week.

Councilman A: The motion that was seconded was two weeks.

Councilman C: Any discussion?

Councilman D: ... I don't think we need two weeks. . . . It is an ordinary renewal.

Councilman A: Connected with the OEDC.

Councilman C: Any further discussion?

Councilman E: ... I'll go along with (Councilman D) on this ...

Councilman B: How long is the lease for?

Councilmen E: Month by month.

Councilman D: Just the same as the others . . . as we have had before.

Councilman A: It is still OEDC.

Councilman D: We shouldn't penalize OEDC just because we have some feeling about it.

Councilman C: From the OEDC letter of request . . . the agreement permits the use of the premises at $800.00/month. . . . I don't know whether it is a month to month basis for one year or a lease for one year.

Councilman B: $800.00?

Councilman A: How big a building is this?

Councilman A: Let the new corporation take over.

Councilman B: . . . I'll go along for a week . . . but I'd like to find out the building that they are in . . . $800.00/month; that should be a $100,000.00 building.

Councilman C: I wouldn't have any idea. . . .

Councilman A: Well let's have that further information.

Councilman D: I am not concerned about its square footage I am concerned about its function and its relationship to the community.

Councilman A: I am concerned about the taxpayer's money.

Councilman C: All right, if it is agreeable . . . this matter (will) be continued . . . for one week).

MOTION PASSED UNANIMOUSLY

THE INDEPENDENT POVERTY PROGRAM

A drawn-out, strained procedure, official separation of OEDC from city hall occurred on May 8, 1968. OEDCI was now designated as Oakland's Community Action Agency. It also had been successful in hiring a staff director who the city manager, the mayor, and the councilmen actively disapproved of because they were afraid of his reputation as an activist-organizer. OEO regulation required that the newly independent poverty board be composed of approximately one-third representation from the public sector. In Oakland, this was interpreted to mean that any mayoral appointment could be a public sector representative.[47] Thus, the OEDCI was still tied to city hall, though the Council no longer served as a routine approving body for

OEDC proposals. But because OEO could grant funds only to an organization that had been officially designated by the Council, the Council remained the sanctioning authority. Furthermore, it could, in theory, remove that designation simply by holding a public hearing for the purpose of removing their sanction from OEDCI.

After the Council had formally released the community action programs, the antipoverty movement fell heir to debilitating intraorganizational strife like that which plagued the ASUO leadership in the foregoing chapter. In a sense, this was perhaps the most sophisticated in a long series of tactics adopted by the Council in its experiences with the community action programs.

When its standard, business as usual buffering routines were no longer adequate, the Council moved to increase its information about and immediate control over the programs. But this centralizing tactic moved the Council to the center of community discontent, and it became a convenient lightning rod. Then the Council members wanted to rid themselves of the community action problems but naturally delayed such a big step. Delay was painful and not especially useful in this case because the Council continued to be the target of the antipoverty organizations' leadership though the Council was not effectively using the delay to search for creative alternatives. Delay may have been an effective tactic in the case of the School Board and the ASUO because the student organization was very unstable but the community action spokesmen, largely supported by OEO monies, had considerably more staying power.

Thus the Council's decision to let the programs become independent was tactically sound. And as soon as the Council removed itself from oversight responsibility, they fell to quarreling among themselves once again and were much less effective against city hall or in the target communities.

Controversies between the OEDCI, the staff, and the TAACs flared over ethnic and economic representation. As in the case of the ASUO, conflict grew between moderate neighborhood activists who believed that the essential purpose of an antipoverty program was to provide needed services for those who would not otherwise have them and the more militant who believed that providing services would not go very far toward curing the complicated cultural phenomenon of poverty. Those who adhered to the latter position advocated employing the grants in part to educate poor citizens to use the community's political institutions as an important step in reducing poverty in populations that lack political skills as well as material wealth. These advocates believed that the educative processes that attend interest-group activities could strengthen confidence and ability to act with authority. Those who were opposed to the advocates' position were inclined to see the advocates as militants acting outside the law and, as a consequence, a threat to life, property, and the stability of the community.[48]

Increasingly, controversies swirling around these polar positions split the community action antipoverty activists into warring factions. Of course, the Council was vocally in sympathy with the antiadvocate, proservice faction. In fact, the mayor was a party to more than one attempt to build a majority on the OEDCI in order to have the increasingly disliked, but strong advocate staff director fired. The mayor eventually became so concerned that he required that any potential public sector representative to the OEDCI must pledge a vote to fire the advocate staff director before the Mayor would appoint him or her to the poverty board.[49]

In spite of increasingly intense feelings regarding Oakland's community action antipoverty programs and the mayor's continuing feud with the OEDCI staff director, the Council was not anxious to burden itself again with the work, headaches, and harassment of these programs. Nevertheless, it is clear that the Council did not like the fact that they had no program control over an "unfriendly" public agency that dispersed several million dollars a year in Oakland.

Table 4.4 lists those programs that have been accepted and released by the Council in the past twenty years. Other than the community action antipoverty programs, the programs released were those that were given to the county as part of a more general assumption of such activities by county governments. The one exception is the city's garbage collection arrangement. The city manager, supported by the Council, decided that citywide garbage collection contracted to private companies would remove a headache from the city administration and ease pressures driving the property tax up.[50] The table suggests that new programs that have an active public interface are placed in the city's organizational structure so as to ensure that the Council will be buffered. The buffering sought is roughly proportional to the degree to which programs are interactive; if a program or activity begins attracting a more active constituency, it is relocated in order to increase the protective layers of insulation. Thus the Council's screens are woven from informal as well as formal strands. The "distant" programs in

TABLE 4.4 "Distant" Programs

Council tends to increase organizational "distance" between itself and agencies/programs that are highly interactive with an active constituency

Interactions with Active Constituency

• Health and Welfare*

                                                              • Community Action Programs

                    • Garbage Collection

                          • Human Relations*

RELEASE THRESHOLD

                          • Model Cities   • Reconstituted Community
                                                        Action Programs

                    • Redevelopment

• Organizational   • Interagency Projects

  Distance   • C.A.M.P.S.

              • EDA/Port Projects
              • Urban Renewal Project
          • Public Service Careers Program
          • Council on Criminal Justice

    • Mayor's Manpower Committee

COUNCIL'S POSITION

*Part of a general assumption of such activities by the County Governments in California.

Table 4.4 are not located in the city hall, but the four least distant are headquartered in city hall.[51]

Citizens who interact with programs most removed from city hall must confront citizens councils, agency staffs, department heads, the city manager's immediate staff, and the city manager himself before their problems, requests, and suggestions reach the Council.[52] However, the Council's relationships with those immediately responsible for a program area become more difficult, complicated, and tenuous as the distance increases. The tendency, therefore, is to cultivate more assiduously informal relationships as distance increases. For example, the heads of the model cities and redevelopment programs are well known and trusted by the Council membership and the city manager.

The Council was not willing to take the consequence of directly removing its sanction from the OEDCI, but it welcomed any opportunity to reconstitute the poverty programs to fit the Council's common form, and accordingly supported the mayor as he sought to convince the

OEO that the OEDCI should not be refunded after its first year of independent operation unless the advocate staff director were fired. The OEO responded simply that the Council had officially designated the OEDCI and the Council could withdraw their sanction at any time.

As it turned out however, OEO was reluctant to refund the OEDCI for fiscal 1971, because its program evaluators felt that the OEDCI was not keeping adequate records. The OEDCI had not been able to close its books for fiscal 1969 or 1970; their books were, according to a reputable accountancy firm, not auditable.[53] The funds were conditionally authorized by OEO before the beginning of fiscal 1971 but the Governor, exercising statutory prerogative, vetoed the OEO grant. Naturally the Council was not pleased that OEO decided to fund OEDCI again. Unfortunately, the governor's veto, though clearly applauded by some Council members, did not solve the problem from the Council's point of view. In order for the gubernatorial veto to become more than a delaying mechanism, the Council still must remove its sanction from the OEDCI, an agency that OEO continued to regard as an acceptable receiving and dispersing vehicle for community action funds. If the OEO declared the OEDCI unfit, then the Council's removing its sanction would be largely pro forma, but so long as OEO regarded OEDCI tolerantly the Council would be assured of vociferous confrontations with target-area leaders if it acted to remove its ratification of OEDCI.

Community action program leaders, reacting to the veto, quickly charged the Council with collusion, maintaining that the Council had secretly persuaded the governor to veto OEO's grant. They complained that the Council was attempting secretly to destroy the community action programs while, because the Council had not moved to withdraw its sanction, publicly implying support for the programs. Ironically, these accusations created such a stir, particularly among target-area residents, that, in order to remove themselves as targets, councilmen began working quietly with representatives from the Governor's Office to persuade the reluctant governor to withdraw his veto and enable the OEO grant to proceed. After some negotiation, getting certain assurances and concessions, the governor withdrew his veto.[54]

Relationships between all parties continued to worsen through 1970. The OEDCI did not receive its full grant for fiscal 1971 largely because it was unable to satisfy the OEO that certain conditions attached to the grant renewal—for example, more thorough record keeping and reporting—were being met. Thus, the OEDCI limped along on a sharply reduced budget through the remainder of calendar 1970. By January 1971 it was apparent that the OEDCI was about to run out of money.[55] The OEO finally very reluctantly permitted the OEDCI to spend the funds that had been authorized but not released pending improved OEDCI control/reporting procedures.[56]

By this time, however, the Governor's Office had received a very critical report from its investigating team regarding the activities of Oakland's community action agencies. The governor vetoed the OEO funding authorization and made it clear that he would not yield.[57] The OEO director had the power to override the gubernatorial veto but chose not to do so. The Council was at last forced to hold a hearing to reconstitute the community action programs in Oakland.

The Council, together with the city manager, very carefully selected a committee from among the manager's personal and departmental assistants to reconstitute an administrative staff for the community action programs. The Council quickly decided that it should redesignate itself as the community action agency for Oakland. It was, however, reluctant to schedule the required public hearing; but however much it wanted to avoid the possible acrimony of a public hearing it seems at this point that it wanted the federal millions in Oakland more. So a hearing was finally scheduled for May 18, 1971. The mayor, wary of possible accusation, condemnation, and subsequent confusion, attempted to have the Council chambers filled with citizens, sympathetic to the city's position, and though he was not able to fill the chamber entirely with partisans, it was clearly a predominantly friendly audience that attended the hearing. Although many of the locally prominent antipoverty advocates or activists attended the meeting, it proceeded with remarkable calm. There was little or no tempestuous condemnation from the floor. In fact, the risk of acrimonious disruption was low because the Council appeared in the guise of rescuer. They were saving a large program that would otherwise have been lost to Oakland. Following a remarkably supportive series of spokesmen from a variety of neighborhoods who brought a variety of predispositions regarding the Council and the community action programs, the Council moved quietly and in an orderly manner to reestablish its more traditional control patterns. It may have been that more than two years of meeting stumbling block upon stumbling block in the midst of debilitating factionism and human error had simply drained the enthusiasm, fight, and hope from many who had supported advocacy. Or perhaps the community-action activists had enough of the difficulties growing from self-rule.

The earlier, more comfortable interaction patterns were reestablished. The Council ensured that the city manager was fully in control of the community action programs' administrative staff. The citizens' board was reestablished to advise and to absorb community-based requests, complaints, and controversies. The Council once again maintained its comfortable distance, routinely reviewing and approving well-screened proposals for new projects, changes in existing projects, staff alterations, and expenditure of the federal monies.[58]

COUNCIL RESPONSE TO THE COMMUNITY ACTION ANTIPOVERTY PROGRAMS

As the community action antipoverty programs became more immediate and difficult for the Council, they instinctively employed a series of coping tactics such as centralization, delay, and removing themselves from direct confrontation. Fundamentally, there seem to be two patterns developing that should be reiterated at this point. First, intraorganizational strife may be reduced by focusing on a visible opponent like the school board or Council. Second, the Council removed itself from the antipoverty arena when it could not find another method for coping successfully and moved quickly back to the center when it had the opportunity and the circumstances were more felicitous.

As the target-area action committees grew increasingly active, that activism, physically through their representatives and psychologically through social contact, spread to members of the OEDC and the DHR staff. In a very real sense, certain activists in the target-area neighborhoods co-opted the city administration's antipoverty program. Those who had been partly responsible for buffering the Council from the vicissitudes of community participation were acting to amplify rather than reduce the Council's interactions with dissident constituencies. Table 4.3 suggests that the Council increasingly found itself in belligerent opposition to the community's poor. Spokesmen for the poor were bringing their discontents and hostilities to the chamber floor rather than to the OEDC. The OEDC began to align itself publicly against Council decisions. The Council delayed; the members did not want to relinquish their power over these programs yet they could not seem to adequately control the programs with their traditional institutional devices.

Naturally as the Council's ambivalent state progressed, the members became less willing, in fact less able, to act regarding the community action programs. This strain engendered confusion and hostility among the Council membership. The public records indicate, as do press reports, that during this period of ambivalence the Council tended to hurl hostile accusations against any likely target, such as the federal offices of the OEO, their regional representatives, and community leaders.[59] The tone of the Council reaction suggests that they were angry and frustrated because their preferred, comfortable routines were being so completely disrupted, and they could not reestablish them. And, rather than using the pain to create alternatives, they were, vis-à-vis these programs, immobilized for a time.

Finally, the OEDC, frustrated by the Council's reluctance to act on important questions, voted to become an independent, nonprofit corporation. The Council fell on this move by the OEDC to resolve the unpleasant stalemate. The Council acted as though it had no prerogatives regarding OEDC's decision. This was, of course not true. Nevertheless, the Council agreed to separation and then acted to slow and confound the divorce proceedings. As a result, the OEDC was not officially independent for more than six months after the Council had first acceded to OEDC wishes. This suggests that this tactic, increasing distance by providing for independence, is not easy for a control-oriented body like the Council. Thus, it would seem to be a last resort choice because it is psychologically punishing and does not satisfactorily resolve ambiguities for the established organization. In common language, we are speaking of a tactical withdrawal.

After separation the Council was never able completely to reconcile itself to this undesirable arrangement—that is, that they were no longer able to affect the community action programs without risking a very public controversy. It would have been thoroughly inconsistent for them to move openly to dismantle the independent community action agency, but they maintained, through the period of independence, a willingness to restore their preferred institutional relationships. When the existing community action agency was functionally dismantled by the OEO and the governor, the Council used the opportunity to rebuild a staff and a citizens advisory board that could be trusted to screen and buffer the Council reliably.

The Council was clearly confronted with a difficult decision problem regarding whether to hold the community action programs or to let them go. Their troubles regarding the community action programs were fundamentally ones of conflicting values. On one hand they valued authority, service to constituencies and active problem solving, on the other they prized absence of conflict, simple clear information, clear choices with innocuous secondary consequences—in short, traditional services. But more than this, the conflicts involved fundamental differences in ideology. The Council believed that the city's elected officials and appointed administrative staff were responsible for deciding about and administering city services—including federally funded programs operating in the city. Citizen participation, beyond the voting act, is expected and accepted so long as citizens air their views, petition relevant administrators, agencies, or commissions, and then accept that body's right to decide about the issue or question. Furthermore, appeal is up to the Council, which is the body legally and traditionally accepted as the final authority regarding the city's public policy.

In contrast, target-area activists grew to oppose this style of governance, at least in respect to the community action programs. Rather than accepting the premise that city officials possessed ultimate authority over these programs, the activists viewed official, particularly Council, opinions only as legitimate inputs in the policymaking process—coequal with those of the target-area representatives, OEDC members, or the OEDC staff. This divergent advocates' posture was unique in the experience of the Council, and the OEO legislation mandating community participation, and administrative interpretation, could be seen as offering support for the activist viewpoint.

Thus, although they clearly disagreed with this perspective, Council members were fundamentally ambivalent regarding which values to respect ultimately in this case; either choice risked unpleasant secondary consequences associated with choosing both sets of values: criticism and guilt for not acting with authority or disruptive, confusing conflict when their screening/buffering processes were no longer functioning adequately and their decisions were not accepted as final. The Council delayed and deferred until it became clear to them that the psychological cost of retaining authority would be intense, and then they let the programs go. They were never able consciously to resolve their fundamental uncertainty regarding which path would be chosen; they acted as though the programs were being taken from them despite efforts to retain it. This may, however, have been a face-saving, conscience-soothing act, because in fact they chose the easier path and, ultimately, the more effective one from their point of view.

The Council's response to the community action programs did not focus on whether or not the programs were laudable. It is likely that, at some level, the Council naturally was suspicious of effective, well-financed organizations that did not accept the traditional political processes in the city. Generally, those in power distrust any kind of organized opposition, particularly hostile opposition. Still, it seems possible that a Council willing to withstand sustained conflict, place solution of community problems first, and act despite painful choices, could have used the energy of organized opposition to enlarge and perhaps slightly redefine the city's active political commuity. In the process, a more creative, effective, widely satisfying program set would have developed. The point is that the response to programs as ill-defined and unstructured as were the community-action programs need not have resulted in withdrawal from responsibility, however tactically effective.

REEXAMINING THE GENERAL CHARACTER
OF OAKLAND'S COUNCIL

Oakland's Council, at least in recent years, has been adept at using other public and semipublic agencies to absorb much of the complexity and pain of public controversy. But, as Table 4.4 demonstrated, the Council has not in general acted to increase the number of independent agencies. In fact, the Council chafes at those agencies—the Oakland Housing Authority, for example, over which they have no formal power or no close informal relationship.[60] Also, the Council, encouraged by strong-minded city managers, has been acting to centralize and simplify the city's administrative structure. In a charter amendment initiated by the Council and manager and approved by the voters in 1968, several semiautonomous city commissions—the Parks and Recreation Departments' Commissions for example—were reduced to purely advisory status. This move in effect strengthened the manager's control over his departments and, at the same time, tightened and strengthened the Council's screening/buffering processes.

The Council's tradition of retaining veto authority but removing itself from city agencies and their constituencies has been, in many ways, successful in Oakland. This technique has enabled an understaffed, inexpert, part-time legislative body to function with little danger of breakdown from sustained overload. In other words, Oakland's Council remains a relatively stable, simple organization despite increasing and increasingly complex problems impinging on the city administration.

On the other side of the coin, this technique has encouraged a maintenance perspective toward city services. This does not mean that the Council will not accept new programs or functions; they have demonstrated that they are receptive when opportunities arise. Rather, the pattern of Council response implies that they employ primitive, perhaps often implicit, cost-benefit criteria when deciding about an action or opportunity. They weigh the need or opportunity to respond to constituency requests and to solve city problems against, first, cost to the city. They obviously prefer projects that will not drain scarce city funds. They may expend a little "priming money" if a return worthy of the investment is expected. They are most reluctant, however, to begin a project/program that requires heavy commitment of city funds.[61] Their second concern or weight on the scale is the probability that their actions regarding a proposal will bring conflict or added difficulties to the chamber floor. If the Council believes that an activity, say appropriating funds for neighborhood service centers, will be expensive and may engender or exacerbate citizen discontent, they would be very unlikely to approve it no matter how laudable the program. If, however, a proposed project, say funding child care centers, would not be particularly expensive but is likely to bring continued or increased discontent to the chamber floor if they *do not* approve it, the Council is very likely to approve the project to reduce the risk of discontent. Naturally the Council tends to agree more readily to proposals that are championed by and will be endemic to the city manager's Departments.

As the assumptions of subjective rationality predict, the Council will reject proposals that are expected to cost the city a great deal or threaten to generate unpleasant personal interactions. If a proposal is not expected to induce psychological discomfort and is not expensive, the Council will yield, especially if a well-argued case is presented or if the psychological costs of refusal appear relatively high. This Council can act in response to a direct appeal, but as this conservative ordering of decision criteria would suggest, their response is usually negative or a delay/negative sequence. The Council's approach to problem solutions, alternative possibilities, and resultant effects clearly reflects their intention to avoid committing nonrecoverable city monies, to retain veto power, and to ensure that there is enough organizational "distance" that they will not "feel" the weight of a program.

But to answer the question set at the beginning of this chapter: How would the Council respond when faced by unfamiliar petitions and uncommon circumstances? The evidence is that they acted, if not gracefully or creatively, effectively. We can see that life is not easy for those who become targets of low-resource pressure groups. Although the circumstances for the policymakers are different from those of the community leaders, staying power is crucial. And it seems that more resources translate into survival potential.

While the low-resource pressure organization deploys its assets to penetrate, disrupt, and threaten grievous consequences, an established institution like the Council invests its resources to develop screening mechanisms to protect it from disruptive penetration and surprise and to operationalize escaping tactics when its screens have been penetrated.

Thus, the Council dissolves amid a formidable array of barriers and alternative targets that reduce its uncertainty about being surprised. Such defenses also increase the likelihood that those who would disrupt the Council's established policymaking process will become confused, frustrated, and disorganized in their attempt. If they persist, at least the Council is likely to be forewarned and have some time to employ other tactics. Finally, the case of the community action organization indicates that if need be, the Council can retreat behind an entire sequence of coping behaviors.

At this point it should be reasonably clear that we have been progressing from the individual citizen's view of the local policymaking process forward to the inner recesses of a city's policymaking apparatus. We are, in this way, attempting to support our hypotheses that individual citizens, pressure groups, and policymakers adopt remarkably similar coping sequences when confronted by the ambiguities and complexities that both confront and confound those who attempt public action. To this point, we have alluded passingly to the rather considerable administrative bureaucracy that is more and more a part of public policymaking at the local level. We now turn our attention to a much more detailed study of several aspects of Oakland's municipal administration. We will concentrate on the methods professional administrators have developed to enable action, survival, and influence on public policy. The following chapters will clearly indicate that resource limitations, staying power, buffering mechanisms, and delay—to name but a few—are just as crucial for those who are developing and implementing policy as for those who want to change it.

The next chapter begins this second phase with a study of the budgeting process in a particularly hierarchical city department. This study suggests that contending, in a business as usual administrative setting, with a seemingly commonplace process—budgeting—is no simple matter. We will see that the budgeting process in this city department is sufficiently complicated that tactics have been developed to limit information needed and prediction required, and a series of screening processes have evolved to protect the top administrators from being inundated by the uncertainties associated with joining operating needs and costs.

NOTES

1. One may argue that any response-nonresponse is an action. This is not a very illuminating approach. Therefore, we intend to define Council activity in a more physical way. A clear "yes or no," for example, implies activity or movement. A "wait" connotes inactivity. Thus, the Council may respond actively or passively.

2. Maintenance legislation is common to all legislative bodies and minimally necessary for the continuance of the government. Reviewing and approving the annual budget is the primary example of such legislative activity. These activities absorb a great deal of time and energy from all legislative bodies.

3. Rarely does an Oakland Council Meeting last more than two hours.

4. See Pressman (1971) and Meltsner (1971: 57-60), for an extended analysis of the well-known politics versus administration problem in the Oakland context.

5. Oakland staff (circa 1970): 2,000 employees (plus), C. M. Salary $42,000 (plus), most department heads $20,000 (plus). In contrast, the mayor about $8,000, Council members about $3,100 each.

6. The directors of and participants in such programs have not always willingly remained answerable to the Council. For example, the Model Cities program in Oakland Planning Committee. They very badly wanted a final voice in the direction and shape of Model Cities development in Oakland. After extended negotiation with the Council, a "dual green light" concept was devised. That is, essentially both bodies retained the power of final veto; both must agree for a decision to be final.

7. Again, the "administrative" function is, theoretically, minimally understood to mean supervised operation of existing programs. Our point here is simply that in Oakland the administrative staff largely defines and directs city programs. In addition, it decides to a large extent what questions that affect Oakland's governmental units will be actively addressed and in what ways. As Pressman (1971) points out, the manager and his department heads act to ensure minimal risk of Council displeasure and disapproval. Nevertheless, considerable administrative latitude and initiative remain, in part, because the administrative side largely defines the problem of the acceptable responses, and because the administrators are relatively more knowledgeable.

8. Of the nine deferrals recorded in Table 4.1, two reemerged in some form for discussion in the Council Chamber.

9. In a study of Oakland, it was reported that 35% of her population was nonwhite. This study, one of the federally funded 701 series initiated in 1966, pointed out that Oakland's nonwhite population made up 48% of the total in 1975.

10. One exception here was a man on the Council at the time who was neither an entrepreneur or a related professional. He was a black, retired YMCA executive.

11. For example, Floyd Hyde, Mayor of Fresno in the mid-1960s, became Assistant Secretary in the Department of Housing and Urban Development.

12. Heinz Eulau interview Number 10607, 1966, p. 7.

13. Eulau (1966: 31) interview Numbers 10601-3-4-5-6-7-8.

14. Eulau (1966: 24).

15. In San Diego and San Jose, 27% and 9%, respectively, voted in a recent municipal election.

16. See, for example, Edward C. Banfield's (1965: chs. 1, 2, 4) analyses of Atlanta, Boston, and El Paso.

17. The voting line-up on this second vote was not the same as on the first.

18. From the Oakland City Council Meeting Minutes of 8/26/1969 and author's notes recorded in that meeting.

19. This analysis does not focus directly on the ideology of recent Council membership. For characterizations of the Council ideologies, see May (1970), Meltsner (1971), and Pressman (1971).

A question asking about unanimous voting was included in a questionnaire administered to seven of the nine Councilmen in 1966. All agreed that voting was usually unanimous. When asked why that was the case, the respondents replied that voting is a routine, approving process. Issues are structured so that they are necessary and obvious.

20. Blumenthal (1969) asserts that: "The White House certainly never thought that the poor . . . would have any part in developing or administering the program. The President, according to his closest aides . . . believed that the local governments . . . would operate the . . . programs . . . (not) . . . separate corporations. Johnson continued in this misunderstanding until shortly after the legislation was passed.

21. The CEP began in 1966 as a pilot project in 19 cities including Oakland. It was a program designed by the Johnson Administration and funded by pooling existing resources from several executive agencies. The program's primary objective was to find jobs for the structurally unemployed in each city's designated target areas.

22. At this time, Oakland's total annual budget was only about sixty million dollars per year. Most of the city budget was committed to salaries, very little was apportioned for capital improvements and that proportion has been diminishing in recent years—15% of the 1969-1970 budget was available for capital improvements. In view of such budgetary constraints, it is easy to imagine the importance of an additional ten million dollars that is not committed to maintenance and is not generated at the expense of the local taxpayer.

23. Other "antipoverty" programs existed in Oakland at this time: The Economic Development Administration (EDA) has been attempting a major public works development program in an effort to reduce minority unemployment—see Pressman and Wildavsky (1973)—The EDA Program, however, is not designed to encourage individuals from affected communities or populations to participate in controlling or advisory capacities. Oakland also received redevelopment and model cities grants from the Department of Housing and Urban Development. These latter programs did include

community-based advisory committees though all programs were administered, evaluated, and approved through the manager's office. Thus, the City Council retained approval or veto authority. Both the Redevelopment and Model Cities programs concentrated on physical rehabilitation. At various times and in various ways, however, these agencies actively considered the problems of participation in political/administrative processes, unemployment, and improving the quality of political and social life in addition to the physical aspects of urban life. (See, for example, Judith V. May, "Two Model Cities: Political Development on the Local Level," ASPA paper, Sept. 1969.)

24. Wayne Thompson resigned as city manager in September 1965. His assistant became acting city manager until the city manager, Jerome Keithley, arrived. Keithley began in Oakland in January 1966. It is generally conceded that Thompson was more sympathetic toward city-operated service programs such as the Grey Areas Project than Keithley.

Keithley resigned in 1972 and his assistant, Cecil Riley, was appointed city manager. There have been two city managers in Oakland since Riley. After Riley resigned, the city attorney was appointed and when he resigned, one of his assistants, a black man, was appointed.

25. This is, of course, further evidence that Oakland's Council looked at the community's problems as though they were business problems. See especially the Council Minutes for 9/17/64.

26. The Industrial Board was to be composed of five members, the mayor, city manager, and one representative from industry, labor, and the "public," respectively. The Board proposal stipulated a large citizens advisory committee. The Council amended the mayor's proposal to include a full-time director recruited specifically to coordinate the antipoverty programs. A small committee of the Council was appointed to work out the implementing details.

27. Kramer (1969: 114) asserts that being chosen to a target-area committee was populations in Oakland that contained an unusually high proportion of low-income, unemployed citizens. North Oakland, West Oakland, Fruitvale, and East Oakland were neighborhoods designated by the Interagency Projects Division in their application for Title II funds from OEO. These four target areas cover approximately one-half of the geographical space that is Oakland.

28. Kramer (1969: 114) asserts that being chosen to a target-area committee was largely a matter of wanting to join.

29. This accommodation may have been for the most part a reluctant submission to constant spurring from the regional office of the OEO.

30. The Executive Committee was expanded from seven to eleven members.

31. This position statement was publicly aired at a poverty forum, November 30, 1965.

32. Request reported in City Council Minutes for 12/21/65.

33. From City Council Meeting Minutes of 1/27/66.

34. See, for example, Council Minutes for 2/10/1966. Alternative methods for reducing local unemployment are imaginable. A city can stress increasing service employment rather than industrial employment. A city could also adopt policies that favor local and sanction suburban employees. *Implementation: The EDA in Oakland;* University of California Press, Berkeley, 1973.

35. John Reading replaced John Houlihan as mayor. Houlihan resigned from office before the expiration of his term. The present mayor, former Superior Court Judge Lionel Wilson, replaced John Reading in 1976.

36. Kramer (1969: 137) reports that the police review controversy extended for some 18 months.

37. See the Oakland *Tribune* 4/27, 5/4, 5/25, and 5/26/1966, and the San Francisco *Chronicle* 5/25 and 5/26/1966.

38. See the Oakland *Tribune* for 5/26/1966.

39. See City Council Minutes for 5/4/67.

40. See for example, Mayor Reading's remarks at the Hearings before the U.S. Senate Subcommittee on Poverty held 5/10/67 in San Francisco, California.

41. Council Minutes for 6/13/67.

42. See Judy May, "Two Model Cities: Political Development on the Local Level," Paper prepared for APSA Meeting in New York, September 1969, for a discussion of the "dual green light" concept.

43. Council Meeting Minutes for 9/5/67.

44. The records suggest that the Council, at this point, did not fully understand their authority to designate (officially sanction) the organization that would administer the OEO/CEP funds. Still, there was no reason for them to believe that the OEDC could simply decide unilaterally that they would no longer allow the Council to "interfere" in these programs.

Clark and Ferguson (1983) argue in Chapter 5 that through the 1970s black community groups declined in salience, race declined as a local political issue, and a fiscal conservatism permeated citizens and elected or appointed officials. Thus black leaders in city hall increasingly resemble their white counterparts as they confront problems of meeting increasing demand with more limited resources. They conclude, "as blacks grew more politically important, black power declined as a political culture."

45. The five-month delay resulted, in part, from the OEDC's determination to hire a well-known poverty organizer and activist to replace Norvel Smith as OEDC staff director. In the end, the city yielded to the OEDC's request and appointed the activist director to serve as interim DHR director until final separation.

46. See for example, Council Meeting Minutes for 12/26/1967.

47. Unrestricted mayoral discretion regarding who could be a public sector representative to the OEDCI was allowed by the OEO through the period covered by this analysis. Eventually OEO stipulated that the Mayor's appointments to the OEDCI must be officials actually in the employ of the City.

48. From the antiactivist perspective, such fears were not totally without foundation. Again, it could be argued that a Council might have acted to prevent the formation of two poles, thus increasing the breadth and depth (effectiveness) of these funds in Oakland.

49. Despite these attempts, neither the mayor nor anyone else succeeded in getting a sufficient number of votes to fire the powerful staff director.

Dorf, R. H. and Steiner, J., "Political Decision Making in Face to Face Groups: Theory, Methods, and an Empirical Application in Switzerland." *American Political Science Review,* Vol. 75, No. 2, June, 1981, pp. 368-380. Dorf and Steiner found that the smaller the size of a decision problem, the probability of majority agreement decreases and the likelihood of amicable agreement increases. Similarly, the more a conflict refers to ends rather than means, the probability of majority decision, or no decision, or decision by interpretation increases, and the possibility for amicable solution decreases.

50. Citizens pay $30 to $50 a year to a private garbage collection concern in lieu of taxes to the city.

51. Similarly, the Parks and Recreation, the Museum, and the Police departments are the most interactive of the city's line agencies. They are all headquartered outside City Hall. The remaining line agencies, with the exception of fire, are located in City Hall.

52. Naturally, any group of citizens can bypass any or all of these layers and approach the Council directly during a formal session. But even in these infrequent cases it would be most unusual for the Council to act other than to shuttle the request, proposal, and so on, back through a program's administrative leadership. In such cases, the Council's relationship with the City's professional staff would have deteriorated considerably, if they did not so include the administrations in the decision-making process.

53. See the Oakland Tribune 5/6/1970.

54. The governor stipulated that the state must be allowed to place an observation/investigation team in Oakland who would compile a thorough report prior to the state's approval of another grant renewal.

55. The OEDCI survived by using excess funds that had not been spent during the previous year and by borrowing from a Community Action Agency in Los Angeles. It is odd that the OEO would guarantee this loan for the OEDCI but would not release the authorized funds.

56. It is noteworthy that, despite a change in federal and regional OEO leadership from Democratic to Republican, OEO continued to support advocacy and service rather than service alone.

57. See Council Meeting Minutes for 2/23/1971.

58. It is noteworthy that a consultant, hired by the City to evaluate the new city administered community action agency, recently blasted the city's hand-picked citizens' advisory committee for being uninformed, confused, torn by factionism, or, in short, inept. He also stated that the agency staff was demoralized and ineffective and that the Council was overzealously guarding the program's purse strings. The staff/board/Council had spent only $400,000 from the present 1.447 million dollar OEO grant. His report concluded by claiming that the city-controlled community action program is essentially no longer operational. In truth, this state of affairs seems to have resulted from long-standing conflicts among the community-action participants rather than from the Council's behavior or City policy. See especially the Oakland Tribune for 3/7/72.

59. See for example, Oakland Tribune 2/4/1970 and 3/3/1970 and *Los Angeles Times* 2/8/1970.

60. The Council's difficulties with the Oakland Housing Authority began shortly after the Council sanctioned the independent Housing Authority in 1939 and continued through 1971. In 1940 and 1971, for example, the Council attempted to remove a staff director that they did not like. In both instances they were not successful.

61. One exception might be the relatively heavy Council commitment to pay for the construction of a large parking garage in the HUD-supported city center presently under construction. It is probable, however, that in addition to the obvious attractions of massive redevelopment of the central business district to a business-oriented Council membership, the Council believed that the revenues from the garage would more than pay for the City's investment. The garage was financed by bond issue.

5 THE ART OF CONTROL
Budgeting in the
Oakland Police Department

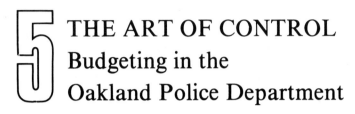

with
David Wentworth
Arnold J. Meltsner

EVEN AN EAGER STUDENT of public policymaking in Oakland might flinch at facing its budgetary processes. Because budgeting is incremental, the process appears clear, straightforward, and unexciting when viewed in the aggregate. City departments—each just another account number—appear undifferentiated in a process that seems to drift along undisturbed by what many view as the urban crisis.

But if one is persistent enough to go below the surface, to get inside a department, he or she can learn much by focusing on its budget. People differ in how they use budgets to achieve particular objectives; various beliefs and values come into play in the process of cutting the budgetary pie. In this respect, each city department has its own peculiar and interesting approach.

This chapter will analyze the budgetary process in the Oakland Police Department, concentrating on the difficulty of managing uncertainty between levels in the administrative hierarchy, and the effect of such management tactics on the budget.[1]

As the previous two chapters have implied, today an obvious trend in urban politics is to decentralize, to "equalize" power if you will, by sharing decision making in the community with experts and novices alike. Amid this clamor to flatten organizational structures, it is novel to examine an organization clinging to a hierarchical operational structure. In police departments the commitment to obedience is a symbol of membership, as well as incentive and reward (Bordua and Reiss, 1966). The tight chain of command is rarely violated, and almost never in an upward direction.

The chief is at the top formally and informally; like powerful people in other fields, he commands. Within the Police Department he makes final decisions on the budget. Although he delegates much of the paperwork and financial computation to subordinates, his signature is not an empty gesture relflecting their hegemony. Surely these people have their own ideas, needs, and attitudes toward police work, and the funds needed to sustain it; and the chief needs their loyalty and cooperation. Nevertheless, despite outside trends toward modifying the hierarchy, the chief maintains control.

Centralized bureaucracy is an efficient way of governing; the chief does not have to bargain away his resources to unruly subordinates. Officers follow because their beliefs are like those of their chief.[2] The chief also gets his way because subordinates, for the most part, are apathetic about the budget; the one issue that unites the rank and file and could threaten departmental accord—major salary increases—is for the most part managed apart from the department's budgeting process by union and management representatives. Under subjective assumptions, this is an axiomatic coping tactic especially among administrators—if something threatens to cripple your organization, avoid it if you can.

Given Oakland's limited revenues, the police budget offers very few incentives for maneuvering or thwarting the chief. On the rare occasion when a subordinate, by detailed documentation and clever argument, can get his or her way, the subordinate must knowingly violate the Department's principles and oppose the precedents of a generation of police chiefs.

These precedents go back at least to 1958, when a chief instituted the two principles that now pervade the Department: (1) cost-consciousness, and (2) need. Generally speaking, cost-consciousness requires that costs be kept to a minimum. Need is defined negatively—that is, need is not how much the item is desired but rather what cannot absolutely be done without. In practice, the two principles tend to become one with cost-consciousness the dominating need. What the department needs is never entirely clear; a subordinate can never be sure that his or her perception of need will be the same as the chief's. What things cost is more easily identified. The principle is to cut costs, minimize expenditure, and be efficient. The chief realizes another benefit by adopting this theme; he gets his subordinates to do most of the routine budget work. Weeding out requests is accomplished at lower levels where intermediate-level administrators reprimand their subordinates if requests seem out of line.

Cost dominates need despite the fact that Police Department administrators usually feel that more people are needed. Police officers are vague when asked to explain specifically how increasing crime rates affect personnel needs; nobody has precise criteria for determining the necessary level of police service. Although there are strong pressures for more personnel—requests for increased human resources backed up by workload statistics on preventative patrol, traffic control, demonstrations, retirement, paper processing, and the like[3]—there are even stronger counterpressures that dampen such aspirations. Obvious revenue and recruitment constraints make it hard to justify requests to city hall for increased personnel.

The pressure to request more personnel is complicated by the Police Department's reputation for efficiency in the offices of the city manager and his finance staff. The manager does not worry about controlling Police Department costs because the chief is cost-conscious. The Department cuts its own budget so that an outsider will not, and thus sets its own priorities and controls its own affairs. The Department's reputation has been maintained for years by a succession of chiefs, promoted from within, and trained to be cost-conscious.

An ideal situation? Yet the chief has limited resources, and appeals for service come from all segments of the political community.[4] Consider his predicament. Requests for new weapons, portable two-way radios, neighborhood centers, expanded training programs, computers, more personnel for tighter patrol and/or community liaison enter from all quarters. But where and how—even if he can decide on his objectives—is he to find the money to answer them? Budget size is largely predetermined and predictable from year to year. The city's constrained budget limits the Police Department to very small annual increments. With minor adjustments, last year's budget is this year's budget.

Thus, the annual budgeting process is largely mechanical, with perfunctory approval given to most basic, recurring items. The personnel category, representing 85% to 90% of the total (see Table 5.1), dominates the budget.[5] The operations and maintenance (O&M) category has remained relatively stable in dollar amount since 1961/1962; as Table 5.2 indicates, O&M has increased only slightly—and far less than has yearly inflation. In the only other category, capital outlay, there is no annual pattern; requests here are not routine but rather vary

TABLE 5.1   Automatic Salary Increases Account for the Growth in
              Personnel Budget and Total Police Budget (in percentages)

Budget Year	Automatic Salary Increase	Change in Personnel Over Previous Year	Change in Total Budget Over Previous Year
1967/1968	3.6	3.5	4.8
1966/1967	3.5	3.9	3.8
1965/1966	3.6	7.9	7.5
1964/1965	3.3	4.6	4.3
1963/1964	3.1	3.3	2.9
1962/1963	4.3	5.2	2.5
1961/1962	4.1	2.2	(0.5)
1960/1961	4.7	4.3	5.6

SOURCE: City of Oakland, Budget and Finance Department, 1960/1961-1967/1968.

with minor equipment or plant items. Capital outlay thus simultaneously shows wide fluctuations but has no effect on the total budget
because it usually represents less than 1% and never more than 3% of the
total.

AN OVERVIEW OF THE
BUDGET PROCESS

There are four levels of the police hierarchy that figure in the
budgeting process: police-chief level (chief); bureau (deputy chiefs);
division level (division commander who is an immediate subordinate of
a deputy chief); and unit level (unit commander who is a subordinate of
a division commander). Division commanders are usually captain, but
can be lieutenants or sergeants. Figure 5.1 illustrates the chain of
command in Oakland.

Figure 5.2 summarizes the budget process in the form of a flow chart;
the process begins when the chief of police receives annual budget
instructions from the city manager (see Meltsner and Wildavsky, 1970).
Instructions, generally similar from year to year, stress that departments
should keep budgetary increases to a minimum above last year's and
warn that the coming budget will be particularly tight. In some years the
chief has sent out his own letter before getting the city manager's.
Several years ago each budget letter was attached to a set of general
instructions regarding the makeup of the budget, but in recent years the
chief's simply has referred to former general orders. The chief's letters

TABLE 5.2   Operations and Maintenance Has Remained Relatively Stable, But Small Capital Outlays Fluctuated Widely (in percentages)

Budget Year	Change in O&M Over Previous Year	Change in Capital Outlay Over Previous Year
1967/1968	6.7	49.2
1966/1967	(1.1)	372.4
1965/1966	4.3	29.7
1964/1965	1.1	86.8
1963/1964	1.4	72.2
1962/1963	(0.1)	62.2
1961/1962	(15.5)	18.7
1960/1961	17.2	76.3

SOURCE: City of Oakland, Budget and Finance Department, 1960/1961-1967/1968.

are nearly identical from year to year, though recently they have included a paragraph calling for careful screening of all requests at lower levels: All command officers are urged to analyze thoroughly all tentative budget requests, paying particular attention to economy and efficiency in the operation of their particular units.

The division commander and subordinates prepare budget estimates by considering what was funded last year, their notions of need, and estimates of future work load. The deputy chief then anticipates the chief's reactions by attempting to cut fat. The chief and his assistants review the budget with an eye to maintaining the Department's cost-conscious reputation and to building consensus among subordinates. Then the chief, the city manager, and his staff meet and cut the budget to fit Oakland's revenue constraint. At each level, police administrators interacted to make budgetary decisions. Table 5.3 summarizes these activities and provides the organizational framework for the remainder of this chapter.

Unit and Division Commanders; The Lowest Budgeting Level in the Chain of Command

Where along the chain of command does the budgetary-guidance process come to rest? Division commanders believe the buck stops with them; as one said, "If you're not a division commander you do not get into budgeting." This is not entirely true because the division commander will seek out well-informed subordinates in order to ease his own work developing the budget.

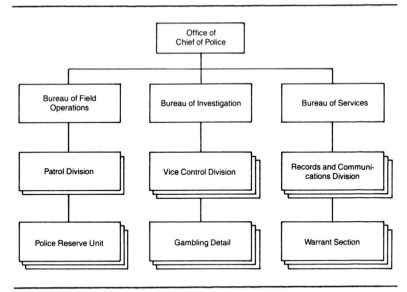

Figure 5.1 Oakland Police Department Chain of Command

For the division commander who wants to do the work himself, unit commanders serve as advisers on specific budget items. For example, in the traffic division or the records and communications division, the division commander relied heavily on his own past experience, on the previous budget, and on statistical information to develop budgets for the units under him. He consulted with subordinates when he had questions, or if an individual came to him with a specific request. Requests from subordinates in the larger units were often quite formal—a written letter describing the request, along with justifications that the division commander wanted to include. Sometimes division commanders assigned lieutenants and sergeants to write justifications for requests. The division commander, however, maintained the initiative and excluded subordinates from broad responsibility for developing the division's budget.

Most unit commanders or subordinates did not care much for the budgeting role, and spent very little time on it; budgeting was thought to be "dull," "routine," and "mechanical." After all, the division commander had the responsibility for developing budget requests at that level. Nevertheless, a unit commander could influence the decision process because he controlled needed information. New division

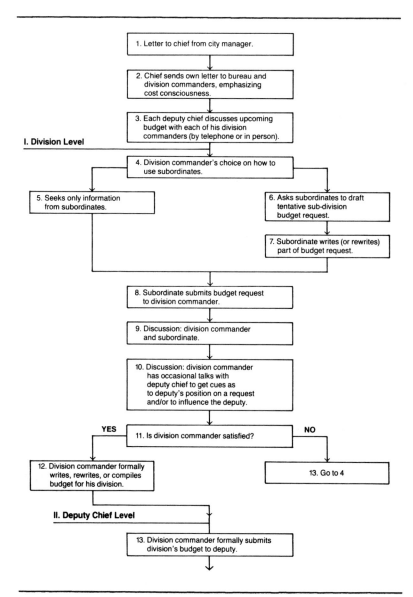

Figure 5.2 Flow Chart of Budget Process Within Police Department *(continued)*

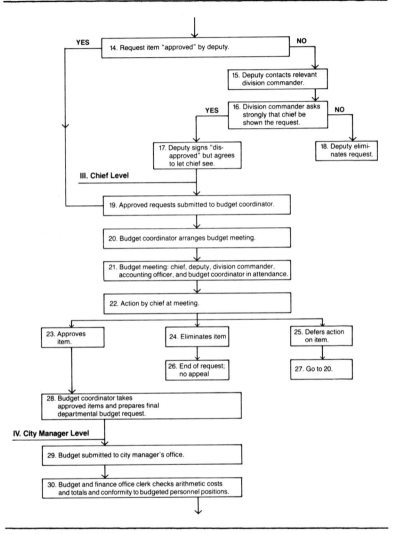

Figure 5.2 Continued

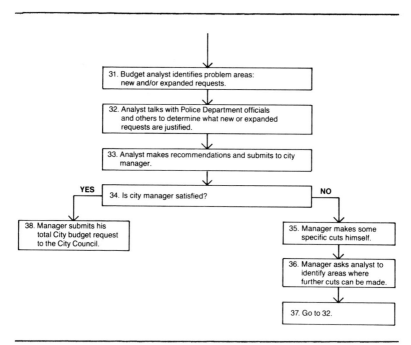

Figure 5.2 Continued

commanders tended to use unit commanders as drafters, but as they became more familiar over time with all division operations, they increasingly drafted the budgets themselves, using the unit commanders merely as advisers on specific items. Unit commanders thus have some limited influence on budget policy.

In the strict hierarchy of the Oakland Police Department, moreover the unit commander could not appeal his superior's decisions. The division commander solidified his position by controlling the flow of upward communication. Formal lines of authority could not be bypassed; no one could communicate directly with the chief or a deputy without prior approval of the division commander. A division commander would see this rule as one way to ensure that his already weak position in the hierarchy would not be further undercut. In the past, the chief had often probed downward, talking directly to subordinates at the unit level. For instance, one chief, when considering buying cameras for the department, contacted a camera specialist in the intelligence

TABLE 5.3 Cutting the Budget: Levels of Interaction

Interaction Levels	Activities Performed at Each Level
Unit Commander or Subordinate–Division Commander	Develop budget estimates: (1) on basis of previous year and cost considerations. (2) on basis of perceived need and workload.
Division Commander– Deputy Chief	Anticipate Chief's reaction: cut out the fat.
Deputy Chief–Chief	Refine for Chief's approval: (1) to maintain department's cost reputation and (2) to build budgetary consensus.
Chief–City Manager	Balance departmental requests with city revenue constraint.

section; he talked to the head of the duplicating shop when considering a new printing machine. Although division heads cannot prevent this, they can effectively prevent any requests suggested by subordinates from reaching higher levels. As a division commander stated, "If sergeants or lieutenants feel an item is necessary and I feel it is not necessary, then there is no request."

Division Commanders and Deputy Chiefs: Cutting the Fat

Some division commanders, on principle, virtually excluded the idea of asking for any increases. Almost all of them reported that sometimes the cost of an item was so great they they could not justify it to themselves—even when it was greatly desired. One division commander stressed that if a new division head was not careful about costs, that division head would get thoroughly indoctrinated about it after a few budget sessions with the chief. The chief's emphasis on cost reinforced his control. Also, because most fat was trimmed from the budget before the chief saw it, he was spared much effort.

A division commander thus placed great emphasis on going by the rules, in order not to attract attention or criticism and also to retain some autonomy. He worked very hard to understand new budget instructions and to fill out detailed forms precisely; he searched out other people in his department for clarification, if necessary, and contacted the budget coordinator, accounting officer, and planning and research division for information and statistics. He justified requests on grounds of what had "always" been done; a new request is defined as a logical extension of existing activity. In short, a rules orientation combined with emphasis on existing procedures protected the division commander from surprise or unwelcome disruption while leaving him some room for creative interpretation and intention of procedures.

A division commander virtually could not defy a superior. But he had one advantage: He spent more time with the division's budget than anyone else. He had time to develop detailed justification for particularly favored requests. Deputy chiefs had much less time to spend reviewing the budgets of each division under them. Even deputies who chose to involve themselves in the budget before it was formally submitted to them could not become completely familiar with all requests, though they would cut new items solely because of cost.

Although the most successful division commander was likely to be the man with a monopoly of technical information who was willing to fight for his requests, he was wise not to fight often. A commander who knew that he was subject to transfer at any time tended to keep requests in line, especially because he knew that no matter what budgeting strategy he adopted, he would get about the same amount of money each year. He knew too that few new proposals were approved. Money is scarce; if he asked for more, he risked antagonizing superiors. The chief's power to make important budgetary decisions far exceeded a division commander's slender resources. And when all was said and done, the typical division commander tended to shrug his shoulders; why worry about where the money will be going in a year-and-a-half? There is a long time-horizon in the budgeting process, and it was a rare division commander who took the trouble to find out how requests fared with the City Council.

The individual deputy, in general, saw himself as an independent spirit: he screened requests from below to weed out the nonessential; he aided his chief by interpreting and communicating his desires downward. Division commanders did not always share this opinion; they tended to see the chief as the principal, the man they wanted to convince.[6] In their relationships with deputy chiefs, many division commanders sensed a degree of autonomy and discretion for themselves, especially on much desired marginal requests. When—during the formal review period for deputies—the deputy asked a subordinate to rewrite a justification, that commander felt that his order came from the chief rather than directly from the deputy. Actually, in formal budget meetings with the chief, the deputy chief did play a supportive role while the division commander did most of the talking to justify requests. However, if the chief reversed a decision, the division commander saw it as downgrading his deputy. Such situations were rare, but they did happen. A deputy recalled one item that a chief approved over his rejection. The deputy had disapproved a $10 request for dues and lunch money for one man to attend the Warrant Officers Association because he felt the meetings were not that useful. The chief, however, knew the situation and approved the item. The deputy said that later he, too, changed his mind when he learned that keeping track of new developments—such as computerizing the issuance of warrants—in this way would indeed benefit an officer in the communications and records division.

From a deputy chief's point of view, consider that all requests formally disapproved by deputy chiefs were passed up to the chief; that the chief rarely reversed the deputy chief's decision suggests that they did have some discretion. When a disapproved request was forwarded to the chief, he usually opposed it because the chief needed the support of his deputies. The division commander, in spite of a somewhat inflated view of his own importance, had to argue powerfully indeed to overcome a deputy chief's opposition. The foregoing examples suggest that a deputy who chose to could increase his leverage in relation to both division commanders and the chief, and become an initiator rather than a passive intermediary. In other words, for an actor who sensed the opportunities for individual initiative, a screening role could be a vehicle for autonomy and authority. The chief needed deputies who were able, reliable assistants who could filter out most nonessential requests before the budget reached him. Without this protection, the chief could easily become inundated and the familiar, comfortable, rigid hierarchy might well become unstable. One division commander estimated that formally and informally a division commander eliminated 20% of the requests; the deputy, another 20%; and the chief, only 1%. Although these figures should not be taken literally, they do suggest that deputy chiefs played a significant role in the Department's budgetary process.

DISCUSSION AND DECISION AT THE TOP

After the review period, deputy chiefs submitted bureau budgets to the budget coordinator, who was responsible for assembling the budget for the chief.[7] The coordinator and the accounting officer checked figures with the city's purchasing department. The budget coordinator did not make any decisions in the budgeting process regarding approval or disapproval of a request (except in his role as a division commander); he discussed any questions with the appropriate division commander or deputy chief, and occasionally asked that a justification be rewritten. Although he was primarily an expediter, he did have some influence because others believed that he was close to the chief. Division commanders, for example, sounded out the budget coordinator as to how the chief might react to various request proposals, and modified their behavior accordingly. Because the budget coordinator was particularly knowledgeable about office equipment, he acted as a liaison with the bureaus and divisions, telling them what was already available in the Department, and supplying information on prices, forms, and procedural details.

The next step was a series of budget conferences with the chief to review the individual division budgets. Bureaus were taken one at a time; initial conferences for all divisions in one bureau were completed before the next bureau was reviewed. The chief, the deputy chief, the division commander, the budget coordinator, and the head of the Department's accounting section attended these meetings. Before the final budget was submitted to the city manager, the budget coordinator followed through on the details, such as rewriting justifications and checking estimates.

Unlike the informal budgeting process at division and bureau levels, the chief's meeting was rather formal and, as a division commander remarked, "You start to sweat a little and get a little tense, for you know that you have to be able to justify your requests. . . . You can't look stupid. . . . The pressure is on!" The first time the chief saw the division's requests was in the conference session; he read each request form, considered it, then either signed it or invited further discussion of it. The division commander did most of the talking while the deputy played a supportive role. If no final decision was made on an item the division commander would be encouraged to make changes and to resubmit the request; occasionally a new conference would also be scheduled. In rare instances, as many as four subsequent conferences for a division were necessary. In these later meetings, debate was limited to the one or two items in a division's budget on which a final decision had not been reached.

The buck stopped at the chief's desk. It was impossible to produce a budget that allocated all resources optimally, for it implied the ability (and the time) to evaluate and compare a great number of alternatives.

The chief was forced to find shortcuts to make the problem manageable. One way of dealing with such complexity is to divide the budget into categories of items and to delegate authority over various drafting functions. Another way is to identify constraints in the external environment that themselves roughly define the size and scope of the budget. The chief developed strategies (fragmentation plus cost-consciousness) that encourage subordinates to limit the budgeting requests submitted to him. In this case, the chief acted to reduce uncertainty for the other actors as well as himself. He divided a complicated budget into more easily comprehended parts and he imposed the general character of the document, cost-consciousness, on his subordinates. In this way, those immediately involved in the budgeting process could readily learn their part and knew what the chief wanted from them.

It seems then that a strict hierarchy focuses the process of uncertainty management on the chief. Though others in the hierarchy, especially those assigned a screening function, can affect this process somewhat, the chief controls it. So rather than uncertainty management involving only intergroup perceptions of ambiguity, in this context, we see that the chief embodies the tension largely in his person. He trades off uncertainty in one area of the budget process for greater certainty in another until he reaches a kind of internal equilibrium that is most comfortable, least painful, or advantageous for him. But he diminishes the collective uncertainties in regard to constructing his Department's budget at the expense of enabling more complicated, ambiguous interpersonal relationships; and though he displays his authority in the budget process, the consequent sociometry clearly taxes it. The chief could have chosen to act differently, say, by not providing clear guidance for subordinates or screening for himself, but then he would be less sure that he could do the job or that it would be a good document that could be adequately defended in competition with others for scarce resources. If he chose such a path, he would ultimately be forced to trade away authority in other areas to enable more personal control over the budget.

The chief's basic philosophy was to eliminate all requests that were not absolutely essential. Need was not defined in terms of cost but was measured by it. Because the past year's budget was a rough indicator of need at that time, increases should reflect a change in need; it was important, therefore, that new requests establish absolute need.

Although the chief reviewed each item, increments got the most careful scrutiny. He tended to approve requests that were less than or equal to the amount in the previous budget, but scrutinized all new requests and all increases. A request twice as costly as last year's was not automatically disapproved, but it alerted the chief to calculate whether the level of police service would actually be lowered without it. If not, the item was rejected.

Considerable emphasis was put on the justification. Division commanders knew they could increase the chances that a request would be approved if they supported it with more detailed statistics. Because the chief recognized that subordinates played the justification game and included irrelevant statistical documentation, he did use other criteria as well to determine whether an item was needed. The chief's long experience was an important factor in his decisions; his recollection of incidents and familiarity with how problems were previously handled was a direct aid for wise budgetary decision making.[8]

Another of the chief's tactics was occasionally to cut an item to show who was boss. This instilled respect for his authority and reminded those so affected to watch costs when they budgeted for the coming year. Another general rule was to drop all requests under six dollars; such inexpensive items either were not really needed or could be obtained informally.

Chief and City Managers:
The Importance of Being Earnest

The strategy of recent police chiefs has been to produce tight budgets; this earns them budget approval as well as a deserved reputation for efficiency and expertise. The ideal is for the city manager and his budget and finance office assistants to recognize "by sheer virtue of past reputation and experience" that the Police Department needs all it requests—that there is "no water in the towel." Contrary to the manager's wishes, the department refuses to list priorities. The chief maintains that "we give the budget a fair shake here" and that everything possible has been eliminated; priorities, it follows, are meaningless. The letter from one chief to the manager covering the 1966/1967 budget stated that "The extent and details in preparation of this budget do not provide for any reductions or deletions, as all estimates have been held to a minimum."

Because the Police Department's budget is by far the city's largest, this strategy of making budget decisions internally has a number of advantages. A loose, padded budget would be indiscriminately cut to accommodate revenue constraints, leaving little or no control over such cuts by the department. These tactics also challenge the city manager and City Council to find any loopholes in a budget that provides Oakland with the bare minimum of necessary police services. Because police and fire functions are among the most visible, politically sensitive city services, the police chief can use the less than adequate budgetary arguments and shift responsibility for complaints from his own shoulders—protecting his, and his Department's, status in the eyes of city officials and the citizenry.

However, the chief cannot completely escape the city's financial problems; the Police Department is but one (even though the largest) of many agencies that must share the city's resources. The chief must always be aware that each agency wants to get its fair share of the budget.[9] Several years ago a chief heard rumors circulating in the city that the Police Department was getting more than its due; he asked the Department's planning and research division to study the charges. The resulting study—covering 17 years—showed that the police budget had declined from 29.5% of the city's general fund in 1947/1948 to 25.7% in 1967/1968 (see Table 5.4). The chief remarked that he felt no obligation to stay within a specific percentage of the city budget, but "wanted to see what the Police Department was doing and possibly to counteract some of the talk going around." It is clear, however, that he could not ignore claims of other agencies on Oakland's resources, and that such demands must affect his own behavior.

BUDGET REVIEW

After the budget meetings with the chief, the final draft of the Police Department budget was compiled and submitted to the city manager. From that time, the chief was the one responsible for getting the budget accepted. Occasionally a deputy went with him to a meeting with the manager, and the budget coordinator and accounting officer also played minor roles, supplying specific information to city hall officials.

The chief acted as a bridge between the Police Department and the city manager's office, which acted on the budget before it was submitted to the City Council. Each side was ignorant of budgetary processes on the other side. Members of the department knew very little of what happened to the budget once it left there. Similarly, city officials, while

TABLE 5.4   Total Police Budget Declined Slightly as a Percentage
of the City's General Fund

Fiscal Year	Percentage of General Fund
1945/1946	28.1
1946/1947	24.4
1947/1948	29.5
1948/1949	27.0
1949/1950	26.6
1950/1951	27.8
1951/1952	24.7
1952/1953	25.0
1953/1954	25.4
1954/1955	25.8
1955/1956	24.6
1956/1957	24.5
1957/1958	26.7
1958/1959	26.7
1959/1960	26.3
1960/1961	26.3
1961/1962	25.2
1962/1963	25.0
1963/1964	25.1
1964/1965	24.3
1965/1966	24.8
1966/1967	25.7
1967/1968	25.7

SOURCE: Figures for the first 17 years are from the Oakland Police Department's
study; for the last 6 years, computed from data in official city budgets.
NOTE: In the police study, percent is improperly labeled as "percent of total city
budget" rather than of general fund. In 1958/1959 the general fund accounted for
73.0% of the city's budget, in 1967/1968, 70%.

expressing confidence in the police budget, knew little about how it was
developed.

The budget completed by the Department goes first to the budget and
finance office where arithmetic totals and costs are checked. Also, it is
checked for conformity to the number of personnel positions approved
by the City Council. The budget is then turned over to a budget analyst,
who evaluates the budget on the basis of his or her judgment and the
finals available. Percentages are calculated to determine how much
items have increased over the previous year and how much of the total
city budget the Police Department budget represents. The budget
analyst then identifies problem areas that, in essence, means changes
from the last year.

In Oakland, the budget analyst is more or less confined to looking at new or expanded requests; the base is not scrutinized. The analyst's responsibility is to ascertain whether an increase in requests actually reflects an increased work load. To do so, the analyst visits the Department, talks with the Department's head, subunit heads, and any other relevant persons. New programs, new personnel, and other proposals that indicate heavy financial requirements receive tags as problem areas.

In the 1967/1968 budget season, the manager at first was concerned about what seemed to be a high Police Department budget request. After an analysis by his budget and finance office, however, he agreed that the requests were legitimate. Later, he complimented the chief, the accounting officer, and the budget coordinator for their excellent budget work.

The police budget is made up primarily of personnel costs, but the precise effect of an additional employee usually is difficult to demonstrate. Revenue constraints, recruiting difficulties, and the incremental nature of personnel requests have tended to keep police personnel requests low. Police chiefs have asked for personnel and have stressed that their request is the minimum necessary to maintain the existing level of police service. The chiefs use their carefully cultivated reputation for conscientiously reviewing all requests at the department level as a lever for obtaining limited personnel increases.

When the Police Department requested seven new positions for 1967/1968, the manager and the budget analyst, who considered them all justified, decided "it was was just a matter of money." The manager decided to approve three of the requested positions. A highly desirable, but expensive, building alteration request for the community relations unit also was denied on the basis of cost.

Members of the Police Department have denied that the chief sets any priorities among requests because the standing argument is that only the absolutely essential is requested.[10] The letter from the chief to the city manager accompanying the budget for 1967/1968 suggests, however, that this is not entirely correct. From experience, chiefs know that they are not likely to get all the personnel they request. Therefore, some statement of departmental preferences can guide the manager. The following excerpt is from the chief's letter:

> In view of the many pressing problems facing the Police Department, it
> seems clear that additional personnel are sorely needed. However, we

have reviewed, carefully, the personnel situation with a concern for minimizing expenditures and with attention to the present status of recruiting efforts aimed at attainment of our present authorized strength. The following personnel needs are regarded as quite critical and these requested personnel are only part of the larger total need.

1. One Fleet and Taxi Detail Officer for the Traffic Division.
2. One Special Program Officer for the Traffic Division.
3. Two Intermediate Typist Clerks for the Warrant Section.
4. One Intermediate Typist Clerk for the Records Section.
5. One Intermediate Typist Clerk for the Personnel Division.
6. One Intermediate Typist Clerk for the Identification Section.

Because the six items are not given in alphabetical order, it can be argued that the ordering reflects departmental priorities. That the city manager indeed used it as a priority list is implied by the fact that the manager approved one of the traffic personnel requests, one of the two typists for the warrant section, and the typist for the records section. He felt all the personnel requests were justifiable but that the city simply could not afford them.

Adding new positions, however, is balanced by cutting old positions. First, the manager decided to cut a patrol officer assigned to the civil defense unit in the office of Oakland's chief of police. One city official explained that the popularity of civil defense is cyclical and could be curtailed without causing political repercussions. Then the manager chose not to budget funds for the auto maintenance-foreman position because this position, authorized the previous year but never filled, had tied up budget money.

Overtime is budgeted as part of the personnel category. In the past, the Department has used salary savings stemming from unfilled budgeted positions to pay overtime expenses. Department members admitted that overtime was difficult to estimate, but they did have certain criteria for drafting overtime requests. Detailed records are kept of the person hours expended in various overtime activities. Although person hours fluctuated from year to year, past figures, in conjunction with subjective judgments, were used to estimate roughly future overtime requirements. Budgeting for overtime is a centralized process. The chief, after informal consultations with subordinates, reviewed statistics on past overtime expenses, added a subjective estimate of future events, and arrived at a figure, but because the criteria were vague, the chief was not heavily committed to it.

The police felt, however, that budgeting for rare contingencies should not be attempted; one recent chief did not believe in budgeting for riots. The general attitude both in the department and in city hall was that funds to cover major demonstrations should be allocated only after the event. This attitude shifted control to the manager and forced the Police Department to maintain strict account of overtime expenditures. The difficulty in predicting overtime needs weakened the chiefs' authority over this aspect of their budget. By putting himself in the hands of the manager, the chief compels him to worry about how to pay for unexpected, expensive, overtime activities. This tactic may tax the chief's overall authority, but in respect to overtime budgeting, his authority cannot be used effectively to reduce the uncertainty, and this method raises the manager's level of doubt vis-à-vis that of the chief in regard to police expenditures.

The Chief Can Make a Difference: Different Coping Styles Having Similar Outcomes Have Different Impacts

The budgeting process of the Oakland Police Department offers some opportunities, though perhaps not many, for the exercise of personal leadership. The three chiefs examined here, Toothman, Preston, and Gain, differed in emphasis and style. Also, the city manager's perception of his own part in developing the budget affects department heads. City Manager Keithley exerted much more leadership than his predecessor. The dominant coalition in city budgeting is small; thus changes in top executives permit shifts in budgeting goals and emphasis within the confines of rather sharp revenue constraints.[11]

Chief Toothman was loyal to his employees but there was no question but that he commanded the Department. Only a few years before Toothman took office, in 1961, the Oakland Police Department had been rocked by scandal, and his predecessor had been brought in to eliminate graft. Chief Toothman, too, was steeped in the reform tradition; he wanted an honest, modernized department. To be effective, he had to take command and make subordinates realize he was boss.

Budgeting was one instrument for asserting his authority and control over administration; he insisted on holding subordinates accountable for requests and expenditures. He felt that requests should be based on need only, and that need should be defined in terms of the traditional police work load. Efficiency and cost-consciousness were integral parts of his reform orientation. Capital outlay- and O&M-requests were drafted by subordinates but always in accordance with his wishes. In personnel matters and for large items such as transportation, however, Chief Toothman did the initiating, thus showing his subordinates that he had control and that they performed only mechanical tasks.

Chief Toothman admitted that he frequently had initiated personnel requests. He kept himself informed either by talking with his deputy chiefs or directly with division commanders. Subordinates knew that the chief was interested in all personnel requests that were being considered. Therefore, they attempted to sound him out. From such direct conversation, or through a deputy, a division commander got cues as to whether he should (1) drop a proposal, (2) explore a proposal, (3) write up justification for it, or (4) definitely push a certain request for personnel. Actually, it was difficult to identify who originated a request, because the chief's feelings were tested before forwarding a formal request; it then became "the chief's request."

Chief Toothman was respected for his experience and knowledge, but he was also viewed as opinionated and uncommunicative. He was a strict disciplinarian—but also a man who would support his men if they were criticized. Sudden personnel shifts, without prior notification, were very effective demonstrations of the importance of complying with his wishes, but such tactics were unpopular, and had some negative results. Although he kept his grip over administration, morale suffered and innovation was stifled. Toothman's arbitrary ways interfered with the communication of cues and expectations, thus confusing subordinates as to how they should act. The Department had to depend almost solely on the chief for new ideas. Thus this chief acted to increase his subordinates' uncertainty regarding what was expected of them; this tactic served to increase his personal control and reduced the need for filters. However, he traded away protection and feedback. He opened himself to overload and error.

Chief Preston—respected, brilliant, but a less experienced chief than Toothman—wanted, also, to run an efficient crime-fighting department. In the one complete budget for which he was responsible—he died after only a year-and-a-half in office—he seemed flexible, open, and reasonable. His tight budget showed that though his influence equaled his predecessor's, his style of leadership was much more satisfactory to his subordinates. They felt that his expectations of them were clearer and more consistent and that he was open to persuasion. Morale was higher because they found Chief Preston listened to them. He differed from

Chief Toothman in emphasizing cost more than need, but the officers accepted his argument that many good ideas were not approved because of revenue constraints.

The Police Department, particularly under Chief Toothman, tried to resist what it viewed as encroachments on its jurisdiction by others; this often led to friction with city officials and agencies. As the Department gradually was subjected to more assertive administrative control by the city manager, Chiefs Preston and Gain adjusted themselves to this change. They saw themselves as subordinate to the city manager and were willing to work with him, working to articulate clearly police responsibilities and needs.

After budget requests left the Department, the chief tried to maximize departmental influence over the subsequent budgeting process, stressing cost-consciousness and producing tight, honest budgets. Generally, the department has done very well over the years, and the chiefs are the first to admit this.

To supplement the basic strategy, and to achieve even greater success, police chiefs have worked to maintain close personal contacts with the city manager during the budget review. This desire, however, has been frustrated by a depersonalizing and formalizing trend in the manager's budget process. The initial review of Department requests was performed by a budget analyst whom the chiefs did not know well. Chief Toothman's strategy was to promote City Council support in order to be able (it was hoped) to override adverse decisions by the city manager and his staff. Chief Toothman's tendency to submit personnel requests based more on need than on cost was a continuing source of friction between him and the manager; the City Council usually followed the manager's recommendations on capital outlay items, but tended to increase personnel and O&M appropriations.

Nevertheless, Chief Toothman disliked this clear shift of influence from the departments to the manager. He complained that during the last several years he had not been given any formal opportunity to appeal the recommendations made by the budget analyst to the city manager. Toothman felt that placing the analyst as intermediary in the process reduced his own opportunity to present his department's needs. Later, Chief Preston also complained that he had no opportunity personally to sell his ideas to the manager.

The city manager used various strategies to cope with Chief Toothman. Sometimes he would wait to notify the chief of his recommendations on the police budget until the last minute, leaving the chief little or no time to respond. Sometimes he would postpone making decisions on an issue. There had been a long controversy about gassing the Department's cars; the police wanted to operate their own gas pumps, but the street department had opposed this proposal. The city manager avoided antagonizing either department by simply never making a decision on the matter. Another example of this delaying tactic is found in the fight, which lasted many years, to enlarge the duplicating shop in the training division. Chief Toothman wanted the department to have its own shop rather than having to use the city's centralized facilities. Gradually, at irregular intervals the Department was granted various items for the duplicating shop, but at no time did the manager issue a final and definitive policy statement on the issue.

As we have already noted, Chief Toothman did not have a reputation in the city for being easy to work with or sympathetic to citywide problems, though his successor, Chief Preston, was more cooperative. Whether because of or despite this, Chief Preston had even more trouble trying to assert Police Department autonomy. Just before Preston took office, a new manager was recruited. The new manager acted to strengthen his position in the budgetary process. He curtailed the tendency of department heads to bypass his authority or to influence his decisions; he made it clear both to the Council and to department heads that responsibility for developing the budget was his alone. In the new published budget format for the city, the column indicating a Department's request was eliminated. Only the previous budget and the city manager's recommendation were depicted; the new manager did not feel that cuts he made from the Department's requests ought to have been public information (Meltsner and Wildavsky, 1970: 33a).

This manager—like his predecessor—occasionally took action without consulting with his department heads to demonstrate his authority. Chiefs generally showed little interest in the civil defense program, but Chief Preston was concerned when, in the 1967/1968 budget, the manager dropped a man from the program. His resentment stemmed not from the action per se but from the fact that he was not consulted. Though responsible for the civil defense program, his authority over it had been eroded from outside without his consent.

The new city manager also limited communication between the City Council and department heads. His policy was for the City Council to deal directly with him rather than going to department heads. By the same token, department heads were not supposed to talk directly to the City Council or to any of its members; the manager often invited heads of the larger departments to the Council's budget hearings to supply him with background information—but it was his, not their, choice.

In the past the City Council had given the Police Department more than the city manager recommended. The old city manager had been upset by the council's tendency to approve positions that could not be filled—which tied up money in the general fund. In fiscal 1967/1968, however, the City Council demonstrated its confidence in the new manager by following his budget recommendations in every aspect.

In short, this man became the primary figure in the budgetary process; he was included in everyone's personal calculations. As division commanders and deputy chiefs in the Police Department relate to the chief, so must the chief relate to the city manager. No longer were chiefs able to assert their autonomy as in the past, nor were they able to bypass the manager and attempt to influence the City Council directly. This city manager was recruited, in part, to fill the need for skillful professional management of the city's scarce economic resources. His policy was that municipal services could be maintained—even under conditions of scarcity—by administrative reform and by more efficient management practices. Similarly, Chief Preston was hired, in part, because he was judged capable of seeing the larger city picture rather than just the narrow interest of his Department, and because he was strongly committed to following the chain of command. See Table 5.5 for a comparison of the budgeting behavior of the old and new managers.

When Chief Preston died, he was succeeded by Deputy Chief Gain. Under Chief Gain there were some changes partly because of his personality and partly due to changed environmental conditions. As deputy chief, his reputation was that of an initiator; as chief he continued his technique of constant probing. He operated on the assumption that there are "no sacred cows in police work." He placed much more emphasis than his predecessors on reviewing existing policies and procedures, and explored possible new programs and sources of funds. Most significantly, he showed a willingness to request sizable increases in personnel.

Chief Gain was extremely cost-conscious and thus stressed management efficiency. Also, operating as he did under the leadership of a city manager active in budgeting, he worked closely with the manager to keep him informed of Department problems and to find solutions quietly, behind the scenes. He knew Oakland had priorities other than the police and that his own Department needs must be balanced against limited revenues. He was sensitive to the city's high tax rate and realized that this should be and is an important consideration in the budgeting process. He even assigned a lieutenant to scan federal programs to which the Department might apply for funds.

TABLE 5.5   Two City Managers' Budgeting Strategies

	First Manager (10/54-8/65)	New Manager (1/66-8/72)
Importance of budget	Low interest. Concentrates his efforts in other areas.	High interest. Means of central control so that scarce resources can be efficiently allocated.
Perception of budgeting role	Somewhat passive. Responds to requests submitted. Examines increments but seldom alters base.	Active. Makes department heads comply with his budget directives. Examine increments first, then search base for items possible to cut if necessary. Claims responsibility for development of budget.
Strategies for coping with the chief	Postpones decisions; reduces personal administrative contact; strengthens bureaucratic intermediary; makes budget cuts.	Postpones decisions; reduces personal contact in budget area; increases personal contact in other areas to work closely with the chief; strengthens bureaucratic intermediary; makes budget cuts. Prohibits direct communication between chief and council; emphasizes chain of command.
Results of manager's behavior	Balanced city budget. Time to pursue non-budgeting activities of greater interest.	Balanced city budget. Central control over budget process in city. Compliance with chain of command. Recognition as final authority on budget by City Council and department heads.

Chief Gain took office in September 1967 with two goals—to improve community relations, and to reduce crime. Gain's first budget, however, departed little from those of his predecessors, though his cover letter to the city manager did reflect a change in tone—a greater awareness of community problems:

> The social and ethnic makeup of Oakland poses a potential for the type of disturbances that have occurred in other core cities; therefore the budget reflects a twofold approach to preclude or meet this eventuality.

He advocated "a community relations effort" to emphasize contact with youths and parents. Also, he saw a need to purchase equipment to cope with a major disturbance if one should occur. He noted that these programs, requiring paper, printing, helmets, ammunition, and the like, necessitated significant increases in O&M expenditures, but pointed to this increase as an exception, like Toothman and Preston before him had done. Gain was careful to emphasize that he was cost-conscious. He pointed out that he was deferring a request for building alterations "in the interest of effecting a savings."

In his first budget (1968/1969) Gain asked for 10 new civilian positions, which was in line with personnel requests in previous years, but in his budget letter to the manager, he laid the foundation for more sizable personnel increases in the future:

> Studied consideration has been given to this area of expenditure. There is an indicated need for additional police officers based upon increased crime rates and demands for police services. However, no such positions are being requested because (1) in spite of extensive recruiting efforts we cannot fill our existing patrolman vacancies; (2) time did not permit of an indepth beat survey to determine needs precisely (we could not of course employ the simplest "standard" of basing personnel needs solely upon increased crime rates); (3) an analysis must be made during the 1968 calendar year to determine the number of positions filled by patrolmen that could be filled by non-police personnel; (4) surveys must be conducted of department systems, procedures, and personnel practices for the purpose of increasing efficiency, upgrading performance and improving the management and operations of the department before we can justifiably request certain personnel increases.

As promised, Chief Gain did initiate a number of studies to review existing policies and procedures and to determine how resources could be used more efficiently and effectively. A Department-sponsored computer analysis of called-for-services revealed that virtually no person hours were available for preventive patrol. Gain sensed a critical need to get more police on the street—to reduce opportunities for crime, and to increase arrests. He adopted a two-fold approach to this problem: transferring officers to tasks for which their training could be more effectively utilized, and requesting more personnel. In December 1968, he announced a long-range plan that would eventually downgrade 27 positions. He transferred officers to jobs in divisions dealing with crime prevention and investigation of citizen complaints and he replaced the three-wheeled motorcyle traffic officers with less expensive meter maids. Chief Toothman had opposed such a change because he believed that the presence of traffic officers deterred crime. Gain also used federal new career funds to hire a number of persons from poverty backgrounds to replace highly paid police officers on routine tasks.

In the police budget for 1969/1970, Chief Gain also asked for more sworn personnel, but it was clear that this sensitive topic would be the subject of negotiation from his budget letter:

> The budget contains a request for thirty-five additional patrolmen and ten sergeants; however, based upon our conversations with reference to the

budget, we will continue to discuss police personnel needs during the period February to June, 1968, based upon the number of policemen needed to combat crime in Oakland, the capability of the city to finance them and the ability to recruit them.

Gain worked closely with the city manager on the difficult problem of financing needs while at the same time firmly registering the person power requirements of the Department. For the discussions that followed the submission of his budget, Gain prepared a report identifying the number of officers needed for various levels of preventive patrol. The city manager, balancing revenue and service considerations, finally agreed to 53 new sworn positions.

The chief continued to ask for more police. Due to successful recruitment in 1969, the desire to have police available for preventive patrol, and the public's concern over the high crime rate, Gain confidently requested 146 new sworn positions in his 1970/1971 budget.

In order to implement his goals of improving community relations and reducing crime, Chief Gain introduced a number of administrative changes, not all of which are directly reflected in the budget. Some changes, such as monies for new equipment and certain personnel allocations, could readily be identified in the budget, but many could not. Many policies, such as written guidelines for gun control and citation release, placing able and progressive personnel in key command positions, training innovations including role-playing and using the best officers to break in new recruits, an open-door policy, and attending community meetings, have been implemented without incurring direct costs.

The differences between the chiefs have been primarily ones of style and emphasis. Each produced a tight budget, but Toothman and Preston differed in their style of leadership; they shared similar beliefs about the police role in society, but Chief Preston was more willing to communicate reasons for his actions. Chief Gain has differed from his predecessors in that he has been more willing to explore new ideas. Although still motivated by cost-consciousness, he has attempted to develop new programs.

The differences in the budgeting behavior of Gain and his predecessors are not only those of personality but also reflect important changes in environmental conditions. As a reform chief, Toothman's primary concerns were honesty, professionalism, and efficiency. Although Toothman always felt more men were needed, budgetary requests were relatively stable. Preston's brief tenure was in a period of transition. Certain professional standards and procedures were not generally accepted, but policies for coping with fast-growing racial tensions and crime rates had yet to be developed. Preston was still learning his job when, after less than two years in office, he died. Gain became chief at a time of increasing racial tension and rising crime rates; it was clear that there were new environmental demands on the Police Department that necessitated adaptive changes in police policies. Gain's policies showed awareness of the new environmental situation of the Oakland police. Traditionally, a police chief's options have been limited by his constrained budget. But, when Gain succeeded to the office, new demands for police services were altering or relaxing traditional restrictions, providing a chief with more opportunity to initiate policy changes.

Regardless of whether one attributes the differences among the chiefs to personal style, different city managers, or a variety of other possible changes in environment, each had to find a way to manage the uncertainties he faced. There were definite similarities among the methods they used; for example, the police leadership, like the Council, attempted to avoid or withdraw from functions or responsibilities that appeared to threaten or that could not be assimilated and controlled comfortably. There also were differences between the chiefs in this regard—remember that they were not alike in their reliance on screening processes. This diversity appeared to influence morale, organizational structure, and process, as well as others' perceptions of the chiefs as persons and department heads. Perhaps more specifically, their choice of coping tactics influenced the shape or mix of difficulties that each confronted as he set out to reach his budgeting goals.

CONCLUSIONS

A budget, of course, is but one tool for implementing policy; the chief did not and should not have relied on it completely. A budget may indicate the number of people in a division, but it tells little about how they use their time. The budget is a control mechanism, but it cannot and is not meant to control everything.

Budgeting in the Oakland Police Department occurs in the milieu of a powerful chief and strong economic constraints. Of course, there are other influences on the budget. Preparing a budget is complex, and people confronted with such a job seek ways to simplify. Various decision-rules, defenses, strategies, and constraints, such as schedules and formats, enable individuals to cope with a complex problem.

Subordinates, linked in intricate relationships, can exercise considerable choice in deciding what to request, or by suppressing information. The chief, though powerful, is not omnipotent and can be both influenced and circumvented.

At another level, however, this apparent modification of hierarchy is partly illusory because centralized control over budgeting is facilitated by prevailing cost-conscious policies. The action of subordinates is conditioned according to the prevalance of cost considerations; they are socialized to the legitimacy of rank and commands. Moreover, disobedience is quite visible and the chief's expectations are clearly communicated.

At still another level, one can see in the Police Department's budgeting procedure the same fundamental approach to managing uncertainty that was evident among the ASUO leadership, community action leaders, and the Council; all attempt to reduce their uncertainty and, failing that, to increase that of others whose personal or institutional authority is either an impediment to or a vehicle for reaching their objectives. This analysis of budgeting in a relatively stable administrative hierarchy, however, did illuminate the buffering or screening process, a common aid in uncertainty management, as a potential resource for those who perform the function.

This chapter offers evidence that individuals in the policymaking process must employ a variety of reasonably sophisticated tactics simply to enable them to cope with routine, recurring problems in a stable setting; one where all members are thoroughly socialized to the proper procedure for each circumstance and role. Perhaps there is more to be learned about this problem of coping by policymakers and the making of policy; it may be helpful to turn to a department that is not so rigidly structured and in which neither the leadership nor the department's members are clear as to what their function in city hall should be or what services they should be providing.

This is a problem that has plagued planning departments and planners in city hall for decades and, again, Oakland is not an exception. The question is how did planners in Oakland cope with the ambiguity of purpose and position in a city government that was trying to focus and streamline its service in the name of efficiency?

NOTES

1. This analysis covers experience with three police chiefs and two city managers: Chief Edward Toothman (October 1961-February 1966); Chief Robert Preston (February

1966-September 1967); Chief Charles R. Gain (September 1967-to present); City Manager Wayne Thompson (October 1954-August 1965); City Manager Jerome Keithley (January 1966-August 1972).

We wish to express our indebtedness to Win Crowther, who conducted many of the interviews on which this chapter is based. We have drawn from many of his insights. A word of appreciation is also in order for the sincere cooperation and interest shown by the members of the Oakland Police Department who were interviewed.

2. The way in which police budgeting is centrally controlled is similar to the way in which the apparently decentralized U.S. Forest Rangers are controlled; see Kaufman (1960). For a discussion of bureaucratic ideologies, see Downs (1967: 237-246).

3. Many of the police were hired in the post-World War II period and when these officers retire, the shortage will be acute. Many people in the department think that preventive police work is being neglected because of the personnel shortage. A recent in-depth study by the Department shows that virtually all of a patrol officer's on-duty time is spent answering service calls from the public and that little time is left for preventative patrol.

4. Studies of budgeting in other cities support the view that there is very little leeway in budgets at the municipal level. See Crecine (1969).

5. From a 1950/1960 Police Department study that indicated that on the average, 86.9% of the budget was for personnel. In accordance with Proposition C of the Oakland City Charter, police salaries are automatically raised each year at a rate equal to the percentage wage-increases of manufacturing production workers in the San Francisco Bay Area. In the 1968/1969 budget, Proposition C was interpreted as only setting a minimum for police salary increases.

6. Tannenbaum (1968: 24) argues that "the averaged judgments by organization members" are reliable measures of control. In this study, subordinates identify the chief as the primary power in the budgetary process.

7. The budget coordinator's primary job is records and communications division commander and he holds the rank of captain. He was assigned an additional function as budget coordinator in 1964 by the chief because of the need to expedite the department's budgeting process. His duties included making the budgetary time schedule and seeing that it was followed.

8. Some functions and divisions are favored over others. Chief Toothman indicated that "the street job" or "the basic police function" must be performed; when money is tight, one must curtail peripheral functions. Thus this chief tended to apply stricter criteria to service bureau requests. Chief Toothman also tended to favor a specialist rather than generalist approach toward police work and, therefore, favored specialists units (such as vice squad, bar detail, and intelligence section) in his budgetary decisions.

9. Aaron Wildavsky (1963: 17) defines fair share as "a convergency of expectations on roughly how much the agency is to receive in comparison to others."

10. See earlier discussion in this chapter's previous section.

11. See Thompson (1967: 124) for a discussion on how the size of the dominant coalition affects the ability of new members to exert leadership in instituting changes.

6 AMBITIOUS DREAMERS The Oakland City Planning Department

CITY PLANNING in Oakland has been relatively ineffective in achieving its own goals or the goals of its clients. There are basically two reasons for this: First, the Department has no clearly defined role, it plays a number of roles and is not sure what role it ought to be playing. Second, planners in Oakland still cling to the idea that effective planning must be comprehensive, which drives them to a negative view of the political process. The values embedded in the comprehensive method conflict with those of political decision makers, and Oakland planners see no clear way to resolve the conflicts. Some see "selling the planning process" as the answer, whereas others hope for unlikely institutional reforms that will put them at the right hand of the city manager. A few are willing to sacrifice the ideal of comprehensiveness in order to acquire some effectiveness in city policymaking. Some want to develop strategies for mobilizing political support on behalf of their plan.

In Oakland the City Planning Department is advisory to the City Planning Commission and is directly responsible to the city manager, who can hire and fire the planning director. However, the latter relationship is not clearly defined, because the Department is not an executive staff. The Department has little interaction with the City Council except through the manager and the Commission. For a time, the Department had an informal liaison with the mayor through his assistant, a former member of the Planning Commission, but it had no contact after this individual resigned. The City Council approves, by resolutions, plans prepared by the Planning Department, but is not bound to follow them.

The Planning Commission, to which the Planning Department staff is advisory, was created by local ordinance. The Commission consists of seven members who are nominated by the mayor, appointed by the Council, and serve for three years. The formal duties assigned to the Commission are as follows:

(1) To initiate and conduct a study of the problems of the city with respect to residential, commercial, and industrial districts, traffic conditions, boulevards, street openings and widenings, public parks, playgrounds and other recreational areas, flood control, subdivision, and, in general, with respect to those matters affecting the orderly growth and development of the city and to make the City Council recommendations with respect to the same.

(2) To consult with and advise the City Council and other city officials with respect to any of the above matters.

(3) To undertake and perform such other duties as may be assigned by the City Council.[1]

Therefore, the Commission is responsible to the Council primarily for land use and physical development. The Commission's responsibility helps to define the physical planning mandate and to guide the actions of Planning Department staff, although the staff has taken on duties broader than those assigned to the Commission.

Another important function of the Commission is to "act as an administrative court for citizens' appeals regarding bureaucratic decisions in administering planning" (Crowther, 1968). This function, as we will see, has important implications for the relationship between Planning Department staff and the Commission.

INTERNAL STRUCTURE OF THE DEPARTMENT

Internally, the Planning Department is divided into two sections: Advance Planning and Planning Administration. The former prepares the general plan, the district plans, and carries out special design studies and projects related to land use. The latter administers the zoning and subdivision regulations.

The professional staff consists of twelve persons, seven of whom have master's degrees in planning from the University of California at Berkeley, and two of whom have such degrees from other universities. Two professional staff members, in addition to the assistant director, work in the Planning Administration Division, and the others work in Advance Planning.

The Department's personnel practices are controlled by civil service, and promotion from within has been the tradition. The result is that most of the planners on the staff have been in this department for a long time; turnover in the Department is usually at the entry level, as there is little movement out of the higher positions. Such stability implies some in-breeding, but this has not resulted in as much agreement about proper functions and roles as one might imagine. However, there does appear to be a good deal of goal consensus within top-level staff, although there is division over means. Goals are vaguely defined, which allows a wide diversity of opinion within the organization on both goals and means without intensive conflict.

This chapter examines the role of the Oakland City Planning Department in the city administration. It addresses itself particularly to the relationship between planning and the political structure in Oakland; the Department's function in and impact on the policymaking process; the Department's propinquity to the public; and the tactics it has developed for coping with role ambiguity.

These issues are interrelated and overlapping; however, they help to focus attention on the Department's ability to influence and to make policy. Of course one would like to have carefully developed, widely accepted measures of effectiveness for planning outputs; but as there are no such universal measures, we must do the best we can on our own. The conclusions in this chapter are rooted in extensive interviews with city, especially Planning Department, staff members.

METHODOLOGY OF THE STUDY

The basic research instrument for this study was a structured, but open-ended, questionnaire. It was administered in the form of indepth interviews with the planning director, the assistant director, the three senior planners, and one associate planner, who were division chiefs. The remainder of the professional staff were given the questionnaire, which they completed and returned. The return rate was almost 100%.

Several planning documents were examined to determine the Department's formally stated goals. These included the 701 document, *Options for Oakland*, the *Central District Plan*, and the zoning regulations. In addition, time sheets for a three-year period were reviewed to determine what the staff was actually doing. The Department's chronological files for the past year and the city manager's files were examined to determine to what extent and for what purposes the city manager used the Department.

Finally, many of the findings are augmented by participant observation. There are acknowledged weaknesses in this method; I hope that the insights acquired through actual participation in the organization are worthy of the biases introduced by the experience.

THE PLANNING DEPARTMENT'S ROLES

Concern about the proper role for planners and the problem of increasing their effectiveness is not new. Robert Walker's (1950) book, *The Planning Function in Urban Government,* attempted to bring planning into the mainstream of municipal politics.

In recent years there has been among professional planners increasing interest in the relationship between the planning function and the decision-making system. Much of this interest has grown from widespread criticism of the comprehensive planning model. The work of Braybrooke and Lindblom, and Banfield has been particularly influential in this regard. Braybrooke and Lindblom argued that decision making is serial, remedial, and incremental and bears little relation to the comprehensive ideal of setting goals, determining alternative means of reaching these goals, or spelling out the possible consequences of various courses of action (Braybrooke and Lindblom, 1963). Banfield, on the other hand, has pointed to the differences between central decision and social choice and has argued that few decisions result from planned choice (Banfield, 1961). Similarly, Norton Long (1958) has viewed the local community as an ecology of games, in which decisions result from a number of role-determined strategies rather than planned actions.

Two recent, notable studies also have questioned the effectiveness of planning and the relationship between planning and politics. Altshuler's (1965) study of the planning process in Minneapolis-St. Paul revealed that politicians usually prefer to operate at high levels of comprehension and predictability, even if it means fragmenting policy choices. His study also elucidates the conflicts between planners and politicians, with both claiming the ability to determine the public interest. Altshuler found that emphasis on comprehensive planning decreased the planning department's effectiveness, because other city departments had a more narrowly defined area of expertise. Highway engineers, for example, could present hard-headed economic arguments for their proposals, whereas planning proposals rested on a vague notion of the public interest.

Francine Rabinovitz (1969) studied the planning and political processes in five New Jersey communities. First, she established a typology of city policies, based on relative concentration of power. The five cities she studied varied as to whether they had effective planning, as indicated by a panel that rated New Jersey cities on effective planning. She then considered possible independent variables that could influence effectiveness: These included the type of policy, the position of the planning department in the governmental structure, and the role of planners in each city. The results of the study seem to show that certain types or roles are most effective in certain political environments, and that planning can be effective in any polity in any position in the administration. In the final analysis, however, Rabinovitz believes it is the interplay between the planners' roles and the type of polity that produced effectiveness or ineffectiveness in each case.

However, there were some major methodological problems in the study, the primary one being that the dependent variable, planning effectiveness, was defined by using a reputational method. This means that some planning departments could be thought of as doing good planning because they produced a large number of attractive plans. It says nothing about whether decision makers are advised by these plans or whether the plans produce net benefits for various planning department clients.

It is difficult to determine the effectiveness of a planning department by examining outcomes because, as Henry Fagin (1970) has observed, planning is two steps removed from action. Planners make recommendations, which may ultimately result in actions.

The problem may also be seen as one of power as causality, as Robert Dahl (1963) pointed out in his classic discussion of power:

> My intuitive idea of power, then, is something like this: C has power over R to the extent that he can get R to do something that R would not otherwise do.

To Dahl, then, power is causation. However, Andy McFarland, realizing that power must be defined more specifically if it is to become a useful concept, uses "influence" to refer to social causation in general and "power" to indicate intended social causation in particular. Consequently, McFarland (1969: 13) modifies Dahl's statement as follows: "C's behavior exercises power over R's behavior if and only if C's behavior causes changes in R's behavior that C intends."

The problem of determining the effectiveness of planning then becomes one of discovering the intentions of planners and linking their behavior to changes in the behavior of decision makers. Empirically this becomes difficult: How does one know when a planning recommendation causes decision makers to do something that they would not have done otherwise?

A second problem is that the concept of effectiveness includes more than power. It also means that planning recommendations should eventually produce net benefits for planning clients other than decision makers. This implies a causal link between proposed actions and intended consequences. The question then is whether planning proposals produce net benefits for the public when they are implemented. In this sense, planners could have influence without being effective.

This short review is intended simply to highlight some of the theoretical and empirical underpinnings, as well as the methodological constraints, that guide this study. It is not a thorough survey of planning and decision theory.

But returning to the primary focus of this chapter—the Oakland Planning Department's profound uncertainty about the role of planning in city hall—the idea of role implies that there are widely shared expectations regarding what those on the staff and, thus, the Department as a whole should be doing. However, little evidence was found of such shared expectations; when we found certain behavior anticipated, then that activity pattern was defined as a role. Of course, the staff member's perception of his or her role and that of the Department more generally influenced his or her response to dissonant expectations and, ultimately, his or her effectiveness.

Perhaps it would be helpful to begin by looking at what the staff actually does. The question, what does the Planning Department do, is often asked by city officials, implying that planning is so esoteric as to be incomprehensible to most. In order to clarify this, I examined the activities of the Department over a three-year period, 1967-1969. Table 6.1 displays the resultant distribution of activities.

The following data give a rough sketch of how the Planning Department spends its time. However, it is an imperfect one because the data were aggregated for use by the staff rather than for use in this chapter. The data also were restricted by the categories used on departmental time sheets, which obscured much detail. Furthermore, not all department activities are recorded on time sheets. Thus, these activity figures should be viewed cautiously.

How Much Staff Time Is Spent Planning?

In order to place the raw data into simpler, more manageable form, and to see how much time the staff spends on planning, the data were aggregated into the following six categories: (1) activities involving actual planning; (2) activities to meet federal requirements; (3) activities producing information; (4) "brush fire" activities; (5) zoning and subdivision control; and (6) other (a residual category). As some projects involved a number of these activities, it was necessary to determine the primary orientation of each project. For example, the 701 Project included aspects of the first three categories. However, it was classified primarily as informational, although there was definite emphasis on plans and recommendations. Table 6.1 depicts the percentage of staff time spent on each type of activity from 1967 to 1969.

Activities directed to planning were characterized by products in the form of policy recommendations. One might disagree that the 701 Project, for example, should be defined as informational, but it seemed that information production overshadowed policy recommendations in terms of time spent and actual output.

The second category—activities to meet federal requirements—is less complicated, although such requirements influenced many planning projects in this period. This category included only projects, such as the Workable Program and Oakland Economic Development Program, in which the Department's primary role was to ensure that federal requirements were met.

Other federal programs, such as the Beautification and Urban Mass Transit studies, which proposed policies or programs, were classified as planning projects.

Information-producing activities were those in which data gathering and analysis constituted the primary emphasis. The 701 Project accounted for the bulk of this activity.

"Brushfire" activities were special projects usually assigned by the city manager. These also often provided information, but were narrowly focused studies in response to specific requests.

TABLE 6.1   Percentage of Staff Time Given to Actual Planning
Compared to All Other Activities, 1967-1969

Activities	Percentage of Staff Time by Year		
	1967	1968	1969
Activities directed to planning	3.4	2.7	15.0
Activities to meet federal requirements	1.7	0.5	1.0
Activities to produce information	49.9	46.4	24.6
"Brushfire" activities	3.1	2.9	8.7
Zoning and subdivision control	9.4	10.3	11.1
Other	32.5	37.2	39.6
Total	100.0	100.0	100.0

Zoning and subdivision control was associated with administering the zoning and subdivision ordinance.

The residual category included housekeeping, public information, and nonproductive activities.

An analysis of Table 6.1 reveals some interesting patterns. First, one student of planning in Oakland argued that the Department was oriented more toward federal requirements than to initiating actions (Vetter, 1968a: 3). However, these data indicate that activities directed solely to meeting federal requirements constitute a relatively small percentage of staff activity. This is not to deny that the staff was heavily involved in federal programs, each of which had requirements to be met. But many of these programs were also used to develop proposals, provide information, and initiate action.

The data in Table 6.1 also suggest that planning activity increased significantly from 1968 to 1969. Although this increase was due in part to Department's participation in a federally assisted urban mass transit study, there would have been a substantial increase just the same. Still, "planning" accounts for a relatively small portion of the total staff activity and is, in fact, surpassed by information production, zoning, subdivision control (except in 1969), and the other category.

Table 6.1 also indicates that brushfire operations experienced a marked increase between 1968 and 1969. This would indicate that more staff time was being spent on a type of activity that the Department downgrades; one observer concluded that the Department disliked brushfire operations, which did not include functions that the staff considered to be real planning (Vetter, 1968b: 40).

Finally, information production consumed the largest percentage of staff time, except in 1969, when the HUD-funded 701 Project was at its zenith.

Remember that data of this sort can be skewed by the federal programs accepted by the Department, especially if they are major projects. A particular program's phasing can distort the picture: For example, the decline in information-producing activities was due solely to the phasing in the 701 Project.

An examination of the roles played by city planners in Oakland is extremely important. If Rabinovitz (1969) is correct that the type of role must be appropriate to the type of polity if a department is to be effective, an examination of the roles played by the planners in Oakland is a good place to begin. We have classified those performed by the staff as technician, broker, mobilizer, and watchdog.

The Technician

It is clear that the dominant role of the Department is that of technician. In the interviews with the staff, it was the most frequently mentioned. The technician emphasizes making recommendations to decision makers, through both long-range forecasts and specific proposals relating to land use and zoning.

However, a large number of staff members mentioned providing information to decision makers and to the public as a major role in the Department. This is basically another facet of the technician role; in this function the emphasis tended toward summarizing factual information rather than advocating certain policy preferences.

The following comments typify the staff's perception of this role:

> We advise the city manager concerning various policies and programs of the city and agencies operating within the city. We make recommendations to the City Planning Commission, particularly with reference to various city ordinances.

> The main function is as an advisor to different levels of activity as far as physical development interest is concerned. The main activity relates to regulatory control. Efforts among these are equally divided. We should be advisory to decision makers.

> The present functions are the following: Doing the expected job of administering the zoning regulations and subdivision ordinance; maintaining a vague and pious master plan, presumably as a guide for the first function; serving as a source of miscellaneous data to miscellaneous people; and doing various quick studies wanted by the manager or mayor, since often no other city expertise exists.

TABLE 6.2   Time Staff Spent on Federal Programs, 1967-1969

	1967	1968	1969
Percentage spent on federal programs	54.3	46.0	37.9
Exclusive of 701 Project	4.4	4.6	14.3

NOTE: Numbers given are percentages of total.

> At the present time, it's generating reliable data, analyzing data and making it available. Coming up with recommendations to the manager. Our data is widely used by OEDCI, Model Cities, etc. Our information is widely used. If they won't listen to our recommendations, they will rely on our data.

The technician's role is also important in the Department's federally sponsored programs. The Department recommends participation in particular federal programs, provides information to the manager about such programs, and helps to fill out federal applications. For example, the Department assisted in the development of the Workable Program, which is prerequisite for urban renewal funds, and also participated in such federal programs as Model Cities, urban renewal, Turnkey Public Housing, Urban Mass Transit, Urban Beautification, 701, and EDA. Table 6.2 reveals that from 1967 to 1969, almost one-half of the total staff time was spent on activities related to federal programs, and that in 1969, excluding the 701 Project, more than 14% of staff time was spent on such programs.

The Department's participation in federal programs provided it a measure of influence; planning recommendations were more likely to be accepted if the federal government paid for implementation.

An interesting variation on the technician role was the idea, expressed by several staff members, that the Department acted as the manager's conscience, reminding the manager of certain responsibilities or suggesting that he undertake particular actions. All too often, however, it seemed that the manager refused to let his conscience be his guide.

The Broker

Rabinovitz (1969: 96-97) described the broker role played by planners in New Jersey as one in which the planner injected new ideas or alternatives into the political process in such a way as to furnish a technically satisfactory solution, and, at the same time, helped to reconcile opposing interests.

In Oakland this was a subsidiary planning role, which operated in two important areas. Brokering was important in zoning questions and when citizens attempted (or were directed) to participate in the city's policymaking process.

In zoning cases granting conditional use permits offers a good example of the broker's role. Basically, these permits allow uses not normally allowed in areas subject to specified conditions of development. This can be a method for reconciling conflict between developers and neighborhood residents, while providing a technically satisfactory solution (Crowther, 1968: 18).

Another way of thinking about acting as broker between conflicting parties would be to view the planners as performing a screening function for the manager and Council. It was particularly clear that the broker role was employed for the purpose of screening when the Department was serving as an interface between concerned citizens and the city administration. On one hand, staff members reported that they would inject neighborhood concerns into the thinking of other departments. On the other, they saw themselves serving to buffer the administration from active citizens' groups. Trying to serve simultaneously as spokesman and buffering agent resulted in difficult cross pressures for the Department and, ultimately, a diminution of their effectiveness. For example, the Department demonstrated an honest concern for the views of West Oakland citizens regarding the need for parks and recreational areas in their neighborhoods. At the same time, there is no evidence that the Department abandoned their traditional supplier-oriented approach; that is, they knew best what services and facilities the citizens of that area needed. In other instances they coincidentally supported citizens' participation in various urban renewal projects while recommending to the manager that, for reasons of efficiency, such citizens' boards and their staff support should be combined, thereby diluting the individual citizen's or his or her group's access and authority.

Perhaps because of such difficulties, the Planning Department was not able to develop the buffering or screening role as a resource to the degree that some in the Police Department were able to do.

The Mobilizer

In a fragmented political system, such as that in Oakland, planners must mobilize public support for their proposals if they are to be effective. This was indeed a part played by the planners in Oakland, although the fact that the city has a strong manager, who can fire department heads, restrains them in this role. In Oakland this can be a dangerous function if the Plannning Department's values differ significantly from those of the manager, Council, and mayor. Therefore, it must be played delicately, somewhat surreptitiously, and within tolerable limits, but it can be played nonetheless.

Rabinovitz (1969: 101) has aptly described the appropriateness of the mobilizer role in a fragmented system:

> In a fragmented city such as Passaic, where there are few guaranteed benefits from the exercise of influence, many actors do not call upon their resources. The consequence of not using these resources is a great deal of "slack" in the system. When someone in the community exploits their available, but hitherto unused, resources more fully and efficiently than before, his influence grows.

How and to what extent, then, do Oakland city planners act as mobilizers? They serve primarily as catalysts to initiate action. The Department may give ideas or information to community groups, which then take action. For example, the Department knew that there were some 100 vacant, single-family houses in the East Oakland-Fruitvale area that could be demolished. The Planning Department saw an opportunity to rehabilitate these dwellings rather than to demolish them. Consequently, the Department went to the East Oakland-Fruitvale Planning Committee to get them to approach the Council on the matter. Because the manager feels that each city department has its own area of expertise, the Planning Department staff felt that he would view a matter of this sort as outside of the Planning Department's sphere of influence. Similarly, a member of the East Oakland-Fruitvale Planning Committee reported that for the Planning Department to present this proposal to the City Council would be a "kiss of death."

The idea of the mobilizer role implies developing a constituency to support planning proposals. However, the Planning Department in Oakland has not been able to develop a broad constituency partly because of the Department's views concerning citizen participation. In the Lowell-Adeline Industrial Triangle rezoning case for example, the North Oakland community appealed to the Department to prepare a district plan for the area, but they refused, saying that they had several high-priority projects under way and, consequently, there was no staff available for this study. At the time, the 701 Project, a citywide effort, was requiring all spare staff time. But the Department missed an opportunity to use neighborhood planning as a vehicle for mobilizing support and responding to neighborhood requests. Why did the planners fail to urge the citizens to go the City Council and ask for more staff to do the study?[2]

The Department missed this opportunity because, first, they were heavily committed to the 701 Project. Originally, the 701 Project was to have included proposals for neighborhood planning, but the manager rejected the idea. Second, the Department tends to see itself more as providing information than advocating the particularistic interests of any community group. Oakland planners see themselves striving to serve the public interest, and the director feels that if the Department becomes involved in neighborhood planning, it will be difficult to balance neighborhood and citywide goals. For example, many neighborhoods want to retain their single-family residential character, thus precluding any hope of meeting the city's public housing goals. Or a neighborhood wants more parks, but may have more than its share already.

These are very real problems faced by planners, and there is no easy way to resolve the conflicts. Thus, in Oakland the mobilizer role is not widely played; when it is, it usually is interpreted in terms of serving as a catalyst rather than mobilizing community support for planning proposals.

The Watchdog

The last major role played by the Department might be called that of "watchdog." The idea is that the Planning Department watches over other departments and certifies that they are acting in the public interest.

Victoria Pohle (1969) in a study of this Department, found that it attempted to be watchdog for the Turnkey Public Housing Program, although it was not clear that the Department was able to play it effectively in this case. In fact, the City Planning Commission told the Council that it no longer wished to review and to make recommendations on Turnkey proposals, because its suggestions were not heeded.

As the Department is not a staff arm of the manager, it has little power to influence other departments. In order to act the watchdog, Planning depends on its ability to convince the manager that other departments are not serving the public interest. The Department's ability to play this role is further diminished if an agency like the Housing Authority is not controlled by city hall.

Within city hall, however, planners can be effective. For example, the Department helped to defeat a proposal from the Traffic Engineering Department for a parking garage in Lakeside Park. In this case the Department joined with others in opposition to the proposed project because the planners did not think it in the public interest to construct a parking garage in one of Oakland's most scenic areas.

"What Are We Doing? It's Just Not Clear"

Thus far, we have argued that Oakland's city planners play a number of roles; however, it is important to remember that the planners are vague about their legitimate purpose. The following quote from the assistant director is indicative:

> We're in limbo. We're not the in-group of the city manager, We have to derive our reason for being from the city manager or the Commission. We should get more attached to the city manager—get his confidence. Now we work in a power vacuum. We do things because we think they're important. In cases where the manager doesn't ask for a recommendation, we work through the Commission. We have a lot of self-activating activities. We seize opportunities when we feel we can be effective. We deal with social, physical, and economic issues. We wonder sometimes where our responsibility ends and someone else's begins. If we were under the manager, we should expand our area of expertise. We could eliminate the more pedestrian things we do and leave them to a line department, but I have mixed feelings about this. At one time we considered long-range fiscal planning and giving up physical planning and land use controls, an area where we have been most effective—the improvement of the physical environment and appearance.

Another high-level staff member put it this way:

> It's random now. Not definite. Not spelled out. We concern ourselves with the physical environment. There are no functions clearly spelled out for the Department. We're advisory to the City Council. Ours is almost what people think of us.

This poor focus is closely tied to the Department's choice of clients, as we shall see in the next section. Before proceeding, however, it may be helpful to examine what the Planning Department staff felt its role should be.

"What Should the Department's Role Be?"

The interviews and questionnaires revealed that most believed the Department should make better recommendations. Two methods for improvement were noted. One was to make more reasoned arguments based on better study, and the other was to become more sensitive to the needs of decision makers and thus to make recommendations that appealed to their interests. In either case, the Department's technical function would be intensified.

Another often mentioned, desirable office was that of staff arm for the city manager; this idea dates to 1941, when Robert Walker proposed that planners become staff to the executive in order to become more politically effective (see Walker, 1950). Both the director and assistant director suggested becoming staff to the manager, and each suggested that the zoning functions could be abandoned by the Department. The director observed that the Department's role in zoning associates it with controversial issues and hinders its relationship with the manager. Moreover, zoning matters constitute a large percentage of the disliked brushfire activities assigned to the Department by the manager. If these were eliminated, the Department could function more as a policy advisor to the manager.

Others among the planning staff recommended more attention be given to educating the public in planning matters in order to gain public support. However, there was wide variation among staff members regarding the advisability of this approach. Some viewed education in terms of providing information to community groups, who would then decide for themselves about issues, whereas others saw it as "selling the planners' viewpoint."

"It's Difficult, But Planners Do Cope"

What conclusions can be drawn concerning the Planning Department's functions? Although it plays a number of roles, the Department staff sees its purpose primarily in terms of the technician, furnishing information and recommendations to decision makers on land use and other physical planning questions. However, this activity seems to be useful only for the Planning Commission. In other words, when the question is what to do, the planners' tendency has been to respond by providing land use and demographic data. They cope with ambiguity about their role by performing the least controversial function of the many available to them. The difficulty with this strategy is that such data do not seem to be particularly useful to anyone in city hall or to the citizens, with the possible exception of property owners and developers. In this situation the planners, although minimizing short-term uncertainty, are performing functions that are not considered helpful.

They rely on a coping tactic that is not likely to lead them to a more purposeful, meaningful existence in city hall. In short, they have not been able to turn others' uncertainty regarding what planners should be doing in city hall to their benefit any more than they have been able to use the screening function fully as a resource. It may be that planners are not particularly adept at managing ambiguity; their raison d'etre, after all, is control of the future. It also may be that the Planning Department in Oakland was more disoriented than, say, the Police Department in that their attention was directed solely to clarifying their purpose. If this was the case, they would be unlikely to enter into a more sophisticated risk management enterprise with "adversary" groups as did the ASUO leaders and police chief. Why follow a difficult, personally threatening path for objectives that are not well specified or understood?

THE DEPARTMENT'S CLIENTS

Problems of a Multiple Clientele

Most of the staff defined their employers as the primary client, so that the manager, Council, mayor, and Planning Commission were viewed as important clients. Most of the staff also felt that, ultimately, the community at large was their client. This latter category included quite diverse groups. The director, for example, identified the Department's clients as the City Planning Commission, the City Council, the manager, and groups in the city, such as the Real Estate Board, the Chamber of Commerce, and various neighborhood associations. To regard such different groups as clients it seems would lead to a kind of organizational schizophrenia. Other staff members mentioned that the Department serves "both conservative and militant groups" or the "community of Oakland." This response may be traced to the planners' perception that they are serving the public interest, rather than particularistic interests, but as Altshuler (1965), among others, has observed, this is an impossibility. No plan can serve the whole community, and this has been among the primary criticisms of general plans; they assume goal consensus in the community. It well may be that part of the Planning Department's inability to define clearly its role results from its diverse interactions with groups having different, often conflicting, expectations of them. A classic response in the face of such conflict is inaction or, in terms of subjective rationality, avoidance.

Yet other problems appear to be associated with several diverse clients. What if the purposes of the WOPC (West Oakland Planning Council) and the Council or manager differed; the Department believed the WOPC to be in the right and, thus, the public interest would best be served if the WOPC were to have its way? Which client would the Planning Department choose to serve? Part of the problem is that the staff, in some ways, began adopting the advocate role, supporting the claims of Oakland's poor, but, at the same time, were subject to sanctions by their employers. However, the traditional view of proper professional conduct for planners has been that they should serve their employer, try to influence him or her to accept their recommendation, and abide by his or her decision or resign. Many of the staff members expressed this view:

> The planner has an obligation to work within the framework of policies determined by the decision makers. He should avoid secretly poor-mouthing these decisions to outsiders. He does not surrender the privilege of recommending changes in these policies, of pushing those values and ideas which are clearly in conflict with basic city policy. There must be a pluralism of thought within city government.

> In accepting employment, he [the planner] accepts a certain amount of loyalty to his client. But he recognizes his employer as an intermediate client, whose client is the public he serves. In an indirect way, the planner's conduct should be in the best interest of the public. There could be a conflict in trying to organize before the employer knows about it.

Adapting to Conflicting Expectations

The Planning Department staff accommodated divergent expectations in two ways. First, it argues that its clients change with the issue. On one issue the Department's client may be the WOPC, on another the Real Estate Board. Of course, there is still the question of who will be the client when there is a conflict between the WOPC and the Real Estate Board. In such a case the Department might try serving as broker in an attempt to reconcile conflicts.

Second, by defining its role primarily as one of providing information, rather than one of advocating the views of various groups, the Department often avoided the client problem; information can be given to all groups, regardless of conflicts. However, at times the Department did more than provide information. It advocated positions that were more acceptable to some of its clients than to others. For example, the Department openly advocated the cause of some low-income groups. Moreover, merely providing information without bias, however subtle, is not possible.

The technician, broker, mobilizer, and watchdog roles all may represent attempts to serve a diverse clientele. The mobilizer role, for example, is particularly directed toward community groups as clients. Of these four roles, however, only the technical function is related directly to city policymakers as clients.

And although it may not have been as promising as some of the others, it has been emphasized by the staff and, thus, was the function the manager had come to expect of his Planning Department. It seems that the planners in Oakland hold values, choose issues, and represent groups that are not supported by and may be antipathetic to the Commission, manager, and Council. But rather than resigning, or fighting in-house to the death, they understandably take refuge in their technical function before a situation gets out of hand.

THE GOALS OF THE DEPARTMENT

The goals of any organization are difficult to pinpoint. For one thing, they may be phrased in such general terms that one is hard pressed to find meaning in them. Second, the stated goals of the organization may not coincide with its activities. And, third, there may not be a goal consensus in the organization. One may apply the first two characteristics to the Oakland City Planning Department but not the third.

Improving the Physical Environment

Interviews with staff indicated that improving the physical environment is the Department's primary stated goal. Improving decision making also ranked high, but the reason for improving decision making generally was to improve the physical environment.

The planning director saw the major goal of the Department as "meeting our charge," meaning the preparation of a general plan and administration of the zoning ordinance. This also related to improving the physical environment.

One of the three broad goals stated in *Options for Oakland* (Oakland City Planning Department, 1969) was to improve Oakland's physical environment. The plan emphasized improving the visual quality of the environment. Therefore, providing a more aesthetic environment was a subgoal that appeared to preoccupy many in the Department.

The *Central District Plan* (Oakland City Planning Department, 1966) calls for preserving and strengthening the CBD in Oakland. In this plan, aesthetics, like orientation, identity, urban character, and uniqueness, are mingled with economic concerns such as intensifying commercial activity in and attracting business firms to Oakland's central business district.

Oakland's zoning regulations also enumerate the foregoing physical improvement goals. One aim, for example, is to "protect residential, commercial, industrial and civic areas from the intrusion of incompatible uses." Another is to "promote safe, fast, and efficient movement of people and goods," and to provide "adequate off-street parking and loading." Still another directs the planner "to achieve excellence and originality in design."

Many other examples could be given to indicate this orientation. These goals are not, however, peculiar to Oakland. Pick up any general plan, CBD plan, or zoning ordinance in the country, and you will find similar objectives. In fact, these are the interests of the modern planner. Our concern for urban environments stems from the Garden City Movement of the late nineteenth and early twentieth centuries. Questions of incompatible use and environmental efficiency gained prominence during the City Efficient Movement in the 1920s. The Oakland Planning staff has been involved in zoning questions because of its position as advisor to the Planning Commission. Moreover, the city manager feels that each department has a particular expertise, and the Planning Department's seems to have been defined informally as land use planning and zoning.

Improving the Quality of Social Life

With the advent of the 701 Project, the Department's goals expanded to include social goals. *Options for Oakland*, the summary of Oakland's

701 Project, aims "to provide good housing for all of Oakland's residents" and "to develop a healthy economy and reduce hard-core unemployment" (Oakland City Planning Department, 1969: 2). Of course, city planners have long been concerned about housing and, recently, HUD required that a housing section be included in all 701 plans. One standard goal of general plans is to provide for a variety of dwellings throughout the city. But *Options for Oakland* focused more on the social problems of providing integrated housing for low-income persons. In this statement, the planners called for an open housing market and sound housing that people could afford.

Oakland became eligible for a 701 planning grant because of its high unemployment; thus, the 701 program also included an unemployment component. In this way, the Department was led to think in terms of economic development and fighting poverty. The focus on unemployment also forced the planners to think about racial discrimination and the relationship between unemployment and education. The final result was that *Options for Oakland* became a social policies plan of sorts, although this was not the initial intention.

The planning director admitted that the opportunity for the Planning Department to develop social goals arose because of a fortuitous tie-in between the 701 Project and the Economic Development Administration. The Department's interest in economic development, however, was not new. Part of the zoning regulations' purpose was to "advance Oakland's position as a regional center of commerce, industry, recreation and culture. . . . To promote the growth and productivity of Oakland's economy. . . . To stabilize expectations regarding future development of Oakland." And the *Central District Plan* was intended to strengthen the economic viability of the central business district.

These, then, are the formally stated goals of the organization and a brief history of their adoption. But such objectives can be adopted for many reasons and do not necessarily reflect the values of the staff. In fact, the Department's actions may contradict such formal ends.

Informal and Latent Goals

Clearly, our true interests are revealed as much by what we do as what we say we should be doing. Basically, informal or latent organizational objectives are those that, although not formally stated or claimed, are likely to guide behavior. For the planners in Oakland, the informal goals primarily were as follows: becoming more effective, enhancing the prestige of the Department, avoiding conflict, serving the citizens' interests, and influencing the policies of city hall. One can readily see that all but one or two of these behavioral guides can be subsumed under the rubric of organizational survival.

Certainly the drive for survival in the organization is not unique to the Planning Department. One could argue, though, that it assumes more importance for the Planning Department than for many other agencies because of the ambiguity in the planners' day-to-day purpose and function.

Several staff members mentioned survival as a goal of the organization. And it is likely that actions that threaten the organization's existence or that of the top personnel will be avoided. Thus, the tendency to avoid controversy goes hand in hand with survival, particularly in an insecure setting. This is not to say that planners eschew all controversial issues but rather that there are limits to the Department's willingness to propose change.

Enchancing the Department's image is another latent goal, and it also is a form of service to organizational survival. David Vetter (1968b: 40-41) noted that the Planning Department emphasized "visible" outputs, which pleased the City Council. For example, much of the staff's time for a three-year period was spent on the 701 Project, which offered a highly visible product and a source of prestige for the Department. Similarly, the Department invested heavily in an American Institute of Architects' competition for a city design award. Subsequently, the Department won an award for its design work, and the planning director suggested to the manager that the city should "blow its horn" about winning.

Perhaps the most important aim of the Department is to become more effective. This is not a new problem for planners; their advice has seldom been taken by policymakers. Moreover, the concept of a general plan has been denigrated, and many planning departments are searching for alternative approaches.

Outsiders' perceptions of the Department also increase their desire to be more effective. The question "What does the Planning Department do?" is heard all too often around city hall. And, too, both policymakers and operating departments' staff tended to view the planners as impractical dreamers. The Planning Department staff felt in general that it could be more effective only if it were to be used as a staff arm of the manager. But this does not seem likely in the near term because, as the planning director said,

> The city manager is concerned with not rocking the boat, while the objectives of the Department are that the boat needs rocking, but this should be done gently so that nobody knows the boat is rocking.

Thus, there is a realization that although change in Oakland is desirable, it should proceed slowly.

Serving the Public Interest

The last informal goal revealed by our study of the Planning Department in Oakland is that of serving the citizens' interest. This is important only in that it suggests that the planners believe that there is a public interest to be served rather than many different, sometimes conflicting interests. Thus, the planners do not admit, at least publicly, that their plans give to some and take from others. Belief in a public or community interest is deep in the literature and culture of our society; such an assumption by practicing professionals is, nonetheless, an effective method for reducing the likelihood of their becoming embroiled in disagreements over the implications of a plan or proposal.

What Should the Department's Goals Be?

Thus far, we have been discussing what seemed to be the actual goals of the Planning Department. It may be helpful also to consider what the staff felt their goals should be. If one examines the responses to a question of needed goals, one finds a general consensus. Most staff members mentioned becoming more effective as the end they most coveted. The following replies are indicative of their feelings:

> The development of power, since no change can come about under the present situation.

> To see that actual projects get built.

> To pursue an active, competent program of public communication.

> To become trusted, consulted advisors to the manager and mayor.

> The selling of planning concepts—get people excited about planning.

> To get the process down to where it means something.

The strategies for becoming more effective differed, ranging from "selling planning" to becoming a staff arm of the manager, but the goal is the same. No one questioned the department's stated environmental objectives; there appeared to be a good deal of consensus on them, although a few staff members favored giving more attention to social goals. In this respect, the Planning Department's conundrum was like that of the City Council in Chapter 4. Just as the Council wanted to maintain active authority over the community action programs, the planners wanted to be more effective. However, neither group was willing to assume the increased risk of public controversy that accompanied attempts to exert more influence in or over their environment.

RELATIONSHIP BETWEEN PLANNERS AND DECISION MAKERS

The Manager

The key figure in city hall is the city manager; he more than anyone controls the administrative departments and the budget. There was general agreement among the planners that the manager did not really use them. A review of the Department's internal correspondence files from April, 1969, to March, 1970, indicated that the memos from the Department to the manager were mostly procedural, policy-oriented status reports, providing information or referring to personnel matters. The frequency distribution among these categories is shown in Table 6.3

Procedural matters, the largest category, included a variety of activities, ranging from approval for conference attendance to procedures for the preparation of an EDA application. Many of these memoranda concerned federal programs, such as the Neighborhood Development, Model Cities, and Urban Beautification Programs. Thus, it seems that despite the planners' feelings, the manager uses the Planning staff heavily at least for technical information in regard to federal programs of this type.

Policy-related communications included recommendations regarding policies or reports that contained policy recommendations or required a policy decision. A proposed sign control ordinance for Oak-

TABLE 6.3   Substance of Formal Communications from Planning
            Department to City Manager, 1969-1970

Nature of Contents	Number	Percentage
Procedural	43	33.0
Policy-oriented	20	15.4
Status reports	24	18.5
Basic information	24	18.5
Personnel-related	19	14.6
Total	130	100.0

land's rapid transit lines, an Oakland Auditorium Study, an analysis of
Turnkey Housing, and comments on proposed deviations from the
Department's plans are examples of such correspondence.

Status reports were readily identified and the federally assisted Urban
Mass Transit Study accounted for most of them in this period. Memos
bearing basic information varied widely: Some simply informed the
manager of attendance at meetings, others described the way in which
the Department had complied with the manager's wishes, and still
others informed the manager of federal programs.

Finally, personnel-related communications concentrated on vaca-
tions, compensatory time, and the like.

If one divides the memoranda into a policy-oriented category and
others, the former account for about 15% of the total. These data
suggest that the Planning Department does not make large numbers of
policy recommendations to the manager.

The available memos from the manager to the Planning Department
between 1967 and 1970 revealed that he employed the Department
primarily for short-term projects, brushfire actions to meet a pressing
need of the moment. Table 6.4 indicates some of the ways in which the
manager used the Planning Department. The planning director, however, observed that formal memos could be deceptive, because many of
the manager's directives to him were given in an informal, personal
setting.

Several interesting patterns are apparent in these data. First, one can
see that the manager uses the Department for brushfire operations more
than for any other purpose. Second, the manager does not formally
request a great deal of information from the Planning Department. In
fact, the conclusion of several Planning staff members that they are little

TABLE 6.4   Manager's Use of Planning Department

Type of Use	Number of Memos
Brushfire activities	4
Staff comment on development proposals	2
Information-giving	2
Information-requesting	1
Getting advice	1
Requesting coordination	1
Request for studies	1
Personnel matters	1
Total	13

used by the manager may be a correct one. It is also clear that the formal communications flow is primarily from the Planning Department to the manager; thus, we can assume that the manager provides the Department with little formal feedback.

However, over the three-year period covered in this study, the Department's major assignments were as likely to come from his requests as from appeals to him (see the Appendix at the end of this chapter).

In short, the Planning staff felt that the Department's relationship to the manager was ambiguous. The director pointed to the Department's ambivalence in trying to serve two masters: the manager and the Planning Commission. Some of the staff comments regarding the Department's relation to the manager were as follows:

We are ignored and little used by him.

He gives only lip service to planning.

He's not long-range oriented.

I don't think [the director] really knows where he stands with the manager.

The manager thinks he can do his own planning.

One frequently voiced opinion regarding the Department's relation to the manager was that the Planning Department was not part of the "management team." This was attributed to planners being different from other people in city hall. As one staff member put it, "Planners don't play golf at the [city golf course]." Moreover, planners were thought to be impractical and "fuzzy-headed."

The Council

The Department had no direct relationship with the Council, and the indirect relationship that it had was not a good one. As the director put it, "There is a great deal of affability, handshaking, and first-naming, but a considerable number of reservations on both sides and a lot of suspicion." Other typical comments by the staff were these:

> To the Council we probably represent a slightly radical, somewhat unsettling presence, which adds little to the conduct of their duties.

> The manager and Council can order work done, and the mayor can ask for reports. None seem enthusiastic about us, and our reticence to strongly and clearly raise issues and make suggestions probably perpetuates our apparent irrelevance, while the occasional, mildly phrased dissents nonetheless raise questions of our loyalty and team play. We have the worst of all worlds—we're distrusted, but not respected.

Part of the problem is that, although the Planning Department's formal goals support an economic development ideology, their adoption was, in part, a strategy to make planning recommendations more palatable to the Council. Informally, the Department opposed a "development at any cost" policy, and the staff's values, which were strongly conservationist, often conflicted with economic development.

Finally, because all Council members at this time were elected at large, the staff raised questions in regard to the representativeness of the Council. They felt that because of this, the Council represented basically middle-class, conservative persons and did not give adequate consideration to the problems of low-income minorities. Several staff members commented that the Council did not like to admit to inequities in city services.

The Planning Commission

The Planning Department serves as advisory staff to the Planning Commission and makes recommendations on zoning matters to it. In a previous section it was argued that the Commission acts to protect developers from unreasonable staff restrictions and to exercise control over physical development. Its members' interests are short-range and topical. The following are representative staff comments concerning the Planning Department's relation to the Commission:

> We have close relations with some of the Commissioners and antagonisms with others.

> We feed information to the Commission on zoning, but we're used for little else. They are fairly sympathetic to planning, but they have a limited grasp of what planning is about. They are topical in their interests. They're interested in individual issues.

> The knowledgeability of the Planning Commission is limited. Most of the commissioners don't know what they're supposed to be doing, and it is hard to educate them.

The Department is closer to the Commission than to the manager, Council, or mayor, and the staff agreed that the Commission usually goes along with staff recommendations. This is partly because zoning is a rather narrowly defined area of expertise and one that planners can claim as their own. Moreover, the Planning Commission tends to approve applications, subject to design review; thus, the planning director judges whether a proposed development meets desirable design criteria. The staff, however, did not view this practice favorably. Rather, they saw it as an abdication of the responsibility for making decisions, and the consequence was an increased staff work-load.

Yet such discretionary procedures actually allow more control over development than do zoning regulations; but the department maintained that the "hold the line" budgeting policy in Oakland restrained them from hiring staff to perform adequate design review. Thus, according to the planners, budget constraints reduced their effectiveness in this situation.

Summarizing briefly, I have argued that the goals of the planners often conflicted with those of the city's policymakers. I further contend that, despite a strong desire to be effective, the Department chose to avoid controversy more often than not. This placed them in a frustrating position. The staff clearly wished for major changes in Oakland's government; alterations in which the present administration would be superceded by one that held values more like their own. In this way, the planners would be released from their "damned if you do and damned if you don't" position without having to tolerate more risk.

But in the period covered by this analysis, the Planning Staff worked in an administrative setting that was not as they would have liked it to be. Thus, they had developed tactics for making the best of their situation, and we turn now to a further consideration of them.

STRATEGIES OF INFLUENCE

The strategies used by the Department to influence others were important determinants of its effectiveness. Moreover, the tactics employed reflected the role the top staff perceived as appropriate for the Department. For example, if the role is understood in technical terms, the likely path would be to develop recommendations for decision makers and to depend on reasoned arguments supporting those proposals. The strategies varied among the Department, but the primary methods used in their attempts to influence are outlined below.

Make Recommendations to Decision Makers

Providing recommendations to the manager, either through inter-office correspondence or through planning reports, was, as indicated, an oft-used approach. I could not find evidence that this strategy influenced policy, but it was not controversial behavior. This same approach also was adopted for the Planning Commission; the staff presented a report to the Commission for each zoning case. One planner admitted that such staff reports often served as "soapboxes" from which they would make broader policy recommendations.

This method, however, yielded no access to the Council. When the Department wished to reach the Council, it attempted to play the Commission and manager against one another, getting one to present the planners' proposals to the Council if the other refused. It is ironic that, although the Planning Department was an important part of the Council's screening network, when it wished access, it was compelled to employ sophisticated tactics just like outsiders.

A variant of the bluff tactic used to influence the manager was to develop support from other departments in order to present a united front. This tactic required enough common stake for other departments actively to support the Planning Department's proposals. This con-sensus was difficult to acquire because most city departments were somewhat hostile toward the Planning Department; they were viewed by other departments as intruders into areas that did not concern them and for which they had no claim to expertise.

Planners often were critical of the proposals and orientations of other departments and tended to be somewhat like a watchdog over them. For example, the Planning Department rankled the Traffic Engineering

Department by opposing the proposed Lakeside Park garage, which the latter was supporting. This approach was expressed well by one staff member who reported that

> the Traffic Engineering Department is not following the Central District Plan, which is Council policy. We monitor the day-to-day operations. We are like a private detective. We watch others, but we can't blow the whistle on them. There is a political role here.

Because planners could not intervene officially in cases like this, their ability to effect the activities of these departments lay in their persuasiveness. Yet if they informed the Council or manager of this nonconformance with city plans and policy, they risked losing needed cooperation from these departments at a later time. But the department could not assure other departments' conformance to its plans except by reporting them. Moreover, in specific cases, such as that of the Lakeside Park garage, the Planning Department was forced to oppose openly in order to stop action. Thus, it is difficult to envision many circumstances in which other departments would join with the Planning Department to present a united front to the manager.

Still, if the "united" approach is as it seems, those wishing to influence policy must at least possess the appearance—or threat—of widespread support; the capability for generating a united appeal would be very important to the plannners. Thus, I found that even though they could not readily get other departments to support their proposals, the Department discovered a way to increase rapport and support-potential from neighboring departments. They formed interdepartmental planning teams that have provided the Department the appearance of wider support through these cooperative ventures.

Two such teams were of major importance to the Planning Department. First, the Advance Transportation Planning Team, composed of staff from the Planning, Streets, and Engineering and Traffic Engineering Departments, was mandated to develop the "design, type, location, and timing of circulation improvements to meet the needs of traffic in any given area." The other, the Resource Allocation Program (RAP) Team, with personnel from the Planning and Finance Departments, was given responsibility for developing the RAP. Moreover, it was intended that the team provide an annual resource allocation study.

Both teams, following their natural instincts for uncertainty management, enabled planners to affect decisions in two major areas of city responsibility: streets and budgeting.

Use Outside Intervention
To Influence the Council

Another strategy for influencing the Council is to persuade individuals to intercede on the Department's behalf. The planners often convinced community groups to support their proposals and then to press the Council to adopt them. This strategy may also be pursued through the press. The *Montclarion*, for example, often printed stories supporting Planning Department interests and maintained a staff member in city hall who was sympathetic to planning proposals. The paper provided strong support for the Planning Department's fight against the proposed parking garage in Lakeside Park and was undoubtedly influential in helping to mobilize the public opposition that eventually defeated the proposal.

This strategy was not employed often enough in the period of this study for us to conclude that the Department's utilization of the screening function as a resource had matured. I noted that the police administrators used the buffering role as a method for increasing influence in that Department's budgeting process; in the case of the Council's response to the Community Action Programs, one could see a hint of this external influence strategy, in which the unit or individual who usually served to screen reversed its role and became a conduit for outside interests. This is clearly a dangerous move, especially so in a situation of mutual ambiguity, suspicion, and antagonism, such as that of the Planning Department. But, if employed skillfully, this approach can result in the screening agents' changing the policy outcomes as the foregoing examples demonstrated.

Educate Decision Makers About Planning

This strategy is based on the belief that misunderstanding rather than conflicting values between planners and decision makers causes ineffective planning. This, however, is not a widely accepted strategy among high-level staff; but it is used, especially for the Planning Commission. The Department schedules periodic workshops to discuss general planning issues that are not linked to specific zoning decisions. The consensus among the staff is that this strategy had not been particularly effective because it required reorienting people's thinking about planning and possible alterations in value structures.

These adaptive strategies grew in an environment in which planners could not resolve the dilemmas engendered by conflicting expectations, objectives, and value structures. We have seen that generally ambiguity and conflict worked against the planners' desire to be important actors in the city's policymaking process. We also have seen that the planners' natural tendency to avoid controversy in this environment (that is, reduce uncertainty about what they were doing) enabled them to continue, but did not really move them toward resolution of the basic uncertainty. However, we also observed that the planners had developed, at least to the embryonic stage, tactics that played more on others' inability to predict the Department's activities or potential activities clearly. These latter possibilities clearly offered the planners better opportunities to affect policy outcomes, although they paid a price in higher risk and continued uncertainty about their role in the city's governmental process.

CONCLUSIONS

In summary, we can identify from the foregoing study two paths by which the planners could become a more active part of Oakland's policymaking process. First, as just noted, they could work to develop strong citizen support for their proposals. This choice uses the screening role to the best advantage. But this is not the easy path; it is arduous work to build and hold support, as the experience of the ASUO in Chapter 3 amply demonstrates. It also is dangerous to stir up controversy for those elements that are employing you to protect them from it. But if it is not the easy path, it is the one that requires the least compromise and provides the most satisfying goal achievements.

The second path leads one to give the policymakers proposals that they will want rather than those one may think they ought to have. In Oakland this means providing them with recommendations that conform to the decision maker's value priorities and that will not cost the city money. This can be a frustrating but eventually fruitful approach. On one hand, it is difficult to determine if one is influencing the decision makers. Basically, you are suggesting that they do what they want to do. On the other, always showing the boss what he or she wants to see will, over a period of time, increase his or her confidence in your recommendations, so that he or she will grow to rely more and more on your opinion, provided that what he or she wants and you suggest does not result in considerable negative feedback. This too is arduous, and it is an intrinsically less satisfying method. It is also the less controversial, safer in the short term, and, I suspect, the more common road. Although the planners in Oakland would not yield completely to this strategy—a particularly difficult one for someone with considerably different values from those of the policymakers—it did become their modal strategy. In other words, most limited themselves to activities that were easy and comfortable for them; they assembled information.

The Planning Department in Oakland has afforded us an excellent view of administrators working under conditions of uncomfortably high ambiguity. Furthermore, although they developed tactics for coping in this circumstance, they were not able, at least through the period covered by this study, to reduce the ambiguities in a way that was satisfactory for them. This disagreeable situation resulted in frustration, seemingly erratic behavior, and rather sophisticated methods for acting influentially despite continuing uncertainty.

The planners' case, then, offers evidence that administrators can exist and at times be quite effective despite continuing doubt about their role. This study also indicates, however, that the planners' methods for managing their doubts were like those of the ASUO leaders, police administrators, and Council members. They attempted to reduce their own uncertainty by narrowly focusing their own responsibilities and, failing that, to increase others' doubt regarding their capabilities and proper role.

The planners in Oakland shared a long experience coping with their role difficulties. Their situation was not a surprising one, like that of the Council in Chapter 4. How do administrators respond when they are unexpectedly faced with a considerably increased collective uncertainty? We turn to this question in the next chapter. The following chapter examines the Parks and Recreation Departments, both of which had a long tradition and well-developed routines to guide their activities. However, the two departments were suddenly and with slight warning merged together by order of the manager. The well-established routines and traditions no longer supplied enough useful information and no new signals were forthcoming from the manager. How did they manage in this surprising, suddenly more uncertain setting?

APPENDIX

Description of Planning Department Programs and Activities

(1) Planning Administration

    (A) *Zoning cases, etc*:

        Investigate and report to the City Planning Commission on all applications for the variance of provisions of the zoning regulations, amendments to zoning boundaries, design review, conditionally permitted uses, and the like.

    (B) *Subdivisions*:

        Investigate and report to the City Planning Commission on all tentative subdivision maps and private access easements that are filed. Investigate and report to the applicant on all preliminary subdivision maps submitted. Interpret the provisions of the subdivision ordinance and work with developers to attain the best design solutions where appropriate.

    (C) *Miscellaneous referrals*:

        Respond or report as appropriate to various departments and agencies on matters pertaining to the zoning regulations, subdivision regulations, and other Planning Administration matters, including referrals from the City Council, City Manager's Office, Industrial Development, Building Department, Real Estate Division, Street Department, State Division of Highways, and others.

    (D) Interpret the provisions of the zoning regulations and the subdivision regulations to those requesting information. Give information as requested on zoning and subdivision cases and on the zoning of specific properties. Review proposals for conformance with the zoning regulations. Provide any other information that might be requested regarding matters handled in the Planning Administration Division.

    (E) *Housekeeping and maintenance*:

        Include maintenance of files and maps and other technical materials not involved with a specific case.

(F)   *Turnkey design review:*

Review of proposals for Turnkey Public Housing to ensure that design criteria are met.

(2) Advance Planning

Major projects

(1) *Lake Merritt Channel Park*

A coordinative effort between the Redevelopment Agency, the Peralta Junior College District, the Port of Oakland, and the city to develop a park. Project uses the state funds for regional open space. The Planning Department became involved at the manager's request.

(2) *Beautification Program*

Coordinating and initiating the city's Beautification Program. Preparation of the application for Council. Working with citizens recommending beautification projects. The Planning Department initiated the program through the manager.

(3) *Model Cities*

Planning Department was part of an interdepartmental task force and was involved in "brainstorming" each department to see what types of programs might go into West Oakland. Also involved in recommending the administrative organization for the program. Worked with the manager in preparing the Model Cities application. Participated on Model Cities planning committees. One staff member worked full-time on land use planning for the program. The Department's participation was requested by the manager.

(4) *Workable Program*

Prepared, in conjunction with the Redevelopment Agency, the sections on plans and programs and relocation. Workable Program was prerequisite for urban renewal funds. Participation requested by manager.

(5) *Neighborhood Development Program (NDP)*

NPD was a new approach to urban renewal in that larger areas may be defined as renewal areas, but only smaller projects can be executed. However, the larger area becomes eligible for renewal grants. Planning Department made proposals for the administrative organization of the program. Also did preliminary planning for NDP areas, but this was primarily a response to Redevelopment Agency proposals. Worked with Redevelopment Agency in developing application. Worked with citizens and Agency to determine NDP boundaries. The Planning Department initiated its participation in NDP.

(6) *Oak Center and Acorn Urban Renewal Projects*

Reviewed and planned changes in these projects. Participation at request of Planning Commission.

(7) *Peralta College Urban Renewal Project*

Worked with manager's office to develop the land package.

(8) *City Center Urban Renewal Project*

Reviewed Redevelopment Agency proposals and prepared preliminary plan needed to meet state requirement. Participation requested by Planning Commission.

(9) *Central District Plan Implementation*

Worked with the Central District Follow-On Committee to get rezoning in the central business district and to effectuate the Central District Plan. Initiated by the Department.

(10) *Urban Mass Transit Study*

Prepared application, in conjunction with AC Transit, to study the public transportation system in Oakland and the East Bay. The study tried to relate employment problems to transportation. Also involved preparation of a demonstration application for new service routing for AC Transit. The program was initiated by the Department through the manager.

(11) *BART studies*

BART impact

Department sought to determine the development potential around five BART stations in Oakland and to see whether public action was desirable to capture the development potential of these areas. Involved roundtable discussions with people from real estate, mortgage investors, planners, and a few community leaders. This was a 701 study and was requested by the Planning Commission.

Sign controls along BART

Department developed changes in the zoning regulations in order to control billboards along BART rights-of-way. This study was initiated by the Department.

(12)   *1970 Census Coding Project*

A program for which the city was given funds by the Department of Commerce working through Association of Bay Area Governments (ABAD) as regional disperse-ment agency to aid in census mailing project. Listed each block-by-block face. Will now be able to get additional information from the Bureau of the Census on block face basis. The Department initiated this project through the manager.

(13)   *Oakland Economic Development Programs (OEDP)*

A response to a requirement by EDA that the Department develop an economic development plan. Was actually only an inventory of all city efforts in manpower de-velopment, education, and business development. This project was performed in response to a request by the manager.

(14)   *Turnkey Impact Study*

Department was asked by the manager, in response to a request by the mayor, to evaluate the physical impact of Turnkey Public Housing on neighborhoods. The study focused on physical factors, such as noise, traffic gen-eration, and maintenance of buildings, rather than on social impact.

(15)   *Auditorium Study*

A study of alternative uses of the Auditorium site, main purpose of which was to keep the land in public use. The study was initiated by the Department through the manager.

(B)   *Miscellaneous special studies*

Numerous short-range special studies initiated by various officials.

(C)   *Services to public*

Provide information on advance and current planning matters to those who request this information. The group served is composed mainly of personnel from public agencies, civic and business people, and students. However, there has been an increasing demand for speakers from neighborhood groups concerned with neighborhood-level planning problems.

(D)   *Housekeeping and maintenance*

Includes maintenance of files and maps and other technical materials not involved with any specific program.

(E)   *Mapping and drafting*

Involves mapping and drafting not allocated to specific programs on time sheets.

(3)   701 Project

(A)   *701 Project*

A citywide program of survey and analyses aimed toward a comprehensive development plan for Oakland. Federal grant was received in 1965. Summary report, *Options for Oakland*, contained recommendations on physical design and development, economic development, and housing. RAP is part of 701 Project. The Department initiated this project through the manager.

NOTES

1. Ordinance No. 192 C.M.S.
2. Portia Shapiro, City Planning Department, Budgetary Process, in Oakland Project files.

7

DISORIENTED
Administration
Reorganization in
the Parks and
Recreation Departments

AS WE NOTED IN previous chapters, in 1966 the mayor and Council were looking for a new manager to replace the one, recently resigned, who had been enthusiastic, imaginative, active, and expansionary. The mayor and Council wanted a man who could slow—even reverse—rising city expenditures. A tough, efficiency-minded man was located and hired. The new manager immediately began looking for ways to "tighten" the city's administration by extending managerial control. He agreed to sweeping alterations in the accounting and record-keeping systems to standardize both practice and form. The idea was to save recording and processing costs and to provide the manager, his assistants, and department heads more timely, complete information about the city's day-to-day activities. The manager, in his search for ways to cut expenses, came to believe that needless duplication and functional overlap existed among his departments. If their activities could be somehow streamlined, money would be saved without obvious reductions in service.

The four departments that reported to semiautonomous commissions were identified as particularly wasteful.[1] They were not cooperating in the difficult job of shifting to timely, standard information reporting. They continued to abuse the accounting system by charging their activities to completely unrelated fund accounts. In other words, these departments had been doing pretty much as they pleased, ignoring the budget, charging particular expenses against any account that had not been depleted. Of these four, the Parks and Recreation Departments seemed especially guilty of overlap and duplication. In fact, Recreation

Department interviews in 1967 revealed widespread departmental opinion that Recreation and Parks should be one department.[2] Significantly, this opinion was found primarily outside Recreation Department personnel.

The manager's plan to trim his administrative ship included the unification of these two departments. A two-pronged approach developed. A charter amendment was proposed that would reduce all city commissions to advisory status along with an ordinance to supersede the existing specification of the city's administrative organization. Essentially this new ordinance required that the Council be responsible for maintaining an efficient, up-to-date administrative organization. In other words, the city manager would in effect be able to organize and/or reorganize his administration at will so long as he had Council approval.[3]

Both propositions were approved in November 1968. The manager acquired substantially increased administrative discretion and four semiautonomous commissions would no longer obstruct his control of city administered services. He began quickly to implement his plans for reorganizing—streamlining—the city's administration. He told the Parks and Recreation Departments that they would be unified. At the same time, the city's maintenance support and supply activities were pooled in a newly created Office of Public Works. The old Streets and Engineering Departments formed the core of the new Office, which included the Building and Housing, Municipal Buildings, and Purchasing Departments. It also incorporated all craftsmen, mechanics, janitors, or gardeners attached to those several departments. Moreover, the city contracted to build an expanded corporation yard in order to centralize maintenance support facilities/activities.

All municipal departments were affected by this combination of changes in 1968/1969. New procedures in the accounting/record-keeping system, the commissions, and the organization of departments severely disrupted former normal operating routines. The Parks and Recreation Departments, however, among all the city's domains, were perhaps most affected by the changes; they inherited all these upsetting innovations simultaneously. Familiar authority patterns or structures and formal as well as informal operating routines were disabled and colleagues displaced. More important, the manager did not follow through after he had directed the Parks and Recreation to reorganize. He had indicated that an ordinance was forthcoming that would provide among other things, elaboration and specification for the new Department. Three years after Parks and Recreation had been told they were to be unified and two years after the fact, no such ordinance had been published. Furthermore, the new department, as we shall see in more detail below, had received little direction in any form. Parks-Recreation administrators were left to cope as best they could.

The following investigation explores the ways in which the leadership grappled with the uncertainties that resulted from these externally imposed, disruptive changes. Their uncertain situation was exacerbated, of course, by a context in which there was no clear authority structure to inform and guide action. We also will attempt to identify consequences of this condition for the Parks-Recreation administrators, services, constituents, and for other areas of the city's administration. But first, it will be helpful to sketch an outline of the two departments before this reorganizing period. The digression will provide information that may enable us to understand more fully some of the difficulties generated by and encountered after unification.

BEFORE UNIFICATION:
SIMILAR WEBS BUT IMPORTANT DIFFERENCES

The Bosses

The size and the structure of the administrative leadership was very similar between Parks and Recreation. In both departments supervisorial staff and line assistants to the level of area director or crew boss numbered between ten and fifteen persons. Each supervisor had two or three staff assistants—accountants, budget analysts, and the like—and program assistants who directed different aspects of the Department's operations. Each program supervisor in turn had function or area directors. In addition to similarity in size and organizational design, the two departments even provided services that seemingly overlapped. Fundamentally they shared responsibility for maintaining the municipal facilities designed for outdoor, leisure, or recreational use.

Within these similar skeins, however, there were important differences of philosophy, emphasis, and behavior. Of the two, Parks had developed a more centralized administrative style. Recreation's approach had been to encourage onsite discretion. It also had a tradition of active and interactive participation in budgetary and most other major departmental decisions. The Recreation Department's supervisor, a man who had occupied that post for seventeen years, was repeatedly characterized as one who absorbed rather than disseminated information. That is, he wanted to feel that he was fully informed about his department's activities but he was not an active director. This style encouraged a feeling among the membership that they were part of a continuing search for improvement and innovation.

Park Department programs, also supervised by a long-term incumbent, were clearly directed by him. This supervisor's habit was to hold a bimonthly staff meeting. In these meetings, problems were voiced to the supervisor while information and direction for planning, decision, and/or solution was returned. The Park Department's administrative style was, in general, more orderly, regular, and routine than Recreation's.

The Commissioners

The semiautonomous Recreation Commission membership was among the first in the city to be integrated, racially and socially. Normally this commission functioned to provide general advice about departmental priorities and policies. They had exhibited an active concern for and commitment to the community's need for usable facilities and healthy diversion. When, the controversial Black Panther Party requested permission, in late summer 1969, to use one of the department's buildings to provide a "breakfast for kids" program in the poor neighborhoods, the commissioners—although they were not disposed toward the Panthers—took a chance and granted the Panthers permission to use a building for what appeared to be a worthy program.

The Parks Commission membership, in contrast, was white, business-oriented, and politically conservative. As one might imagine, they placed heavy emphasis on horticultural and agricultural occupations. Their concerns were that the city have well-manicured, "green" boulevards, and many, well-designed, clean, healthy park areas. They exhibited a tendency to provide minutely detailed advice to the supervisor and his assistants but in fact they appeared to have slight impact, serving largely to ratify the supervisor's priorities and policies.

The Constituencies

Both Parks and Recreation had, relative to their sister departments, an extensive network of active constituents. They were clearly the two departments with the most lively public constituencies before the burgeoning of human resources and antipoverty programs in the city. In Recreation, the district supervisors, program directors or, perhaps, the supervisor responded to common requests for use of a recreation center, playing field, or special equipment. Less common requests—from questionable groups—were forwarded to the Commission for decision. The following instances exemplify the kinds of questions that reached the Commission for decision: a group of golfers wanted a recent municipal green's fee increase rescinded; a neighborhood association requested that the department set aside "green areas" under certain high-voltage power lines; and last, the Commissioners enlisted another neighborhood organization to help them solve continuing "patron control problems, both in the building and on or near the grounds" of a recreation facility.[4] In sum, the Recreation Department administrators tended to forward unusual decision problems to the commission. Although it naturally delayed decisions, the Commission seemed willing to make hard choices. Specifically, the Commission delayed the most difficult problems, such as the Black Panthers' request, until they were reasonably sure that their decision was defensible or that further delay would lead to greater problems.

Most users of Recreation services or facilities did not have much in the way of personal influence with the commissioners. They were, for the most part, the city's younger, undereducated, poorer, black and brown citizens. They did not have the information, skill, presence, self-confidence, formal positions, and informal acquaintance network commonly required to exert influence effectively. Ironically, these constituents, because of this poverty of resource, have been influential in the city's recreation policy. Both the school and police administrations had come to regard municipal recreation programs as effective deterrents against disruption and crime in the city. Thus the local school administrators and police have become strong, though usually covert, allies of the Recreation Department's largest but most personally disadvantaged constituents (Dahl, 1969: 14). The influence of the young and poor was further increased because in the 1960s different federal agencies' combined contribution to recreation for the sake of the ghetto dweller accounted for 15% of the department's yearly budget.

The Parks Department's active publics were, as you might guess, different from those of Recreation. More than 50 garden, breakfast, and/or service clubs regularly and formally used the municipal park facilities. In turn, the membership of such groups could be relied upon to vigorously support the department's programs. Although the supervisor energetically "sold" the Parks Department's project to the Council, most felt that constituency influence with the commissioners and the council members was the important factor in getting their department's request approved.

Parks' administrators generally were able to employ this outside influence strategy more successfully than the Planning Department administrators because their clientele groups possessed most of the requisites for power. In 1967, for example, the department requested additional capital improvement funds from the Council in order to rebuild an aging and heavily used lodge in one of the larger municipal park areas.[5] The petition was disallowed during the 1967 budget hearings. The Parks' supervisor, seeking to get the funds reinstated, reported to the Council that the popular lodge would have to be closed because it was no longer safe for public use, thus eliminating a popular Parks service. He went on to argue that revenues from a new lodge would completely replace the city's cost within 20 years, and then the lodge would become an important revenue source for the city. Finally, user groups, encouraged by the supervisor and commissioners, made an impassioned plea for a new lodge before the Council. The Council relented, the funds were restored, and the lodge rebuilt.

Clearly, the Parks' constituents possessed more traditional political capital than the Recreation Department's. They were neighbors, fellow clubmembers, professional acquaintances, and friends of the commissioners, councilmembers, and the administrative leadership of the city whereas Recreation's constituents more nearly resemble clients in the professional sense. Parks—in contrast to Recreation, which must rely on formal institutions for financial and political support—leaned on an informal set of like-minded people: clubs, neighborhood associations, professional organizations, and individuals often contributed money to support a particular project. A large building and garden center was built in one of the city's most attractive parks with the help of a $100,000 donation from a large garden club. In return, the department allowed this club to use the center for their meetings and waived the use fee.

The Parks Commission, then, functioned more as a powerful and supportive lobby for Parks administrators than as a decision-making body. The Parks administrators did not often forward decisions to their Commission. Moreover, the Parks Department did not seem to be confronted with hard decisions such as whether or not to allow the Black Panther party to use its facilities for a formal program. Rather, they faced routine requests that came from friendly, supportive, homogeneous constituencies.

Interdepartmental Relationships

We move now to the relationships and routines between each of these two and other city departments. Generally, each had quite similar feelings about and interactions with others in the city family. But their respective internal responses to parallel situations was not the same.

Those in both departments reported little contact with city hall, especially the Manager's Office. Moreover, no one, other than perhaps the supervisors, knew the manager's feeling about their shops or programs. The supervisors saw the manager infrequently, normally in defense of a budget request. The analysts from the Budget and Research Department would see the supervisor or the departments' budget or administrative analysts, but others had very slight contact with their colleagues in the city. In fact, a very clear "we-they" consciousness had developed between both departments and other city offices. In Recreation, perhaps because the times and thus powerful institutional allies were favoring recreation programs, this separatist feeling was not accompanied by resentment, frustration, or hostility. Recreation's commitment to widespread participation in the search for improved services was benefited, even enabled, by a sense of independence from city hall.

Parks, on the other hand, reacted to this division with suspicion and hostility. They too, as we indicated, had powerful supporters. But Parks did not see their situation as one offering opportunity for experimentation, self-direction, or increased participation; on the contrary, they constantly were looking for direction. Perhaps this perspective developed because their alliances generated more problems for them than those of Recreation or because they were a more centralized department. Before unification, Parks administrators felt—whatever the reasons— that the city administration was not experienced regarding or concerned for Parks. After unification, this habit of expecting clear direction was to raise considerable difficulty for most parks administrators.

Both departments had developed under the commission system a practiced juggling act as part of their fiscal record-keeping procedures. From the viewpoint of a city manager or his finance department such practices were travesties of accepted municipal management practices.

Ironically, when the city administration increasingly committed itself to electronic data processing in order to improve fiscal management, the Parks and Recreation Departments sharply complained about the paucity, due to difficulties with the city's electronic data processing (EDP) system, of timely, accurate account information available to them.[6] It seems likely that the Parks and Recreation administrators were actually grousing about the threat that strict, machine-centered accounting and record-keeping procedures might pose for their unorthodox financial practices. Although it is probably true that the introduction of EDP altered the "game," it also seems likely that—considering the city's difficulties with EDP (detailed in the next chapter)—the departments' opportunities for fiscal latitude increased. Just one administrator among those interviewed in both departments seemed to grasp the possibilities presented by a nascent, uncertain, and error-prone EDP operation and acted to take advantage of them; the others acted as though the system was in fact constricting their activities. In short, their response was rather like that of the Council when faced with the question of independence for the Community Action Agency. Although the Parks and Recreation administrators clearly did not want to yield their fiscal independence to an EDP system, they behaved as if they had no other choice when confronted by it. The fact is that computerized record keeping at this point in its development presented as many—perhaps more—opportunities for fiscal maneuverability in city hall. Again, it appeared that most administrators, like the council members, chose to withdraw rather than continue with more difficult, perhaps dangerous tactics for managing their uncertainties.

Parks and Recreation had both developed informal operating procedures (other than simply budget related) that further expanded their discretionary power. Purchasing/supply activities, for example, had been especially personalized. Over the years an extensive acquaintanceship in both public and private sectors had evolved and was relied upon to furnish supplies at a fair price, promptly, and without extensive paperwork. A similar net provided for those maintenance and craft services that the department itself could not perform. Again, the emphasis was on good work at a fair price, promptly, that did not require much documentation. Such informal activity was threatened by the city's growing commitment to EDP because one of the products of an EDP system is substantial increase in the amount and regularity of documentation flowing from the departments to EDP central. The city's EDP operation, however, had not become sufficiently established at this point to seriously cripple these departments' nonstandard procedures, but the creation of a central maintenance/supply support division did disable them.

In the preceding paragraphs we have attempted to provide a brief sketch of the Parks and Recreation Departments before they were unified. A look at their many functional and procedural parallels accompanied by clearly different leadership styles and attitudes about the nature of their respective roles is important for our understanding of the problems experienced by those in the unified Parks-Recreation Department. They provide clues about the structure and style of the new department's administrative leadership.

Before we begin to weave these threads, it may be illuminating to elaborate more fully the unification process and the resultant organization.

IMPLEMENTATION: "AT SEA"

Our discussion began with the manager's announcement in late 1968, that Parks and Recreation were to become one department. However, he made no immediate move to implement this reorganization. The two continued separate—though increasingly apprehensive—existences for many months after the official decision. At first the manager divulged no information about the merger—when it was to occur, what the resultant administrative structure would be, who would fill the new positions, or how the present service mix would be changed. Then, after a year of this lame-duck operation, the departments received the manager's directive to merge. He directed that the incumbent Recreation Department Supervisor take over as supervisor of the new department. The Parks supervisor was transferred and became the director of the city's new Museum Department. The manager indicated that his office was preparing an ordinance that would specify the new administrative structure in detail. But as the time for completion of the merger approached, there was no ordinance. Thus, on January 2, 1970, when Parks and Recreation became one department, there was no official Parks-Recreation administrative organization nor was there a directive regarding the mix of services that the new department was to provide, other than that it was to take over management of the civic auditorium. There were, however, constituencies to serve—users of the

Parks-Recreation facilities and/or services who must be answered. In short, the Parks-Recreation functions could not just stop and wait for further direction. The cautious supervisor, probably anticipating official directives from the Manager's Office, "arranged" his department's administrative personnel but did not formally or publicly announce their positions, titles, or functions.

Time passed and no new direction emanated from the Manager's Office; still, the supervisor did not publish internal organizational or operating directives. It was clear that, after several months in a nebulous condition, this unusual situation was weighing on members of the new department.

Fall 1970—The Bosses, "Becalmed"

More than eight months after unification, the supervisor was still delaying decision about formalizing the new organization. The other administrative leaders in the department were cross-pressured—in fact, nearly immobilized—by the ambiguities generated by the manager and supervisor's lengthy delay. They had few guides for decision-making but, as we have noted, constituency expectations, requests, and demands required that they continue to provide most of the traditional services. Correspondingly, the administrative leadership felt that they had lost most decision-making power and thus were no longer able to provide acceptable service. The result was frustration among those who had spent most of their professional lives in the city's Parks or Recreation departments. Nearly everyone alluded to poor morale since reorganization. More than one talked of this as "simply another move by an insensitive central management to move decision-making power from agencies in the field to enable increased administrative efficiency."

Despite administrative disorientation and frustrating sense of impotence, Parks-Recreation nevertheless continued to offer service at some level. But the fact is that on one hand the administrators felt that they were not able to shape or reshape their new department; on the other hand, they were not being told what to do. For example, one administrator responded that regarding questions or problems relating to structure or operating procedures, "the question is what to do, and the answer has been do little." A second said that he was "waiting for the dust to settle so that he could see." Yet another replied that in terms of administrative leadership, he did practically nothing; he functioned narrowly and on the strength of his particular professional expertise. One particularly caught the flavor of the department's administrators in this period when he said that they "stick very close to their own bailiwick." One thing is clear: the manager had effectively fettered these heretofore relatively autonomous departments.

The Commissioners, "Abeyant"

The new Parks-Recreation "Advisory" Commission simply echoed the administrators' disoriented, do-little-attitude.[7] Table 7.1 indicates that the Commission's activities, controlling for reduced responsibilities, declined substantially after reorganization.

Constituents, "Reacting to Interrupted Services"

So, too, constituency relationships deteriorated markedly. The administrators interviewed in this period indicated that reorganization had stripped them of their ability to respond to constituency requests effectively, and as a result they were feeling pressed by their constituents.

Centralizing support services, which resulted in the dismantling of the departments' cleaning, repair, maintenance, and purchasing capabilities, was responsible for much of the constituency pressure. Normally many constituents' requests required one or more of these services, and the department could no longer respond to them easily and directly. They were required, in accordance with the pool concept, to submit formal requisitions for service or supplies to Central Services. A request from Parks-Recreation would be assigned a priority and lumped with similar requests from other departments. This procedure, involving new administrative forms, considerably extended the time from request to action. Moreover, the Parks-Recreation administrators had no control over the quality of support service provided. They argued that upkeep had not been adequate since reorganization and the formation of Central Services. In their opinion, the general condition of Parks-Recreation facilities and grounds was deteriorating. In fact, many supplies and services that the departments had offered were no longer available because the informal maintenance/repair/purchase nets were not usable. That is, some of the craftsmen formerly employed by the Parks and/or Recreation Departments could not or would not satisfy the more complicated contractual procedures required by Central

TABLE 7.1   Parks Commission 12-Meeting Sequence, March-April 1966,
1967, and 1970: Controlling for Alteration in Commission
Responsibility

	1966		1967		1970	
	Decisions* Action	Delay/ Defer	Decisions Action	Delay/ Defer	Decisions Action	Delay/ Defer
Routine	16	3	15	0	2	0
Nonroutine	4	1	4	1	0	1
	= 24		= 20		= 3	

NOTE: Commission activity drops substantially after unification and alteration to
advisory status. This tabulation excludes discussion of budgetary and department
personnel items. Those responsibilities transferred from the commissioners to the
manager after reorganization. The years 1966 and 1967 were chosen randomly from
those between 1962 and 1969. March and April were usually two of the busiest
months.
*Routine decisions are simply those that, after inspecting the minutes of Commission
meetings for a five-year period, seemed to come to the Commission repeatedly.
They were recognized as common requests by the commissioners and acted upon—
usually yes or no—with a minimum of discussion and hesitancy. Nonroutine are,
of course, all others.

Services. Similarly, certain kinds of supplies were lost because the
purveyors didn't conform to the city's more formal requirements. In yet
other cases, support services' personnel simply did not know whom to
contact for a particular need, or they determined—perhaps er-
roneously—that it should be addressed by city staff in order to save
money.

The Parks-Recreation supervisor reported that reorganization to a
new department had generated a flood of requests, many of which had
been submitted to one of the parent departments or commissions and
rejected. He confessed that he was so overloaded by these demands that
he had given insufficient attention to forming his new department. But
Table 7.1 suggests that he was not passing these requests to the new
advisory commission in order to free his attention for the problems of
developing guides for his administrators. In any event, the department's
constituents and the Manager's Central Services organization combined
to increase Parks-Recreation's frustrations.

Interdepartmental Relationships, "Stormy"

Parks-Recreation contact with the Manager's Office, as the preceding
paragraphs indicate, did not increase or improve after unification. The
"we-they" feeling persisted among personnel. The department is several

blocks removed from city hall and several miles from the Corporation Yard, home of central services. One disgruntled Parks-Recreation administrator claimed that the city manager had not even been inside their complex. Yet EDP and central services required more—especially formal—contact between themselves and Parks-Recreation personnel. This necessity for more formal, less physically and substantively satisfying contact added yet another measure to the irritation of the Parks-Recreation administrators.

In general, the administrators resented the disruption of their established routines and their diminished autonomy, particularly at the shops' service level. Their resentment was exacerbated by their belief that this accumulation of changes upsetting their lives was not, in any sense, improving Parks and Recreation services or saving the city money. Still, they, understandably, were not inclined to endanger their careers by acting on their own initiative to diminish the negative effects of these changes. The P-R situation at this point nevertheless offered a chance of substantial reward for someone with imagination and willingness to accept the risks of unilateral action. At least one administrator, however, was imaginative and willing, and was by all accounts the most influential and successful member of the department. It was said that the supervisor relied on this man's judgment more than any other.

1972-PARKS-RECREATION IN PERSPECTIVE: "ADRIFT"

The Bosses

An ordinance specifying the city's new administrative organization still had not been published two years after unification. After more than two years in this nebulous administrative milieu, the question is this: What had developed in Parks-Recreation? What adjustments, if any, had been made by the administrative leadership? Perhaps the most obvious development was that the parent Recreation Department simply absorbed the Parks Department. One of the higher level Parks-Recreation administrators who had been in the Parks Department quipped, "I am all that remains of the old department." The same men had occupied the top positions in Parks-Recreation since its inception and two years after reorganization they naturally had a greater sense of permanence and stability in their positions and, more important, of the entire department's composition. The department personnel realized that all the higher posts, save one, were probably going to continue to be staffed by Recreation Department personnel.[8] Moreover, they had begun to realize that a leader's personality and experience are particularly important in a context of ambiguous, emergent administrative form. All agreed that the new Parks-Recreation supervisor responded to a dearth of direction from the manager by allowing—perhaps encouraging—the transposition of his old department into the new. The widespread feeling was that the Parks-Recreation Department was more an expanded Recreation Department than something new or an offspring of two parents. In short, the supervisor had responded to the dearth of direction by focusing on procedures and services with which he was most familiar and entrusted them to employees he knew best. The supervisor's choice of method for managing high-order uncertainty resulted in difficulties for his subordinates, particularly those who had responsibility for Parks functions and/or personnel. The old Recreation Department, as we have argued, had pretty well run itself; its formal and informal routines were well established, and the field supervisors were encouraged to run their own shops and to participate in the search for new methods of providing services. The recreation supervisor and Commission had screened the department, as well as the Council and manager, from difficult, potentially disruptive constituency requests. Table 7.2, together with the supervisor's admission that he had been inundated by more than double the usual number of constituency requests, suggests that he (and, increasingly, the Commission) devoted considerable energy to screening requests. However, this drain continued to leave the department without active leadership and formal or well-established informal operating guidelines. Those who had previously served under this supervisor reported that, though they missed their in-house and rather informal support net, flexibility with their budgets, and current fiscal status information, they were not so disturbed by unification as the former Parks personnel were. These administrators were acquainted with the supervisor's personality and administrative style, yet they too continued to be frustrated by their department's lack of structure.

Former Parks personnel were in an even more difficult situation. Their experience had been in a centralized administration; the Parks supervisor had more actively directed his subordinates. Furthermore,

Park's philosophy had been different—it was more conservative and less active than that of Recreation. In sum, they were poorly equipped to deal with this more ambiguous situation. Moreover, the nature of the Parks Department's service necessitated that they rely more heavily on their informal support, particularly supply, network. And, too, Parks had more freely manipulated their budget. After unification they found these supports gone; they had, in effect, become part of the city's recreation department and they understandably did not much like this situation. Every Parks employee questioned mentioned at some point that he or she found the personality of the Parks-Recreation supervisor baffling and frustrating. One said that "because of the personality of the supervisor, parks and park facilities were becoming more recreationally oriented, less parks-oriented." Another argued that "many of the problems experienced as a result of the reorganization would have been largely alleviated if the supervisor had seized the initiative—been willing to play quarterback." Generally, there was a pervasive malaise in the parks related areas of the Parks-Recreation Department. As one man said, "the idea of parks has pretty much dissolved in this city." Some of this feeling is undoubtedly the kind of murmuring that one would expect from those whose professional lives had been severely disrupted. Three of the top four administrators in Parks-Recreation entrusted with responsibility for parks functions and personnel retired early, in each case considerably before the mandatory age.

The Commissioners—"Rebirth"

When the Parks and Recreation Commissions were stripped to advisory status and amalgamated, either the tenure of three members expired or they resigned. One commissioner was from Parks and two from Recreation; thus a seven-member board emerged from the two five-member commissions. There were no other personnel changes associated with the reorganization. Yet, Table 7.1 above suggests that for some months after unification the Advisory Commission was for the most part idle. Table 7.2 indicates that the Commission was beginning to function once again in its advisory and screening capacities. But the Commission, particularly in its weakened form, could do little to provide an increased sense of structure or leadership for the Parks-Recreation administrators. The Advisory Commission may have been stagnant because in addition to losing most of their formal powers, they

TABLE 7.2   Parks-Recreation Advisory Commission 8-Meeting Sequence
            March/April 1970 and 1971

| | 1970 | | 1971 | |
	Action	Delay/Defer	Action	Delay/Defer
Routine	2	0	4	0
Nonroutine	0	1	3	4
		= 3		= 11

NOTE: The P-R Advisory Commission is beginning to function again, relieving
constituency pressures on the supervisor. Conceptual construction follows that of
Table 7.1.

had little influence with the manager and were not in the habit of
advising their department except through the supervisor.

The Constituents—"Parks Users Are
Looking for a Sympathetic Audience"

The Parks-Recreation supervisor at first was absorbing the pressure
from the extensive and divergent constituencies of both departments.
The data suggest that he has begun to pass some of these demands to
the Advisory Commission and others to his subordinates. Delayed
responses and generally less well-kept facilities occasioned by a newly
formed central support services have generated more complaints, but
the less autonomous Parks-Recreation Department cannot respond as
had Parks and Recreation, engendering more complaints. The rather
different nature of the Parks constituencies, together with the shift in
focus away from traditional Parks philosophy and the displacement of
Parks personnel in the reorganization, lead one to expect that Parks
constituents would be the most complaining, most demanding. These
constituencies—the garden clubs, breakfast clubs and so on—were the
least familiar to the supervisor and he would likely feel less competent to
deal with their requests. On one hand this situation surely would
contribute to his frustration and feeling of ineffectiveness; on the other,
one might expect that a subjectively rational man in this position would
be most likely to slough off. Actually, all eleven items that appeared in
the 1971 sample depicted in Table 7.2 were parks-related questions
brought by parks constituency.

Interdepartmental Relations—
"Improving, but Still Frustrating"

Last, we return once again to interdepartmental relationships two years after unification. It was conceded that both a formal and an informal interaction web centered around Central Services is slowly emerging. The consensus was, however, that the problem of supply, custodial, and other skilled support was still a frustrating one. Nevertheless, Parks-Recreation contact with other parts of the city's administration is increasing. One administrator who has thoughtfully observed Parks-Recreation since unification maintains that the Parks-Recreation supervisor has not had much contact with other departments, especially Finance and Manager's Office. He continued that the supervisor, in his desire to control an ambiguous situation, has not been cooperating with city directives, policies, or the manager. Neither has he been communicating with his assistants. The administrator went on to illustrate, saying that the supervisor encourages indiscriminate fiscal reporting, such as was widely practiced when the departments were under the semiautonomous commissions, to enable continued flexibility despite concentrated attempts by the auditor, finance director, and the manager to eliminate the procedure.

THE LESSONS I: "THE PAIN CONSTANT"

We have acquired, at this point, some insights regarding the ways in which the Parks-Recreation Department's behavior altered in the face of a surprising, sizable increase in their uncertainty about role, product, market, and client.

Most Parks and Recreation services continued but the feeling among the department's administrative leadership was that the service was no longer of acceptable quality, and that they were unable to do anything about it. As a result, frustration increased dramatically and morale dropped.

The new department's leadership group tended to act not as administrators, but more narrowly on the basis of a particular professional expertise like accountant, horticulturalist, or practical engineer.

In short, they quickly adopted a posture similar to that of the planners; they fell back to a meager, noncontroversial set of activities. Those problems that could not be solved in the framework of this limited perspective were ignored and if that was not possible, the Parks-Recreation administrators, like the Council, withdrew from the decision arena and acted as though the set of difficulties—and their consequences—could not be affected by their choices.

Constituencies responded to the uncertainties enveloping the department—unaccustomed delays, and loss of certain supplies, repair capabilities, and kinds of care—by pressing more vociferously for a return to previous levels and quality of service. This, of course, further exacerbated the administrators' malaise. Three of the top six leaders in the new department retired early thus underlining the seriousness of this malaise.

Part of the problem for the Parks-Recreation Department was that reorganization crippled, at least temporarily, their powerful outside-influence strategy. Constituencies that had found the Departments to be excellent conduits for their interests found their access to the city's policymakers choked off by the careful, almost timid atmosphere that accompanied the Parks-Recreation administrators uncertainties. The result was that both department administrators and clients were befuddled and frustrated when their traditional, mutually reinforcing relationship no longer worked.

The Parks and Recreation reorganization experience, at the very least, instructs us that major changes in long-established, stable organizations are likely to be painful—perhaps unavoidably so—especially for those who have been thoroughly accustomed to old structure and routines. One Parks-Recreation administrator interviewed said thoughtfully that "many people prefer to work by rote—they feel more comfortable in settings in which (the procedures, responsibilities, and authority patterns associated with a) job are well established."

Some undoubtedly prefer the opportunities, challenge, and freedom of the more amorphous administrative setting to the well-established one. One or two such administrators questioned in Parks-Recreation seem to have reacted to the reorganization period as a challenging, exciting, and not particularly painful one. One reported that in the absence of clear directive to the contrary, he had done as he wanted and spent money as though the department had it. Most of us, however, are not comfortable without pretty clear guidelines against which to evaluate our performance.

The experience of the ASUO leaders, the Council, the Planning Department, and the Parks-Recreation Department demonstrate that, particularly for those who are responsible for choice, the necessity to work and act in an amorphous setting results in frustration, dissatisfaction, and apprehension.

THE LESSONS II: GETTING BY

A few organizations—notably research and development types—are relatively amorphous, almost by definition. Their leadership is guided by few established routines and authority may shift among the relevant experts rather than accrue to a structure of offices. In this situation action tends to be based on or justified in terms of professional expertise. This is precisely the behavior observed among many Parks-Recreation administrators. But they were not encouraged to adopt the collegiality that usually attends an unstructured context and reduces the members' disorientation and anxiety. It seems possible that attention to building supportive interrelationships by the manager, his assistants, the Parks-Recreation Supervisor, or his assistants could have eased the pain of reorganization. There was, as we have noted, a rather considerable variety of philosophy, style, training, and experience among the administrators of the two departments that might have been fruitfully shared, particularly before implementation. But there is no indication that such preparation was considered. These opportunities were not exploited and the different experiences and viewpoints acted to intensify resentments, poor internal communications, and disquietude. So, too, the Parks-Recreation experience demonstrates that, although extraorganizational, professional expertise may serve as a behavioral guidepost, it also provides a ready excuse for not acting when the ethical or substantive professional guides do not apply. The latter is exactly the circumstance that existed between the manager and Parks-Recreation supervisor and his subordinates, and the division or field leaders and their shops.

Similarly, the Parks-Recreation supervisor chose a limited coping response and continued in his professional capacity as director of Recreation. The remaining Parks-Recreation leadership chose to follow this same path. One division chief said, "Until we receive direction from higher authority, we will rely on commitment to professionalism in our new shop."

In sum, it seems that the administrators did not explore seriously strategies that might better have enabled them to adapt to their unusual situation; in short, they were not working to find pathways that would enable them to move away from their effective, but in the long run inadequate, coping responses (e.g., avoidance, delay, and professional fall-back).

Ironically, it seems in situations like that of the Parks-Recreation administrators, there is little to lose and much to gain by choosing an unknown direction or using ambiguity as a weapon. It may be that the bureaucratic experience to which we are constantly subjected conditions most of us so that we are not able seriously to contemplate using collective ambiguity as a tool, just as we employ information to cope with our environments. In retrospect, it appears that the ASUO leaders, thinking they had little or nothing to lose, were able to use more sophisticated tools to manage their uncertainty.

By way of conclusion, let us direct our attention to an obvious, though not trivial, question: Was the frustration and pain worth it? In short, was anything gained by the Parks-Recreation reorganization?

Not one person in Parks-Recreation thought the unified department, supported by Central Services, was saving the city money. Many believed that costs had gone up because support services personnel did not know where to buy repairs or supplies as cheaply as had the personnel of the Parks and Recreation Departments. A few thought that Central Services might prove more efficient after they "smoothed out," but two years was not enough time to realize its benefits. Table 7.3 indicates that unification of Parks and Recreation had not saved the city any money in the two-year, postorganization period. The combined departments' $5.6 million becomes $6.1 million in 1971—growing at 5% a year. In addition, remember that several Parks and Recreation supply and maintenance support personnel were transferred to the support pool.

The Parks-Recreation Department seemed to be paying little more attention to city directives and policies than had the Parks and Recreation Departments before, but if the manager had exerted more direct, personal influence, the new department—anxious for guidance—would almost certainly have responded. The manager's style, however, was not a direct one. He tended to authorize formal instructions, usually of a general nature, and issue direction through

TABLE 7.3   Pre- and Postreorganization Expenditures

Fiscal 1968 Parks expenditures	$2.3 million
Fiscal 1968 Recreation expenditures	3.3 million
Total	5.6 million
Fiscal 1971 Parks-Recreation expenditures	6.1 million

assistants. He remained almost invisible to the Parks-Recreation personnel; they received directives sanctioned by him but they did not see or communicate with him.

The reorganization seemed to have developed in ways that no one really intended or expected. Why? It is too easy to assert glibly, that the manager, his staff, and the Parks-Recreation administrators simply did not do their "homework" despite sufficient warning. However, there may be some truth in this assertion—one that was voiced repeatedly by administrators during our years of interviewing and observing in the city. But it does not appear that more thoughtful, intensive preparation could have alleviated all of the difficulties encountered in the reorganizing period.

Preparation requires time and energy from busy people. It is expensive. Moreover, how much preparation is required to ensure that major problems will be avoided? How do we know that all the "important" questions have been asked? Here lies the crux of the administrators' dilemma. Our understanding of the complicated, delicately arranged institutions in which we are born, educated, work, play, die, and with which we regulate the relationship between institutions and each other is relatively crude. Furthermore, we suspect that the personal costs of improving our understanding of these complex social units—if indeed it is possible—are more than most of us can afford. In our Parks-Recreation example it is doubtful if there would have been substantially increased reward for attempting more thorough preparation.

Furthermore, the Parks-Recreation experiences suggest that it is very difficult to specify realistically the implications in public organizations of a deceptively simple concept like efficiency. Which, on the face of it seems more efficient—the old, relatively flexible, informal, and redundant Parks and Recreation Departments or the new (in theory) more rigid, carefully controlled Parks-Recreation Department? Some might argue that one can more easily understand and improve efficiency in a simpler setting. Yet, in the general city reorganization, of which Parks-

Recreation was only one part, the movement was toward more complicated organizations. Redundancy was decreased without reducing size, thus increasing the organizations' complexity (Landau, 1969; LaPorte, 1969).

Parks and Recreation is an excellent example, then, of the unintended consequences that can result when major decisions are undertaken and the underlying concepts are no longer adequate for the situation. Confusion and uncertainty result while the administrators follow their natural inclination to search for information in order to clarify and reduce uncertainty. In a situation such as that of Parks-Recreation, information search was not rewarding and the adminstrators were compelled to act according to the information that was available; that is, they acted as they had before reorganization or in accordance with the norms and guides of their particular professional expertise (March and Olson, 1983).[9] However, if neither old routines or professional training and experience informed them, they were effectively immobilized.

It should be clear that there is no easy answer to the kinds of questions raised by the Parks-Recreation chronology. Certainly, thoughtful preparation is needed before attempting to modify sophisticated organizations. Also, we must act from time to time in organizational settings like low-resource pressure groups, that are not carefully controlled by someone in higher authority or brightly illuminated by extensive networks of formal and informal procedures. Finally, we must accept that we must act, aware that we cannot know enough. Therefore, the results are likely to be somewhat surprising, perhaps distasteful or incorrect. For the individuals affected, such experiences are almost certain to be painful ones. We will return to this theme in an expanded and more formal treatment in the concluding section.

We began several chapters ago examining the citizens' knowledge of attitudes toward and responses to government in Oakland and its effect on their lives. In subsequent chapters we moved ever more deeply into the inner recesses of city hall as we traced the city's policy process from the perspective of disinterested citizen, through citizen activists and elected officials, to mid-level administrators. In each case, our objective was to elucidate response under conditions of high-order uncertainty.

One can see through the progression of these cases that, though the individuals, organizational setting, and character of the problems confronted were quite different, there has been a remarkable similarity of response among them. From the residents to the Parks-Recreation Department administrators, avoidance, delay, and withdrawal have become common. So, too, anxiety and frustration mark those who are caught in ambiguous dilemmas. In sum, the foregoing studies uncovered a variety of rather sophisticated tactics for coping under conditions of uncertainty; and we have seen that such methods do not appear to be unique to certain types of people or to particular organizational structures.

Before we proceed to summarize the findings, and it is hoped, to extend our understanding of the tactics employed to cope with different types and levels of uncertainty, there is yet another case that promises to be fruitful. In this next study of Electronic Data Processing in city hall, we will see that a poorly understood technical process nearly crippled the city. In many respects, this next chapter will bring us full circle from a review of citizens cynically eyeing a government they do not understand to the decision makers cynically viewing a sociotechnical process—one that is at the very core of their policymaking process and which they do not understand. How did they respond to this situation?

NOTES

1. The four were Parks, Libraries, Recreation, and Museum.

2. This analysis is rooted in more than 50 interviews about the Parks, Recreation, and Parks-Recreation Departments collected from all levels of administrative leadership in these departments and associated departments in the city. The interviews were acquired at three different time periods and include many second and third repetitions. The first set, about 30 in number, was gathered by Portia Shapiro from Parks and Recreation in 1966 and 1967. A second set, including interviews of interested administrators outside the department, was collected from Parks-Recreation in the fall of 1970 and a third was collected in the summer of 1972 by the author.

3. The next section will illustrate that it has not been difficult for the manager to obtain Council approval for his decisions.

4. From Commission meeting minutes of June 25 and August 26, 1969. Quote from meeting of September 24, 1969.

5. The request amounted to an additional $84,000 in the capital improvement budget for fiscal 1967. This was considerable sum for one department to request from an economy-minded Council and manager that looked for possible paring of capital funds.

6. Chapter 8 is devoted to further analysis of EDP in city hall.

7. The Parks-Recreation Advisory Commission, like the Department, was not composed of new members but an amalgam of members from the semiautonomous Parks and Recreation Commissions.

8. Former Parks employees were, of course, especially sensitive to this situation. Even former Recreation workers, however, noticed the problem and felt that it was not a particularly healthy condition.

9. March and Olson assert that any reorganization will be rapidly attenuated unless there is persistence. Such persistence must come from a belief in the values served by the organization. In the case of Oakland's Parks and Recreation Department, there was some attenuation but long-term persistence was fueled by the city manager's belief in the possibility of markedly increasing efficiency.

8

A HOUSE OF CARDS
EDP in City Hall

THE PURCHASE OF EDP hardware, like the acceptance of the OEO community action programs, has produced few expected and many unexpected results. This analysis, like many of the foregoing ones, will point to some real, and perhaps unforseeable costs of unexpected secondary and tertiary consequences of a program decision.[1] This study also demonstrates that the best, most imaginative advice and ideas are likely—given a routinized setting in which the less imaginative stay and rise according to their seniority—to come from young, entrance-level members of the management hierarchy.[2] They are, at least in Oakland, more widely educated, and like the ASUO leaders feel that there is little to lose if they are mistaken. Yet they are closer to the root of a program or problem area. Such beginning-level administrators may be able to act in the context of a problem-laden program while remaining emotionally detached from it. They do not, in most cases, share in the decisions about the program or the responsibility for it. Their relatively advantaged position stimulates searching criticism and imaginative alternatives. But if, or when, one of these lower-level officials voices his ideas, suggestions, or criticisms to superiors, his comments are usually edited or filtered out because the more senior administrators are not rewarded for passing work, trouble, or criticisms to their bosses. The tendency at the intermediate and senior levels is, as our analysis of the Planning Department suggested, to forward only the best estimation of what the boss wants to see rather than what he should see.

EDP—THE ADMINISTRATIVE CONTEXT

Oakland's administrative organization set provides a variety of specialized services and employs well over 3,000 individuals, many of whom are rather well-paid professionals. A sixty million dollar annual budget supports these more than 3,000 full-time employees, and the greatest portion of the budget is committed to salaries and institutional maintenance. Oakland provides a wide range of services common to large cities. It provides, in addition to police services: parks development and maintenance, recreation services, and a large planning staff; fire protection, a large libraries system, an excellent museum, housing inspection, appraisal, and certification functions, and a large public works operation including design, construction, maintenance, and repair of public facilities. These are obviously diverse services requiring a variety of specialists operating in rather specialized suborganizations. So, too, many people providing many different services requires well-developed coordinative structures. Oakland has, in addition to a well-staffed city attorney's office, a city auditor suppported by clerks and accountants, a well-staffed city manager's office and large Personnel and Finance departments.[3] We turn now to a more detailed exploration of the official and the informal relationships among the coordinative suborganizations and between the service or public-oriented and coordinative or control-oriented subsets. The instance of the introduction of EDP hardware and processes will be used to highlight decision behavior in a nonroutine problem area.

The city manager's departments are, in certain respects, parts of a highly routinized bureaucracy. The C.M.S. Ordinance outlining the formal structure of the city manager's departments states that the basic form of organization shall be a hierarchical arrangement of Offices, Departments, and Divisions. The city manager is at the apex of this hierarchy. The ordinance goes on to describe in detail the responsibilities of each office and department and also outlines work schedules and salary structure. This detailed official description also contains elaborate operating guidelines.

One finds that the second- and third-level administrative leadership has been rather stable in Oakland. Promotion to these levels is usually according to seniority, which means longevity. Table 8.1 displays the department and division heads who have moved from their positions for reasons other than mandatory retirement from 1962 to 1972. Table 8.1 illustrates that despite a considerable administrative reorganization, the

TABLE 8.1   Middle-Level Management Positions in the City
Manager's Departments Are Stable

Stable: No shift in department head other than retirements, which were routinely filled by an immediate subordinate.	*Unstable:* One or more nonretirement department head shifts.
1962 to 1972	*1962 to 1972*
1. Accounting Department	1. City Manager**
2. Police Department	2. Finance
3. Fire Department	
4. Parks & Recreation Depts. (leadership reshuffled in reorganization)	
5. Libraries	
6. Public Works	
7. EDP*	

*New division since reorganization.
**Staff has expanded but remains essentially intact.

only significant shift has been that of the city manager himself who, instead of shifting or promoting an "old hand," handpicked a man from another city to head the critical, reorganized, and expanded Finance Department.[4] A stable leadership and detailed official descriptions of structure and process clearly imply a routinized setting.

Stability among personnel, especially among departmental leadership, also suggests, however, that extensive informal processes will be present. And there are indications that strong informal (non- or counterofficial) procedures exist among the city manager's departments in Oakland.

The city manager, considering a charter reform plan in 1968, informed the Council that an administrative reorganization was necessary, in part, to weaken existing informal processes that worked to enervate his organization. Before this reorganization was approved by the voters in November, 1968, several departments—Parks, Recreation, and Libraries, for example—reported to semiautonomous commissions even though they were formally responsible to the manager.[5] However, such departments often were able to circumvent the manager's authority by working through their commission to the Council.

Further indications of the ubiquity of informal organization can be found in several interviews about Oakland's transition to and experience with electronic data processing (EDP). In the intensive interviews collected in 1968 and again in 1972 regarding this program, office and department heads and assistants, administrative and budget analysts, and consultants cite long-held, unofficial departmental procedures as exacerbating the problems of transition to EDP.[6] For example, one senior administrator in the Finance Division told the author that some departments and sections operated largely by fiscal management procedures and processes that were almost one hundred years old and that specific knowledge about the workings of these systems was deeply buried in the divisions. Often only one or two individuals in a division would know about a certain procedure or process; they possessed a specialized knowledge that had been passed from one person to another and modified by each for decades. In fact, the finance director himself complained that, despite attempts to codify and standardize departmental record-keeping for machine processing and storage, people in the departments continue to use their personalized, informal procedures.

EDP IN OAKLAND

It is true for those who live and work in or study complex organizations that frequent personal interactions involving problems that are not readily solved with existing routines is antithetical to the idea of bureaucracy (see Crozier, 1969: 187-198 for a similar argument). Intensive study of the organizational setting as well as three years participant observation has convinced me that the city manager's departments in Oakland, like the City Council, are rarely confronted with problems that cannot be routinely solved, deferred, or ignored. But, attempts at transition to EDP have presented the manager's departments with a sequence of difficulties that have not been subdued by routine treatment.

Oakland acquired an automated data processing capability in 1942. At that time the city purchased machines that would punch, sort, and tabulate cards. This semiautomatic mechanical system—together with manual posting—served the city's information needs until 1962. By this time, it was reported that the city was beginning to have difficulty maintaining accurate, timely information—particularly fiscal information. The city auditor had become convinced that the city must replace and streamline this old, overburdened machinery. But, the Council was very cost-conscious; the property tax, though diminishing in relative importance, is still the City's largest *single* revenue source.[7] The property tax rate is high in Oakland, and before Proposition 13, it was nearly double the average for California cities.[8] The City, therefore, was sensitive about and not inclined to support proposals requiring large expenditures. Additionally, it is evident here as elsewhere when most of a city's budget is committed to rising personnel costs, the capital improvements budget absorbs most of the paring. It is simply easier— less painful—to go without a given repair or replacement for "one more year" than to cut Civil Service Personnel or to raise the tax rate. The Auditor, knowing the Council's feelings about large capital replacement expenditures, believed it was not likely to approve the purchase of new tabulating equipment for his office. But he thought that the Council might be persuaded to *lease* electronic data processing equipment. The Auditor counted on the Council's knowing little about EDP and on their being attracted to this technology that was connected, in the popular mind, to sophisticated, efficient, comprehensive, forward-looking management techniques. In other words, the auditor had decided to explore the alternative that seemed to him most salable to the manager and Council rather than to make an attempt to evaluate several alternatives based on other criteria. Everyone questioned who was working in city hall at the time of initial transition to EDP recalled that the auditor had set out to build a case for EDP. There is no personal or documentary evidence that he seriously explored other possibilities. The auditor's problem seems to have been one of providing the Council with a feeling of certainty about the nature of the City's fiscal-management information problem and the relative merits of his remedial proposal. If he were to present the Council with several possible alternative solutions, he probably would achieve precisely the opposite result—increasing their sense of uncertainty about the solutions and getting nothing he had requested. Thus, the auditor may have chosen to focus on EDP alone mostly as a matter of tactics, though it is possible that he also was caught in the web he had spun for the manager and Council.

The auditor began his preparation by directing his systems and procedures analyst (the chief of his tabulating equipment division) to study the processing needs of the city manager's department (Bledsoe, 1968: 39). The analysts's subsequent report argued that reporting with existing tabulating equipment was not satisfactory. The statements generated by the existing data processing equipment were difficult to interpret, not sufficiently detailed, and reached the departments too late to be of real use.[9] The study went on to state that each department ought to receive timely, readable information covering their personnel, payroll, retirement status, inventory accounts, cost accounts, appropriation accounts, budget status, and so on. These reports were being produced by the existing system but, according to the analyst's commentary, not satisfactorily (Bledsoe, n.d.: 4). Lastly, the auditor's analyst recommended that an independent consultant be commissioned to provide a more detailed study.

Following this recommendation, an Oakland-based public accounting/management consulting firm, Thompson, Dechow, Johansen, & Reich, was engaged to do a feasibility study.[10] The consultant's contract negotiations with the city spoke only of exploring the possibilities of placing a computer in city hall.[11] The report, forwarded to the city manager, claimed the EDP would cost the city relatively little initially and that by July 1, 1967 "all costs of acquisition and installation [would be] recovered" and that the city would "begin to realize annual cost savings of about $60,000" provided the computer is "processing and storing personnel records, inventory costs, appropriation and revenue accounting, permits & licenses, and coordinating the City's traffic signals."[12] This extremely favorable report, added to the auditor's enthusiasm for and the Council manager's unfamiliarity with EDP, convinced the City Council to approve the installation of a computer in city hall.

Some of the staff assistants to the city manager argued that if the installation was to serve all departments' data processing needs it should be placed as a special unit answerable directly to the city manager.[13] The auditor did not object to this, but the city manager was not willing to request the $26,000 consultant's fee in his budget or to include the funds necessary to establish an EDP section in his office. Also, the very optimistic consultants' projection aroused suspicion among the city manager's staff; someone on the staff wrote another management consultant firm for their opinion of the Thompson study. This second firm reported that, in their opinion, the Thompson cost-savings projections were very optimistic, perhaps overly so (Bledsoe, 1968: 9-11). The manager forwarded the second consultant group's opinion to the Council, stating that he did not believe that an EDP installation would result in any personnel savings. Thompson et al. stoutly maintained that considerable personnel savings was possible, and the auditor continued to reassure the Council that the project was proceeding on schedule. Thus, it is quite clear that though the city manager would not openly object to a computer in city hall, he did not want to be responsible for the decision that placed it there.[14] Curiously, the consultants' letter to the city manager, in January 1962, proposed that the computer be placed in the Auditor's Office. The city attorney ruled that it could legally be placed in the Auditor's Office, and, moreover, that it should be placed there.[15]

Data have been collected regarding EDP placement in municipal governments. It is clear from these data that placing EDP in an Auditor's office is not common. Furthermore, Table 8.2 indicates that from the data processing managers' perspective, this location is the least congenial reported. But the consultants', auditor's, and attorney's proposal set was the one that reached the Council for decision. Characteristically, the Council was passive approving or vetoing rather than probing and requiring alternative proposals to be forwarded to them before making a final decision. And, as the auditor had expected, they did not veto a proposal that promised a sophisticated new machine which would update and improve City operations and save money at the same time.

The hardware requirements had been specified by Thompson et al. together with the auditor and bid requests had been forwarded to equipment firms; six firms responded. The consultants informed the Auditor that the bid from National Cash Register (NCR) was lowest— based on dollar per hour cost of leasing the hardware.[16] Thus, an NCR (Model 315) electronic data processing system was leased. On the one hand, hardware cost projections were based on an assumption that six basic functions could be programmed and operated in accordance with the design specifications using 63 hours per month hardware time: payroll, personnel and retirement records, inventory accounting, cost accounting, appropriations, revenue, and permits and licenses. On the other, the cost projections required productive use of the computer for at least that number of hours each month. In short, the cost projections as they stand—without considering variables that were exogenous to the consultant's calculus—were very delicately contrived.[17]

It seemed at first that the auditor's plan for renewing the City's information—especially accounting—system had been successful. He began implementing his plan late in 1961, and by mid-1963 the stage was set: Delivery was expected in July 1963, and programming was to be completed in October 1963; it was expected that EDP would be fully operative by March 1964 (Bledsoe, n.d.: Appendix A). The auditor had carefully designed his proposals so that the Council, given their passive nature, would be unlikely to veto. His position, which did not require

TABLE 8.2   Placing EDP in the Auditor's Office Is Not Common
           and Is Not Perceived as a Good Location*

Location in Organization		Data Processing Managers' Attitude	
		Good Location	Other Than Good Location
Finance	42 cities	24	18
Controller	15	7	8
Manager's office	14	13	1
Auditor's office	9	4	5
Mayor's office	6	5	1
Administrative board	5	5	0
Data processing board	4	–	–
Central services	3	–	–
Other	3	–	–
Total	101		

*Adapted from Kansas City, Missouri, Finance Department Survey, June 1969.

going through the manager's hierarchy, was peculiarly favorable for
bringing EDP to Oakland. If such a proposal had emanated from the
Budget & Research, Public Works, or Planning Departments, for
example, it seems likely that it would have been screened out before
reaching the Council. This seems particularly likely considering the
hesitancy among the manager's staff regarding EDP.[18]

The tone of the auditor's EDP proposal and the Council's reaction to
it indicate city administrators and the Council saw the decision to
lease an NCR as a sophisticated economizing plan rather than a
commitment to transition to EDP per se.

LIVING WITH EDP: IS THERE A PROBLEM?

The auditor, after getting approval to start an EDP system, found
himself required to start the system moving before he could test the
credibility of his carefully built savings argument. His first request was
for three new programmers to begin in July 1963. The computer was to
be delivered in January 1964, and parallel operations were scheduled
until July 1964. Obviously, projected personnel savings could not be
realized before that time. The auditor's initial problem then was to hold
start-up costs down so that realization of projected savings at or close to

the predicted time, 1967, would be theoretically possible. In order to sustain this possibility, despite a first-year departmental budget increase of 34% (see Figure 8.1), the Auditor argued that one-time start-up costs incurred before the EDP system was fully operative should not be counted in the cost-savings projections.[19] He then went on to submit a $140,000 EDP budget for fiscal year 1963, warning the Council that the figure was likely to increase to more than $170,000 in the next fiscal year. However, the auditor immediately countered this warning with the argument that the city would save $194,000 during that period because his office and the Police Department could close down their tabulating equipment. In other words, the auditor promised the Council $20,000 per year savings after fiscal 1964. This tactic saved his fiscal 1963 budget though it was 50% more than the Thompson et al. projection for 1963 Bledsoe, 1968: 11).

Obviously the Council was willing to spend a little more money if they were convinced that the investment would save the city money in the near future. This auditor clearly was skilled at convincing the Council to increase its investment in his department. It is also likely that he suspected he would not be in the Auditor's Office to account when predicted savings failed to appear because he left for another job shortly after successfully defending this first EDP budget and committing the city to a leased NCR computer.[20]

Almost single-handedly, this Auditor had generated and guided Oakland's acquisition of EDP equipment. In general, he was adept at expanding the responsibility, function, and prerogative of his office. He appears to have been an exception, the unusual administrator who, like the activist in the Parks and Recreation Department, better understands the advantage that inheres in a situation clouded with uncertainties. Such individuals are able to turn uncertainty to their advantage by pretending to know more about the substance of a problem than their peers and thus often have their way because they resolve, at least temporarily, the ambiguities of the problem for others. The essence of this tactic is that the supplicant works carefully, skillfully, and assiduously to allay any uncertainties the policymakers may feel.

The man who replaced this auditor did not share his ambitious vision of the Auditor's Office although he had worked with him for some years. Moreover, he was not as knowledgeable about or as committed to the EDP transition plan as his predecessor.[21] The "new auditor" stated in an interview that Oakland's accounting and fiscal management-information system did need revision in 1961, but "the city" had rushed into the NCR plan without adequate thought, information, and preparation. In fact, he said, he was not particularly desirous of keeping EDP in his shop. He announced that an EDP service should be "established as a separate City department with direct responsibility to the City Manager" in order that it can be "responsive to all departments on an equal basis."[22] Obviously, the new auditor did not oppose the recent administrative reorganization that placed EDP services in the manager's Finance Department. Since that administrative reorganization in 1969, the new auditor has been a frequent contributor to the list of criticisms of EDP. For example, since transferring to the Finance Department, EDP has been a disaster he reports.

The point is that after the initiating auditor left, no one in the city really supported or was committed to EDP. Thus, because he left before the EDP equipment had even been delivered, the presence of EDP in Oakland was, in a real sense, an externally imposed perturbation. And we have another example of the Council accepting (failing to veto) a complicated program before it began to understand its implications for the city. There were expectations of the EDP program just as there had been for the Community Action program, but it was not long before the Council and administrative leaders discovered that the expectations had little to do with reality.

In both cases the Council was consistent in that it expected to improve the fiscal health of the community and the municipal government. In the Community Action example remember, the Council hoped for job training, job development, ultimately, business development. In this situation, the Council expected that EDP would hold back the rising cost of municipal services thus slowing the rise in property taxes and making the city more attractive for business as well as residential development. But it seems that to date neither program set has saved the city money or encouraged commercial development.

In any tradition-laden, routinized organization, a certain amount of grumbling will accompany any innovation, especially a poorly understood technique that threatens to eliminate personnel. In Oakland's case such mutterings appear to have been justified. For one thing the chronology of EDP in the city departed substantially from the projected schedule. The initial EDP budget exceeded the consultants' cost projection by 58%.[23] In fact the consultants' cost projections were never less than 50% too low (Bledsoe, 1968: 12). The initiating auditor, however, had so projected his savings that first-year start-up costs were not included. Figure 8.1 indicates that no savings accrue between fiscal years 1961 and 1967.[24] Figure 8.1 does indicate that the acquisition of

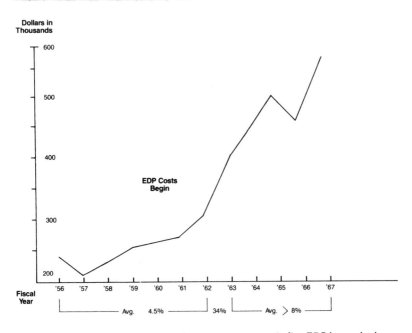

NOTE: The auditor's budget both shifts and turns upward after EDP is acquired.

Figure 8.1

EDP shifted the auditor's budget curve sharply upward. Similarly, it seems likely that EDP costs were responsible for almost doubling that department's average budget increment. Moreover, Thompson et al. had projected that EDP would eliminate 27 persons from the city departments, adding only 3 to the Auditor's Office. Between 1961 and 1966 EDP requirements had swelled the Auditor's Office from 37 to 50 persons—more than four times the projected increase. At the same time, there is no evidence that more than 20 persons were released from other city departments. The city's budgeted expenditures expanded routinely—minimum annual increment +4%; maximum increment +14%—through this period. It is true that department heads jealously protect their personnel allowances in any large bureaucracy. The tendency is toward growth.

The sophisticated savings argument had been advanced that EDP would save by reducing future expansion, but, rapidly increasing EDP costs and "normally" expanding city expenditures suggest that the slowed growth proposition is an unlikely one.

In spite of these increases in personnel and other costs, the promised citywide savings may have been realized. Advocates of EDP might still defend the "savings arguments," because it can be argued that monetary expenses are only one element in the set of EDP costs. The initiating auditor conceived the EDP transition plan ostensibly to stem rising data processing expenditures and to encourage more accurate, complete, and timely reporting to all departments. Again, Figure 8.1 indicates that the switch to EDP did not curb rising monetary costs. But what about the promise of better reporting? There is complete agreement that the quantity, quality, and timeliness of the city's information regressed after Oakland adopted EDP. An administrative assistant who has worked in city hall for many years related that the city's reporting, record-keeping, and information storage system took a giant step backward when they made the transition to the NCR-315 system. He claimed that reports continued to be late and in hard-to-use formats; in addition, they were usually incorrect. In short, they were unusable. He went on to say that the city's data processing has not recovered from the step backward despite ever increasing investments in EDP. Similarly, an administrator in the Finance Office wryly offered the opinion that blindly tossing a dart over his shoulder toward a table of random numbers was as likely to provide a correct, up-to-date fund balance as that which the computer offered. In fact, he recently hired an accountant to manually review departmental records in the hope that more accurate fund balance information could be developed. This administrator stated that until the city's EDP could do simple bookkeeping functions accurately, it would never grow into a full management information system. All interviewed who had interest in, responsibility for, or need for EDP services—more than twenty administrators, elected officials, or consultants—reported that the city's information had not improved as a result of the transition.

Thompson et al. projected and the initiating auditor promised that six major applications would be operative by July 1967. Furthermore, all cost-savings projections were based on the assumption that the six would be fully operative in the EDP system. An EDP status report from the city treasurer to the manager, dated July 31, 1967, states that only three of the six functions had been converted to EDP.[25]

Table 8.3 indicates that nearly double the projected personnel and machine requirements were needed to perform less than one-half the

beginning six applications. The treasurer's—or finance director's—
report to the manager goes on to say that "Appropriations Accounting
and Budgetary Control . . . [are] not the integrated overall program
originally anticipated." The initial design specified daily disbursements,
reconciliation and monthly expenditure, cost, and summary reports.
The NCR system was not issuing, in July of 1967, payroll or general
warrants; reconciliation was done by hand, and those interviewed stated
that monthly reports were still late and error-filled (Bledsoe, 1968: 13).
All interviewed agreed that administrators simply no longer had "base"
information, and thus all fiscal decisionmaking was "seat of the pants or
rule of thumb." Moreover, no one really knew if these guesses were off
and, if so, by how much, because there is no reliable fund balance
information.

The EDP design had stipulated that personnel information and
retirement master files would automatically be updated at the same time
that the payroll was being processed. But retirement personnel records
were still being manually posted several years after the transition to
EDP. It is predictable that such performance, in view of the promises
given three or four years before, would begin to generate concern among
a cost—thus information—conscious manager and Council.

There is no evidence that the Council, three or four years after the
transition to EDP, was fully informed about the nature or extent of the
problem. Rather, the Council characteristically was fairly well-screened
from all but the iceberg's tip and that was carefully rounded by the new
finance director and manager. Neither of these men was in the city at the
time of EDP adoption and they naturally had no wish to begin their
tenure by unduly burdening the Council with "administrative" problems.
And too, the administrators may not have realized the number and
severity of the EDP difficulties. Still, the new manager realized that the
city was having problems with its EDP services, because it was included
in his comprehensive administrative reorganization plan. But the new
manager, like the one before him, did not want direct responsibility for a
complicated, expensive technique he did not understand. But he apparently believed that EDP could yet contribute to increased administrative
efficiency. The new manager, shortly after arriving, recruited a finance
director from another city. The new finance director-treasurer—before
reorganization—was chosen, at least in part, because he had successfully guided a transition to EDP in another city. Thus, he was considered
knowledgeable regarding EDP and an advocate of EDP in city government. And the new manager's reorganization proposal directed that EDP

services would be removed from the Auditor's Office and placed in the Finance Office.

The new finance director arrived after the reorganization had been approved by the voters to find himself confronted by an EDP system whose performance was not even close to that expected by the Council and department administrators. Furthermore, there seemed to be no hope of achieving significantly better performance from the NCR system in the near term. But the new finance director, faced with rising EDP costs and diminishing data, obviously needed better performance or good reason for high cost and apparently poor performance. According to one administrator in the Finance office, the city was still altering its accounting procedures because the specified automated accounting system still was not operative.

It has been said that the difficulty with the NCR-315 system was, in large part, erroneous data. Reports were not trustworthy, audit was difficult, and budgeting was increasingly guesswork. The new finance director became convinced that new hardware that used a more common programming language—COBOL: Common Business Oriented Language—and provided more manufacturer's support was needed to realize the initial or design goals even though the NCR system at this point was not being utilized two full shifts per day, five days per week. National Cash Register had not provided much programming support.[26] The new finance director had been impressed by the amount and quality of "software" or programming support that IBM Corporation promised. There is no evidence that the finance director actively explored other possibilities like dropping EDP, resuscitating tabulating machinery to support the NCR system, turning to time-share, or hiring a software firm to upgrade the NCR system's performance.[27]

The basic assumption seems to have been that a more powerful computing system—mainframe—automatically provides better performance. And, too, transition to a different yet more sophisticated EDP system provides, at least in the short-run, explanation for inadequate data files and late, erroneous reports. Thus the new finance director decided that the city must have an IBM series 360, model 25 EDP system and that the choice could not be subjected to the vagaries of a formal bidding process. He successfully persuaded the city manager that his machine would save the city money and help solve present EDP problems (Meltsner, 1968). In sum, the new finance director used basically the same arguments to justify an IBM system as the "initiating Auditor" had used to get the NCR system. So too, the new city manager

TABLE 8.3   EDP Projections Overestimated Performance
and Sharply Underestimated Costs

I.	Applications projected for July 1967	I.	Operative July 1967
	1. Appropriation accounting and budgetary control		1. Appropriation account
	2. Payroll, personnel and retirement records		2. Payroll (only)
	3. Permits and licenses		3. Inventory
	4. Inventory accounting and control		
	5. Cost accounting		
	6. Revenue accounting		
II.	Computer hours projected to perform these six functions	II.	Required July 1967
	1. 63 hours		1. 100 hours
III.	Number of personnel projected to operate the NCR -315 system.	III.	Required July 1967
	1. 13 individuals		1. 21 individuals

used these arguments successfully to persuade the City Council to approve new hardware and to permit the city to contract with IBM without a bidding process (see Table 8.3).

Of course the acquisition of the larger, newer, more sophisticated IBM 360 again shifted data processing costs sharply upward. Table 8.4 indicates that EDP costs rose substantially faster than total expenditures for the same period. The IBM-360 was leased in 1969 and EDP costs increased nearly 88% that year. The increment returned to "normal" the next year but the base shifted up in fiscal 1969 just as it had in fiscal 1962 (see Figure 8.1). The increased EDP costs were not just increased hardware costs. Consultants' fees cost the city many thousands of dollars between 1961 and 1967. Thompson et al., and later Lybrands, Ross Bros. and Montgomery, received a considerable portion of that money. The Remington-Rand tabulating system required 10 support personnel in 1961, by 1967 the NCR system required 21. In 1971, the IBM system required 38. Again, there are no indications of compensatory savings in other departments to offset these increases.

Oakland's per capita spending for EDP was $1.80 in 1970.[28] The city, responding to a HUD information systems survey in 1970, reported twelve different computerized applications in their information network. (U. S. Department of Housing and Urban Development, 1970: 111-112). Among 77 cities reporting, 48 listed EDP per capita expenditures between one and three dollars. The average number of applications for

TABLE 8.4   EDP Costs Shift Upward Dramatically as the City
            Transitions to IBM Equipment

	EDP Costs: Total in Thousands / % Increase		Total City Budget: Total in Millions / % Increase	
FY 1967	257	/ —	47	/ —
FY 1968	316	/ 27	49	/ 4
FY 1969	592	/ 87.5	56	/ 14
FY 1970	694	/ 17.4	61	/ 9

these 48 cities was $1.95 (U. S. Department of Housing and Urban Development, 1970: Table 8.5). Thus, Oakland's EDP performance compares slightly on the low side of the average.[29]

But, Table 8.5 suggests that, although EDP is not cheap for any city, Oakland's cost application is relatively high. The table indicates that Oakland's cost is considerably higher than comparable cities (see explanatory note on Table 8.5). The second highest cost application is that of San Jose, which reports a computerized traffic control system in their costs. Oakland's design specifications, drawn in 1962, included a traffic control application. To date, that function is no closer to operation than it was in 1962.

There is no doubt that an IBM-360 system was more sophisticated, versatile, and powerful than the relatively old fashioned NCR-315. Has this new equipment helped the city to remedy its record-keeping, accounting, and reporting difficulties? An administrative analyst, with considerable experience in Oakland, argued that the city's information system had taken a step backward when the NCR was adopted and that it had not recovered this lost ground before they moved to the IBM system, a move that resulted in further regression. After acquiring the IBM system, the city moved from having late, shoddy, incorrect reports to having no reports at all. The city auditor, in a report of city expenditures, said, "in the routine audit . . . we found it was not possible to verify that all transactions were charged against the proper fund and appropriation and recorded accurately in the general ledger accounts because the accounting records were not up to date."

A partner in the city's perennial independent auditing firm, Lybrand et al., confirmed that his firm had not been able to close the city's books since its transition to IBM equipment—a period of almost three years. He indicated that it was almost inconceivable for a close-out to extend so long. The finance director admitted that the EDP system he had

TABLE 8.5   Oakland's Dollar Cost/Application Is Relatively High
           in FY 1970

City*	Cost (in thousands)
Sunnyvale	26
San Jose	43 – includes automated traffic control
Long Beach	40
Burbank	8
Anaheim	33
Oakland	49

*These cities were selected because they are traditionally used by Oakland's Budget
and Research Department for fiscal comparisons. Again, these comparisons are sug-
gestive at best because there is no way of knowing which applications are successful
and which are in a hopeless mess. Data from U.S. Department of Housing and Urban
Development (1970).

developed for another city would have that city's records prepared and
an independent audit would have been completed fifteen days after a
fiscal year's end. He reported that Sunnyvale, California, had its records
ready for independent audit 24 hours after a fiscal year closed.[30]
Everyone agreed that even in the old manual record-keeping systems,
the auditors would have finished by October at the latest. One
administrative assistant reported a conversation between two accountants from the County Auditor's Office and himself in which the
county employees claimed that they would expect to be put in jail if their
records were found to be as confused as Oakland's. Vital fiscal
information has simply been lost since the transition to the IBM system.
The city hired Lybrand et al. again in 1971 to help it manually
reconstruct departmental records to build the general ledger so that
Lybrand et al., in their role as independent auditors for the city, could
close the books for fiscal years 1970 and 1971.

Little knowledge of the city's record-keeping and accounting problems had, until very recently, got beyond the city manager.[31] In fact, the
manager himself had been compelled to accept the consultants',
auditors', and finance director's explanations and proposed remedies
because he was not knowledgeable about EDP. Similarly, the Council
had been forced to accept the manager's explanations and proposed
solutions regardless of increasing EDP costs. The idea of a screening
process is clearly two-edged. On one hand, the Council cannot become
overburdened with detail; on the other hand the nature of the process
ensures that problems and difficulties will be deleted from each
administrative level to the next. In this way, error may be induced

through several levels so that by the time one nears the highest administrative levels or the Council, information about problems is sketchy and often misleading. Thus, the Council had been so effectively screened from EDP-related problems that they were unpleasantly surprised when one of Oakland's weekly newspapers printed a story, in March 1971, that the city had millions of "surplus dollars stashed" that were not being used.[32] Although the *Montclarion's* article was not aimed directly at the city's EDP system, many of the newspaper's remarks come uncomfortably close to the EDP problem. The article questioned why the independent auditors had not qualifiedly closed the books since 1968. The *Montclarion* wanted to know why the city had not published a detailed "Report of Financial Transactions" since fiscal 1968. The article's charge of a large fund reserve was especially threatening because our data suggest that the city may not have known what their fund balances were. The *Montclarion's* article generated a detailed, seven-page report to the Council from the finance director. His reply focuses on the "politics of a coming councilmanic campaign, charter changes, and subsequent accounting system alterations," but EDP and erroneous records, late reporting, and incomplete ledgers were not mentioned.[33]

The City Council and administration had barely recovered from this narrow escape when they were threatened again, this time by the state government. California returns some of the revenue from gasoline tax to municipalities for street repair, improvement, and construction. Oakland's share of the state's revenue was approximately five million dollars in 1969, 1970, and 1971. This was approximately 50% of the Street & Engineering Department's budget for that period. In June 1971, the state controller wrote to the city, via the mayor, stating that gasoline tax revenues would no longer be forwarded to Oakland until "the city can produce adequate verifiable record expenditures and can demonstrate that it is in a position to prepare adequate and timely street reports." The controller goes on to say that the city's books for fiscal 1970 and 1971 are totally inadequate. The loss of five million dollars "free" revenue stunned a cost-conscious manager/Council. Frantic hand reconstruction of needed information and some quiet negotiations with state offices resulted in the renewal of gasoline tax funding to Oakland some four months later.[34]

Once again the city narrowly avoided a major crisis. A budget analyst, who no longer works for the city, said that he finds it incredible that the city administration had been able to keep the lid on an increasingly explosive situation for so long. Except for these incidents, however, the Council and to a lesser degree the manager have been screened from data processing problems despite increasing pressure for action from the departments, the independent auditors, and state officials. In 1968 the new finance director responded to similar pressures by convincing the manager and the Council that new, more powerful, sophisticated, and expensive hardware was the answer. Four years later, he was again arguing that the city's EDP system was overburdened. Moreover, the finance director spent thousands of dollars for more core storage, tape drives, discs, and printers to expand the capabilities of the IBM-360 system. None of these expensive additions was projected four or five years earlier when the city was persuaded to switch from NCR to the larger, more expensive IBM equipment. Yet, the existing EDP installation did not begin 24-hour operation until 1972, though it still operated little more than five days per week.[35]

The finance director, however, felt that if they were to catch up with the accounting and other management information requirements that had been backlogging for three years and, at the same time, improve and expand Oakland's EDP-centered management information system toward the one designed and promised more than ten years before, a much bigger main frame was needed. The requests for proposal were forwarded to several firms. The finance director's request was for a system that was bigger by a factor of five than the IBM 360 system.[36]

THE ELUSIVE GOAL: WHAT HAPPENED?

The development of computer-centered information processing and storage in Oakland has not proceeded as promised, projected, or anticipated. What happened? Why have projections consistently failed to approximate reality; why have expectations been consistently violated? There appear to have been several fundamental oversights, misconceptions, and misjudgments committed repeatedly throughout the period chronicled here. The interviews indicate that many who are, or have been, involved in the transition to EDP were cognizant of such oversights.

Some were administrators who did not feel that they could voice critical opinions or offer recommendations that implied censure of superiors' policy decisions. Others argued that their judgments would not reach or would not be given credence at the highest administrative levels. But this was not true at all; one of the manager's highest level administrators, for example, indicated that traditional, unofficial, and peculiar record-keeping and accounting practices continued to sabotage the EDP system. Yet there has been no concerted campaign to educate department personnel, especially service-oriented personnel, away from their traditional practices. In fact, an administrator in the Parks and Recreation Department reported that supervisors tended to discount the instructions of those sent to train them in EDP reporting procedures because they readily perceived that the technicians understand little about the particular operations and problems of those in Parks and Recreation. Such half-hearted attempts to convince departmental personnel to abandon traditional record-keeping practices and follow procedures demanded by the EDP system had precisely the opposite result.

Thus, EDP continued to falter and obvious fundamentals, such as structuring incentives to reward thorough training and cooperation of all involved in an EDP network, continued to be overlooked. An administrative assistant remarked that when he came to Oakland in 1969, he knew nothing about EDP but that the city was transitioning to hardware systems that demanded new accounting procedures. He located two elementary textbooks on EDP management and quickly discovered that the city had made or was making nearly every cardinal mistake cited by them. The reference texts, he said, recommend long-term parallel operation. Oakland has repeatedly chosen not to maintain parallel operation.[37] Nearly all interviewed mentioned this failure.

Another reason that EDP faltered in Oakland is that expenditures for EDP have been justified from the first in terms of cost savings. This argument is a particularly difficult one for a public sector organization to justify. There are no widely accepted output measures; consequently EDP impact on future cost reductions—reductions in the rate of increase—is most difficult to assess.

This same administrative assistant also said his references specified that considerable investment in planning and coordination be put forth before a change in administrative structure, information processing, and accounting procedures can be successfully executed. He is convinced on the basis of his experience as an administrative assistant in a service-oriented department, that little or no attention was given this problem.

This means that a city's administrators who are most involved with record-keeping and information-processing procedures and policies, such as the department heads, auditors, finance director, and manager, must begin to think in terms of making the personal investment necessary to learn considerably more about EDP before acquiescing to campaigns that result in committing them to it. If they had expended the effort to learn, then they would have been in an excellent position to judge what additional information-processing capabilities their city really needed, what technologies were available that would satisfy these needs, which ones the city could have reasonably expected to operate, how much this would have cost, and, finally, what steps were needed to assure that departmental personnel understood and cooperated with the requirements of the new system. But rather than proceeding more slowly, investing in preparation and education, administrators commonly leave these preparatory considerations to consultants who, as I indicated above, did not really understand the city's needs or capabilities and apparently served to provide support for the administrative leaders' proposal.

The administrators' reluctance to take the initiative in the beginning may have resulted from a general inexperience among city administrators regarding EDP. Few cities had EDP capabilities before the early 1960s. Yet the absence of informed, coordinative effort and its negative effects continued over the years. The hesitancy of either city manager to take clear responsibility for the direction of EDP certainly reduced the likelihood of effective coordinated effort. The administrative arms that have attempted to develop the EDP system had neither the persuasive force nor the official authority to elicit the service-oriented departments' complete cooperation. Also, the apparent need to justify the EDP machinery's cost as rapidly as possible worked against a patient, thoughtful transition.

Still another cardinal violation of good transition procedure was responsible for delay, error, and frustration. The NCR-315 data processing system needed a somewhat peculiar, little known programming language—NEAT—to make it work. It was difficult to find programmers already trained in this language, in part because the city's pay scale was not sufficiently generous to attract them.[38] National Cash Register agreed to train certain Oakland employees in the language. But those so trained would then develop a program or perhaps one or two subroutines and, thus experienced, move on to a better job. In the process of program building, it seems that no record was kept of how a program worked even though personnel turnover was high. When the author of a program left the city, the program usually had to be rewritten when its modification, correction, or expansion became necessary. This delay-causing problem was due entirely to inexperienced EDP management and only recently has been overcome. Nevertheless, this lack of careful documentation in a context of rapid programmer turnover further delayed the maturation of the city's EDP system.

Generally, these instances of fundamental misunderstanding suggest that no major decision process pertaining to EDP included a thoughtful, serious analysis of the supporting organizations—the sources of input data—though in each instance those involved have ruefully acknowledged this failure after the fact. Specifically, EDP seems to have intensified the tendency to informal practices. Furthermore, the natural chafing between coordinative-oriented and service-oriented departments was dramatically increased because of the city's EDP program. The coordinative departments chastise the service departments for not cooperating and providing timely, complete, correct information to Computer Services. The service-oriented departments respond that the coordinative ones do not understand service needs, do not provide them with useful output information, and generally get in the way of their providing needed services. Also, the sharply increased requirements to document and forward information to EDP in unfamiliar formats for which the service activity gets no usable return further distracts them from their proper function—provision of services. Thus, the service-oriented departments become increasingly disaffected with the coordinative and circumvent them by operating informally. Clearly, the city's and the consultants' failure to anticipate this reaction contributed to incorrect prediction and projection.

It is obvious that the city's EDP transition expectations, fostered by the consultants, were at best myopic. The administrators continued to act as though the Council would not support investment for long-term, perhaps nonfiscal dividends. Such an assumption has never been tested regarding EDP but every decision examined reflected it. Such unquestioned assumptions resulted in a single-minded, unimaginative approach to EDP. But the administrators' assumptions regarding the Council, however crippling, do not of themselves explain why the city endured more than ten years of increasing information difficulty without doing something about it. No remedial decision examined implied any movement away from the initial approach, which assumed that more sophisticated, powerful information-processing machinery would markedly improve the city's recordkeeping, reporting, and management information. Rather, each remedial step reinforced the existing tack and, thus, proliferated the problems associated with it. Although there has been every appearance of decisive remedial activity—physical change, increased expenditure, and "weighty decision"—in fact, no new concepts are to be found in the EDP decision series. The administrative decision makers have been able to see but one road and the Council can see that road only if it is illuminated by the relevant decision makers.

Once again we see that coping tactics, however natural or instinctive, are not always appropriate for the problem. It is certainly easier and less personally risky to obtain approval for increased expenditure toward an existing "solution," hoping that intensification will solve the problems, than it is to sell a new approach. But, even if there were individuals who would risk open, official objection to an existing approach and voice alternatives, the "screening effect" would be likely to render such proposals ineffective. About two years ago, two administrative assistants did circumvent the official hierarchy by sending a five-page memorandum about the EDP problem directly to the city manager. They proposed, among other actions, firing the finance director and hiring a software firm to assume all the city's EDP. There was no evidence that their argument had any effect on decisions about EDP and, therefore, that the risk incurred by circumventing the administrative hierarchy was justified.

Similarly, a city accountant, reportedly talented, hardworking, and relatively knowledgeable about EDP systems openly tried to convince the new finance director that the transition to an IBM-360 system in the manner and length of time specified by the finance director, could result only in disaster. The finance director did not actively respond to the accountant's argument and the frustrated accountant left the city.[39]

CONCLUSIONS

First, the fact of the transition to EDP casts some light on the context of bureaucractic innovation. In a bureaucratic setting, screening assures that, in most cases, negation quickly accrues to nonroutine proposals.[40] In a bureaucratic setting, individual reward structures overwhelmingly favor the status quo. Civil service systems, for example, hinder rapid salary increases and position advancement. In most bureaucratic settings there are sanctions for initiating or experimenting if unexpected difficulties or failure result. One can easily be shunted aside on an already slow career seniority ladder, and at the same time lateral mobility may be severely reduced.

Through these last chapters we have seen that the bureaucratic setting is not well-suited for coping with more than episodic, moderate levels of uncertainty. Moreover, in those contexts that were confronted by long-lasting, uncommonly bewildering situations—for example, the Planning Department or the Parks and Recreation Department—bureaucratic structure was remarkably diminished. Perhaps this is part of the reason that the initiating Auditor presented EDP as a better way to do the same, traditional functions rather than as a technique for doing new things.[41]

The initiating auditor was particularly well-placed in the organization for this kind of entrepreneurial activity. He was not responsible to the city manager directly, and he enjoyed relatively direct access to the Council. Remember, the manager and his staff tried, albeit somewhat half-heartedly, to block the auditor's EDP plan but perhaps because of his unusual position the manager and his staff seemed ambivalent and did not respond with the same force or alacrity that they would have had the plan come from a senior budget analyst or planner. In other words, if someone is so placed that official reaction to them is ambivalent or slow in forming, the likelihood of successfully initiating a project, program, or other change is substantially increased. Remember, in the case of the Council and Community Action, the official reaction to the poverty council's wish to hire the advocate poverty organizer crystallized slowly and he was employed. Similarly, one would expect precisely the reverse reaction in a nonroutinized, say, small group setting. The longer the membership hesitates, the less likely a change is to be adopted. The more bureaucratized the organization, and the slower the official reaction to a proposal, the more likely it is to be implemented (see Table 8.6). The foregoing chapters, together with this study, lend support to Crozier's finding that the supervisors—especially in the service-oriented departments—resent the changes to their comfortable routines. Their response is one of cantankerous opposition. They may be very subtle in their opposition, but they can effectively sabotage the innovation's intended result (Crozier, 1964: 202).

EDP is usually acquired with the intention that it will be an aid for management. This was certainly true in Oakland; the interviews indicated that all respondents had expected that the technology would provide management with more complete information. It is never clear,

TABLE 8.6 Organizational Setting

		Highly Bureaucratized	Less Bureaucratized
Official or Group Reaction	Slow	Innovation likely	Innovation unlikely
	Fast	Innovation unlikely	Innovation likely

however, what information is needed to provide more control; apparently everyone expects that when an EDP system is operating "as it should," it will become obvious what data are needed to improve the management process. Improvement in this regard usually means altering conditions so that the administrators can control the activities of their organization more ably. In Oakland, however, EDP has unintendedly served more to decentralize than to centralize. It had, over the ten-year period, eroded rather than strengthened management strength vis-à-vis service-oriented divisions. For example, one former budget analyst interviewed argued that, because the computer had provided no information that anyone could use, the department heads were the best source of information available about their operations, and no one could generate similarly reasoned and strongly defended refutations of their claims. In general, the less a supervisor knows about his subordinates' operation the more that supervisor is dependent on them.

Once a sophisticated, little understood technology like EDP has been injected into a bureaucratic setting like that in Oakland, it is unlikely that the problems that arise will be effectively solved by the administrators. As we have indicated, advice or suggestion is screened out rapidly because it challenges the status quo and threatens superiors.[42] The example of the competent accountant who left because his corrective advice threatened the new finance director's EDP program is illustrative. This more negative side of the screening effect may, in part, explain the city's tendency to spend, repeatedly, thousands of dollars for advice from independent consultants.

The irony is that the independent advice does not come from a strictly independent analysis. It is clear that, from the first, the city's consultants acted to marshal support for the initiating auditor's proposal. In fact, the expensive independent advice neither improved nor changed through the ten-year period. For example, a report, in November 1969, from the consultants who had drawn the design specifications for the NCR, reviewed the city's transition to the IBM-360 system. It indicated that the consultant group, probably acting to defend its credibility, was still chastising the city for not finishing what the consultants had designed in 1961. It goes on to comment in some detail regarding what must yet be done in order that the original plan be fully implemented.

In short, after nearly eight years, the city and the consultants were starting over again—same advice, same goals, and a *new machine* (Lybrand et al., 1969).

Furthermore, there is no evidence that the manager, department heads, and most other administrators are not still attracted to EDP in general as a tool for the indicator of efficient and up-to-date administration. The interviews and the city's activities since 1962—including recent acquisition of a new minicomputer by the Police Department to supplement their EDP needs—indicate that in the city administration, the belief was widespread that the difficulties of the previous years had been a result of pecularities in the Oakland context rather than problems inherent to EDP.

This analysis has suggested that the city has, from the beginning, overemphasized the EDP hardware and neglected the department's social networks in the long sought computerized management information system. One administrator in the Finance Office has stated that the city's biggest mistake was and continues to be, concern for and subsequent focus on hardware elements to the detriment of social elements in the information system. Those responsible for EDP decisions in the city focused on the promises of the machinery itself giving scant attention to the person-machine interfaces—the effects people have on the machines and vice versa. The evidence we collected for this study clearly indicated that the demands of the hardware elements often adversely affected middle- and lower-level administrators who responded by subtly refusing to cooperate. In short, the EDP system suffered from poor integration between people and machines. Overall effectiveness was much less than promised or expected; in fact, it was lessened each time more sophisticated hardware was introduced.

One young administrative assistant stated the problem well when he said that there was a very old fiscal management tradition buried deeply in a variety of departments and sections. There were many idiosyncrasies about that traditional system known by one subspecialist or another, but no attempt was made to uncover these quirks. As a result, the design of many EDP programs, reports, and accounting procedures did not account for departments' needs and were not helpful to departments.

Thus it seems that many of Oakland's problems regarding EDP resulted from misidentification of or misconception about the complex social organization that is the Oakland government. Nothing seemed to work; schedules could not be met; data were inaccurate, ill-fitted, irrelevant. The administrative leadership—rather than attempting to redefine or to map their organization more accurately—turned to more powerful machinery, arbitrarily redesigned informational procedures and processes, and restructured their organization in an attempt to make EDP work in Oakland.[43] In fact, it appeared that the administrators, like the Council with Community Action, could not understand the basic problems because they did not have enough information about or experience with EDP technologies.

In this chapter one can observe coping tactics like those noted in previous chapters. For example, the Council and many high-level administrators relied on screening techniques to help them cope, in the short term, with the problems EDP raised for them. The result was that the city's difficulties probably were more intense and longer lasting than they might have been. Naturally the policymakers most responsible for the choices wished to be reassured and the auditor, like the police administrators in their budgeting process, worked assiduously, carefully, and skillfully, to minimize the decision makers' feeling of uncertainty about EDP.

This EDP analysis has traced a decision process under conditions of great uncertainty, which resulted in decision makers reinforcing. . . or trying harder. . . to implement an initial solution or choice rather than to reevaluate and, perhaps, elect another alternative. The formal and informal costs are too high, particularly in a highly routinized setting, for widespread adoption of an informed trial and error approach—say one based on a Bayesian algorithm. Of course such a tack is possible only if there exists enough understanding to make some guesses about alternatives and outcomes; that is, if the policymaker is near the middle of the uncertainty continuum outlined in Chapter 1. This can be, as has been suggested in the foregoing chapters, an unrealistic requirement.

Traditional bureaucratized or any highly routinized organizations by definition are not capable of withstanding unusual or unexpected levels of ambiguity. Accordingly, the Council did not respond to the community action programs with its customary demeanor. The Planning Department was perhaps the least bureaucratized department in city hall, and the new Parks and Recreation Department did not quickly and surely establish a fresh routine.

At this point, it is clear that the adoption of coping tactics like those outlined in Chapter 1 under conditions of high order uncertainty is widespread. It is also obvious that such coping tactics though natural and useful in the short run are not always functional for policymakers or their organizations in the long run. Thus in the next chapter, after a brief recapitulation, we will turn to the possibility of constructing and implementing policies that build on instinctive coping behavior yet provide for strategic movement toward long-term adaptation.

NOTES

1. It seems reasonable that, given the limitations outlined in this study, most of what happened in the case of Community Action and in the EDP chronology was quite simply unforeseeable. It is ironic that screening processes filter out much of what may be helpful along with that which may be disruptive, tedious, or demanding. See, for a similar analysis, Crozier (1964, pp. 178-194).

2. To the degree that seniority accrues to longevity in a single organization, it will become more routinized or rigid because the best people leave for faster opportunity leaving the less imaginative to rise more slowly.

3. California has more cities with the professional manager form of government than any other state in the nation. It is, therefore, a very attractive location for those trained for and aspiring to positions in local administration. Thus, Oakland, one of the larger cities in California, attracts some very intelligent, well-trained, and aggressive young people.

4. A completely accurate picture of stability in this period is somewhat complicated by an extensive administrative reorganization in 1969. The reorganization was a centralizing, formalizing or routinizing one and resulted in little personnel change in these middle-level positions.

5. The various commissioners are appointed by the mayor subject to Council approval and serve specified terms. The commissions are atrophied relics of the commission form of government which was displaced by a manager form in the late nineteen twenties. Until the reorganization in 1969, these commissions still approved departmental budgets and passed on many of their requests.

6. Members of the Oakland Project of the University of California, Berkeley collected many interviews from administrators, auditors, consultants, and others who have had, at one time or another, interest in the mechanics of the city's fiscal machinery. Most of the interviews referred to in this chapter were drawn from those collected by Mike Bledsoe in 1968 or the author in 1972 and 1976—both members of the Oakland project.

7. See Meltsner (1971: Table 2, p. 19). Meltsner indicates that the property tax accounted for 76.6% of total revenue in 1945 and 1946 and only 47.1% in 1965 and 1966.

8. Oakland's property tax rate was, in 1968, $3.14/100.00 assessed valuation or about $50.00/month for a property assessed at twenty thousand dollars. The statewide average for 1968 was $1.84. From Meltsner (1971: Tables 2-3, p. 24).

9. From an interoffice letter cited in Bledsoe (1968: 4).

10. Thompson, Dechow, Johansen & Reich is now part of an internationally dispersed firm of accountants/management consultants, Lybrand, Ross Brothers, & Montgomery.

11. Thompson et al., letter to Martin Huff, Auditor, Sept. 6, 1961, in Bledsoe (n.d.: 6).

12. Thompson et al., letter to City Manager, Wayne Thompson, January 17, 1962. These savings are projected from reduced personnel costs. The supposition was that the computer would eliminate redundant work hours applied to the old information system.

13. The auditor is elected at large in Oakland and his Office is not strictly part of the city manager's departments. His function is to serve and to check the department's fiscal management practices.

14. Actually, the manager was favorably disposed toward EDP; he was simply convinced that it would not save money in the near term.

15. There is no evidence of collusion, but Thompson et al. has served, at least since the early 1950s as Oakland's independent auditor.

16. The other five firms were IBM, GE, Burroughs, Remington Rand, and RCA. RCA's bid was lowest but they were disqualified because they did not follow the instructions for proper bidding (Bledsoe, 1968, Appendix C).

17. The NCR-315 was leased for a fixed $76,140/year or $6,345/month. There was a provision for extra hours usage, but the cost per hour was higher (Bledsoe, 1968: Appendix C).

18. One might argue that the activities of the manager and his staff vis-à-vis the auditor, the consultants, and the Council were attempts to perform a screening function for the Council though the auditor is peculiarly difficult to screen from the Council. Regardless, the manager and his staff simply did not know enough to convincingly refute the auditor's/consultant's projections.

19. Bledsoe (1968: 11). Table 8.3 indicates that they were one-time only in that they set a higher level curve for the Auditor's Office.

20. Martin Huff, the initiating Auditor, left Oakland in July 1963 to become Executive Director of the State Franchise Tax Board.

21. Alan Brizee, appointed to fill the post vacated by Martin Huff, continued in the Office through the 1970s.

22. Letter from auditor to city manager, April 5, 1971.

23. $88,000 projected—$139,000 requested and granted.

24. Consultants' fees were first paid in 1961. After fiscal year 1967, EDP was no longer in the Auditor's budget.

25. The city manager, Wayne Thompson, left in 1966. He was replaced in early 1967 by Jerry Keithley who served as city manager until September 1972. The new manager was no more anxious than the old to have the immediate responsibility for EDP, but he was more actively interested in the function and progress of the installation. The new manager also appeared to have more understanding of and belief in the possibilities of EDP as a powerful management tool.

26. The NCR installation in Oakland used a relatively uncommon programming language—NEAT—and the only support National Cash provided was to arrange for Oakland employees to be marginally trained in the language.

27. A year or so later a software firm, Cybernetics Inc., was hired to program one or two transitions to the IBM-360/25. Also, two young administrative analysts reported that they had searched extensively but informally for usable program packages. They said the search had not been successful.

28. Per capita figure based on EDP costs of $694,000 in fiscal 1970 and a population estimate of 380,000.

29. The HUD study does not indicate to what degree an "application" is working usefully so it is difficult to know how the cities really compare.

30. See Table 8.5 for a cost comparison between Sunnyvale and Oakland.

31. Most of the EDP commentary in the city's files is on interoffice letterhead and treated as confidential.

32. *Montclarion,* March 10, 1971.

33. From the Finance Director's "Comments to Council Work Session," April 6, 1971.

34. As implied in the previous chapter, Oakland had influence in the state capitol through this period.

35. For example, the April 1971 "Computer Utilization Report" documented 497 hours computer use time for the month. This amounts to approximately 24-hour shift operations for 20 days.

36. The request was for a system that would have 250,000 bytes core storage and could be expanded to 750,000 bytes. This is 15 times bigger than the IBM 360-25, which was limited to 48,000 bytes. By today's standards, these all are small EDP systems.

37. The NCR transition plan allowed for six months parallel operation. This was the longest formal parallel activity to date, but parallel operations have clearly been developing unofficially in the service departments and the Budget and Research Department in order to keep the city going. That is, most departments reportedly keep separate records by hand as well as supplying EDP input information and using its output.

38. Many of those interviewed believed that the city's awkward, rule-bound, personnel-civil service system was largely responsible for inadequate personnel support of the EDP operation. And poor support in turn was responsible for many of the problems experienced in the EDP installation.

39. It is possible that in this case the Finance Director was persuaded by the accountant and, thus, did not wish to respond negatively but believed his public commitment to more optimistic projections prohibited active agreement with the accountant's position.

40. See Victor Thompson, *Modern Organization,* Alfred A. Knopf, New York, 1961, pp. 61-62 for a similar argument.

41. Crozier (1964) reports similar findings.

42. See Victor Thompson (1961: 91) for a similar analysis.

43. Actually some redesign of the informational processes and procedures was required in order to adapt the information processed to the limitations and constraints imposed by various hardware changes.

FROM COPING TACTICS TO ADAPTIVE STRATEGIES

A RECAP

Perhaps the most remarkable finding that emerges from this research is that, despite diverse contexts, persons, expectations, and experiences, the reactions to higher order uncertainties across the seven studies do not follow from assumptions of an idealized rationality. However, the responses are somewhat predictable.[1] Every case demonstrated several layers of adaptive technique and each began with the same fundamental avoidance and delay tendencies. It is apparent that individuals discard avoidance and delay tactics only when forced by great need or compelling circumstance.[2]

Each study was itself unique and interesting. In Chapter 2, for example, a cross-section of Oakland's citizens responded to questions about their city and its government. There are few studies in the literature on city governments that reveal citizens speaking generally about their lives in relation to their city and its governmental institutions. In Chapter 3 a low-resource pressure group exemplified the problems for and strategies available to citizens who have few resources and wish to influence public policy. The study in Chapter 4 presented an informed view of the city's elected officials torn between long-held routines and procedures, and community activists, armed with disruptive tactics, who did not respect the established routines. Chapter 5 offered an extremely rare analysis of the decision-making process among high-level police administrators. This analysis depicted different styles of police leadership as the chiefs struggled to balance the need for control, discretion, and information. The Oakland planning department, portrayed in Chapter 6, presented a poignant and timely examination of the widespread confusion regarding what planners ought to be doing. An administrative reorganization, examined in Chapter 7, highlighted the parks and recreation administrative leadership struggling to cope with severe vocational disorientation. Lastly, the case in Chapter 8 offered a detailed view of interaction among the city's policymakers as they endeavored individually and corporately to adapt to successive waves of surprising consequences engendered by the introduction of EDP into city hall.

Taken together, these studies have given us a glimpse of the complete municipal policymaking spectrum from citizens' reaction to policy outcomes to the inner recesses of city hall where the choices that become a program, a service, a tax, and so on, are made. The seven cases also provided insight into the processes of uncertainty management, even though it is difficult to observe individuals caught in the upper half of the uncertainty continuum partly because of strong individual and cultural forces acting to reduce ambiguity. Thus this research yields an uncommon comparative view of adaptive responses to uncertainties in policymaking and the outcomes.

In general the research indicated that, although coping strategies might appear somewhat direct and unsophisticated from the macro perspective, some very subtle tactics can be observed in a microanalysis of administrative processes.

Summarizing briefly, Chapter 2 revealed that Oakland's citizens knew little about their city government. If they were well-to-do, they thought Oakland was a pretty good place to live; if not, they were less sanguine. In general, the people of Oakland cope with their uncertainty about city government and its effect on their lives by planning to leave if the cumulative burden becomes too great.

Chapter 3 indicated that, if a group of citizens is to have an impact on public policy, a considerable investment will be required; the fewer the traditional resources such as money, professional relationships, business acquaintances, and such, the greater the time and effort required to become informed, build a following, achieve access, and be heard. A low-resource pressure group, for example, copes with inadequate knowledge by working very hard and using intuitive judgment to play its following against the policymakers.

Chapter 4 demonstrated that screens or buffers protected the Council from most disruptive and ambiguity-producing activity. When the screening processes collapsed, the council reacted like others, attempting to avoid or delay making a choice when the members could not guess what the consequences would be.

Chapter 5 suggested that police chiefs played their cards very close to their vest in order to maintain control that is crucial for the stability, thus effectiveness, of a hierarchical organization. They needed information to get what they wanted from the manager and Council without yielding discretion to them. Though the chiefs used screens to protect themselves, this research demonstrated clearly that the screening function can be a resource for those performing it; such persons can manipulate a screening function to increase others' uncertainty vis-à-vis their own. Generally, the chiefs absorbed the ambiguity associated with control, balancing the city's senior policymakers against their immediate subordinates.

The case of the planning department in Chapter 6 illustrated that individuals who have been caught in the higher uncertainty levels for some time tend nevertheless to choose the least controversial path available. Moreover, they remain disgruntled and frustrated. The planning department, however, displayed the most sophisticated and largest number of coping strategies among those studied. The members had developed methods for working around their own and others' obvious confusion about what a planning department in city hall ought to do. The fact that the confusion was liberally spiced with suspicion further added to the planners' difficulties. Yet the evidence suggested that the planning department might have been more influential if they had not hobbled themselves by choosing avoidance and limited response as their modal strategies.

Chapter 7 followed the reorganization of the parks and recreation departments. Their well-established operating guides were abolished and the departments' administrative leaders had no clear idea what choices of activities were possible or what the outcomes might be. This case, more than the others, revealed intensification of delay and avoidance tactics to the extent that activity in some areas all but stopped. Though this was not the only case in which the limited response was manifest, it was clearly revealed in this chapter. As the parks-recreation case clearly demonstrated, the fall-back often is a sophisticated method for not confronting the problems that are causing great ambiguity.

Lastly, Chapter 8 traced electronic data processing in city hall from its acquisition through several levels of development. In this study, the screen or buffering tactic is revealed as an effective though dangerous method for coping with uncertainty. EDP had become a very serious problem in Oakland before the Council and even the manager were fully alerted, because they were so effectively buffered in regard to EDP.

Their response, when they were informed, devolved basically to a reinforcement of the existing solution. This is the institutional analog to the professional fall-back tactic: If a choice, however generated, does not resolve a problem, if alternatives or their outcomes cannot be identified with confidence, and if lower order, less sophisticated tactics such as avoidance or delay are not possible, then the tendency is to intensify the previously attempted solution.

Active Tactics, Accompanied by Frustration and Anxiety

The hypotheses forwarded in the first chapter hold that the first layers of the coping hierarchy are the most frequently encountered and are basically passive. This research suggests that passive responses tend to be more successful for those with institutional or personal resources to expend for protection. Screening processes and organizational and geographical distance are notable examples of passive coping techniques widely employed by those responsible for choice in formal organizations.

But what of the less frequently observed coping techniques such as limited response, withdrawal, reversible choice, and the like? In Chapter 1, it was suggested that adoption of these active coping tactics normally would be forced by insufficient resources or a breakdown in the screening process. What have the foregoing studies demonstrated with regard to adopting and maintaining these more difficult active techniques?

In Chapter 4, for example, there was no evidence in the history of the community action programs in Oakland that the programs would spawn adversary groups. This was, at least from the Council's point of view, an unintended and surprising development. Though they did not like it, the Council members did not know what to do about this situation. Despite ideological divisions, it is difficult for a revenue-hungry government to refuse several million dollars' annual aid. The Council, however, was not willing to risk either offensive or defensive tactics, and the members appeared unable to estimate confidently the consequence of choice so they remained immobilized, unwilling to react to the tactics of target-area activists.

In this case, the Council clearly was concerned that any action might generate greater demand, more anti-city hall feeling, and, thus, increased support for the low-resource group that was pressing them. In short, they sensed that disagreeable or costly consequences were possible, but they did not know how likely. As many have observed, few people wish to risk expensive, perhaps disastrous, results if they cannot estimate with reasonable[3] confidence what the outcome will be or how likely it is to be undesirable. The Council, like the P-R leadership examined in Chapter 7, tended to be made up of older men whose personal stake was, for various reasons, greater and their flexibility reduced. In other words, the Council members too shared beliefs, principles, and substantial personal investment in a career or way of life that increased the apparent cost of error in any uncertain situation.

Long before the OEDC became an independent organization, the evidence indicates that the Council could not control or outmaneuver community action dissidents. In fact, they often were not able to predict the effects of even trivial or routine decision. The evidence in Chapter 4 demonstrates (see Table 4.3) that the Council was compelled to continue making a great number of decisions regarding community action programs. But they increasingly assumed a professional demeanor toward the antipoverty programs rather like that embraced by the P-R administrators toward the new department. Instead of embarking on a tactical path that might have used the widespread ambiguity surrounding these programs to improve their position relative to the activists, or perhaps using it to guide the development of the programs, the Council members fell back to thinking about the programs in terms of such ready measures as square feet of office space rented, eyeglasses dispensed, job trainees graduated per dollar of grant money, and the like. This kind of response was very uncharacteristic of the Council in this period. A careful search of the record indicated that the members normally referred a question involving technical details to the manager for his recommendation.

The continuing necessity to make numerous decisions regarding the programs obviously was increasingly painful for the Council; the limited tactic was not working for them. This seems to have been an important factor in their relinquishing control of the antipoverty programs. Similarly, several early retirements among the P-R leadership appeared to result, at least in part, from their painful experience.

In some circumstances, withdrawal is not possible regardless of whether punishing consequences appear likely. The ASUO student leaders could not leave the public school system in Oakland, and the police administrators could not carry out their responsibilities if the budget did not meet their needs. The question then becomes the following: What does the decision maker perceive his or her stake to be in the outcome of the decision process?

Part of the dilemma about the question of stake, exemplified by the EDP study in Chapter 8, is that we are attracted to sophisticated technologies that seem to promise that the fruits of science can solve our toughest problems, and this very magnetism renders us rather easy targets for any reasonably persuasive salesperson. It is not difficult to sell a very costly EDP machine that is not really understood. This is precisely when the trouble begins. At this point there is a considerable monetary and social stake in a device that does not seem to perform as the buyer optimistically believed. In fact, the study of EDP in Oakland suggests that the introduction of a complicated, poorly or incorrectly understood technique in a traditional administrative setting can easily result in confusion and less effective management. This is not an all inclusive antiscience or antitechnology argument. Rather, it is like asking if an electron microscope is worth the cost for someone who does not understand its capabilities or limitations. After the disappointing investment, why not simply admit the mistake and give up the innovation? Part of the answer is obvious; some middle- to upper-level administrators are likely to have committed themselves, personally and professionally, to the new technique, and it is naturally difficult for them to admit a very costly error. Such candor can stifle, even wreck, a career.

Part of the answer is less obvious. It is difficult to back away from the symbols of modern management and admit that one is not sophisticated or "up-do-date" enough to employ them. Moreover, many appear to have greater faith in modern technologies, despite high cost, ineffective performance, and so on, than in other persons, simple devices, or procedures.

When the stake is perceived to be high and a withdrawal option is not available, the situation begins to appear quite threatening. At this point, the use of ambiguity as a weapon is likely to be the most effective tactic open to the policymaker. The student leaders in Chapter 3 and the police administrators in Chapter 5 adopted it with some success. One P-R administrator used it skillfully and the planners appeared to be moving toward adopting this approach.[4] In general, the use of ambiguity as a weapon requires the use of tactics intended to increase others' uncertainty regarding one's capabilities, legitimacy, following, knowledge, information, and the like. The result is that criteria for judging a choice are rendered suspect, which reduces the probability that a decision will be questioned or that, at least in the near term, punishing consequences will follow.

Whatever the reasons, if ambiguity cannot be employed as a weapon, the stake is high, and the consequences may be unfavorable, then an easily reversible choice or a reinforcement routine become the most likely coping tactics to be used. The planners in Chapter 6, for example, had developed many roles and, if the role adopted for a particular situation was challenged, they could readily shift to a different one.

Though the planners were frustrated as professionals among a confusing plethora of roles, this appeared to be a very effective coping behavior in city hall.

Another effective and not infrequently observed tactic is that depicted in Chapter 1 as the reinforcement subroutine. Use of this coping behavior was most clearly demonstrated in the history of EDP in Oakland. In this case, the EDP question was drawn out for many years by investing more in EDP whenever punishing consequences threatened those responsible for it. With normal personnel transfer and turnover, responsibility for the choices can be diffused to the point where nobody is personally affected by punishing consequences. For example, when EDP difficulties did finally spill out of city hall, Oakland's government in general was regarded as culpable. Thus blame was sufficiently diffused so that no administrator's career or department's standing was threatened directly.

Finally, as Figure 9.1 indicates, it is possible that a policymaker will find him- or herself in a situation that does not yield readily to natural coping tactics. When this happens, immobilism engendered by panic may result. Under such extreme pressure, the most likely action is to loop back in the hope that withdrawal or flight is an option that was not open or chosen when the decision maker passed the first branch to it.

The experience of the Council in Chapter 4 was an example of this situation. The Council was reduced to the point where it was not able to act with regard to the OEO-sponsored, antipoverty programs in Oakland. In the beginning, withdrawal was not perceived by the Council members as an available option. After a time, however, the Council found no satisfactory method for coping with the antipoverty-sponsored activities, and it determined that withdrawal was legally permissible and did so. Similarly, the experience of some P-R administrators and certain officials responsible for EDP decisions provided further evidence that policymakers can be immobilized by conditions of high uncertainty, regardless of strong need or demand for active choice.

Though the cases chronicled in the preceding chapters imply that many naturally attempted to avoid choice under conditions of great ambiguity, the evidence suggests that few could do so. Moreover, it seems likely that more decision makers will find themselves in similar predicaments more often. Each of these studies—and perhaps that of EDP most starkly—suggests that many in city hall believe that innovations are needed and that attempts will be made to implement new, often untested, poorly understood techniques. This research indicates that weakly perceived, incomplete alternative sets or paths and costly information search decrease the likelihood that an information search will reduce the level of uncertainty. Furthermore, often needed skills and understanding cannot be acquired quickly, and the cost of mastering new procedures, machinery, or political situations usually will be high. The evidence in the foregoing cases suggests that few municipal officials are intellectually or emotionally prepared to adapt to high levels of uncertainty.

This summary of the coping tactics identified among the several cases has yielded information and insight regarding responses to high-level uncertainty. What can be inferred from this analysis that may provide succor to beleaguered administrators and officials in city hall?

Characterizing Uncertainty in a
Formal Decision Problem

There appear to be two basic dimensions along which individuals or groups of individuals can be arrayed in relation to a decision problem. A difficulty may be unique to an individual, or he or she may suspect or vaguely "know" that others have faced similar questions. Perhaps professional colleagues, acquaintances, or on-the-job associates have encountered such difficulties once or many times, or the individual affected may have faced similar situations once or many times. In Figure 9.1, this is labeled the *experience* dimension or component as it affects uncertainty.

The second dimension in Figure 9.1 is labeled *theory*. This is not intended just to denote grand, philosophical abstractions but also technical training and know-how that may have developed—at some point—from highly theoretical formulations or very mundane experience. In short, this dimension reflects a formal training and education component as it affects uncertainty. This vector too can be visualized as progressing from no training or education through vicarious to personal knowledge. This means that someone confronted by a particular problem may have no acquaintance with theories—including analytic techniques or algorithms—that appear pertinent. Alternatively, he or she may know of techniques or trained specialists who he or she believes possess perceptions and capabilities that are relevant to his or her problem. Finally, he or she may possess the necessary education or technical expertise.

The three categories characterizing each dimension should not be viewed as discrete points on their respective vectors. They are simply intended to specify more clearly the modal characteristics of an essentially infinite number of possible points in an "uncertainty space."

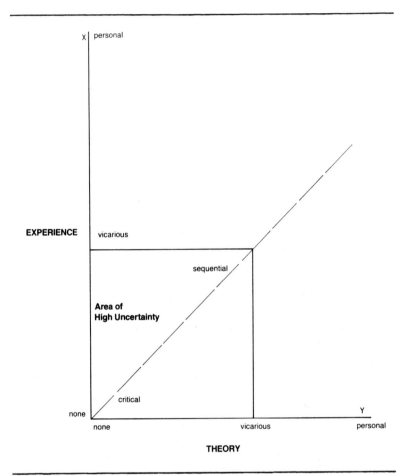

Figure 9.1 Degree of Uncertainty Is a Function of Experience and Theoretical Understanding

It is readily apparent in Figure 9.1 that the degree of uncertainty varies as the decision maker's position in relation to each dimension changes. It is hard to imagine an adaptive process—where the decision maker actually moves out of the area of high uncertainty—that does not necessitate movement along one or both of these two dimensions. If he or she is immobilized there is no movement and no adaptation; if the decision maker flees or withdraws, the problem is no longer demanding a decision. Although withdrawal can be an effective coping technique, it is difficult to think of it as adaptive behavior because the policymaker has not mastered uncertainty; rather, he or she has refused to confront it. It might be well, at this point, to relate coping tactics to adaptive movement and to reiterate the obvious qualification that uncertainty is meaningful only if the decision maker regards the outcome or consequence as nontrivial.

Basically, the coping sequence outlined in the first chapter is directed to surviving in situations of great ambiguity. If adaptive movement along either vector results from coping behavior, it is very likely an unintended byproduct of an individual's or an organization's attempt to maintain itself. Delaying can provide time, search yields information, surviving itself increases experience, and so on. The foregoing research, however, offers slight evidence that such techniques are chosen deliberately to increase understanding—and thus reduce uncertainty. Rather, the evidence suggests that a coping sequence is tactical maneuvering in reaction to high-order uncertainty. In short, coping as a tactical and adaptive movement is, at root, strategic; the idea of strategic development connotes greater anticipation and investment of resources than tactical maneuvering.

The area of high uncertainty—which is approximately circumscribed by the "weak side" of the vicarious area on both dimensions—occupies roughly one-fourth of the decision space. This suggests that most decision problems are not likely to be characterized by high uncertainty. So, too, one need not be in the high area of both vectors in order to avoid the shaded area. A problem defined as critically uncertain—as Figure 9.1 indicates—is one that is unique to the decision makers' experience or sufficiently unusual to him or her that any effective solution will appear enormously costly and perhaps insoluble. However, a question need not fall in the critical classification in every respect in order for a decision maker to feel its sting. Many if not most problems require a set or series of choices. Each decision might be visualized as a node in a path; if any node is found to be critically uncertain, the solution process is likely to stop or, at the very least, become painfully difficult at that point.

Toward the outer edges of the high uncertainty area and spilling over into the area of medium uncertainty, decision problems may be more appropriately characterized as sequential.[5] Sequential uncertainty tends toward the vicarious region on both dimensions and may be high- or mid-level depending on the degree of difficulty encountered acquiring experience or formal knowledge either personally of from others' contribution. Sequential uncertainty is characteristic of situations in which, on the one hand, a decision maker is confronted by difficulties for which he or she has no training or experience. On the other hand, the decision maker is reasonably confident that others have been faced with similar questions or that a body of knowledge exists that can illuminate and inform the situation. Here too, if search is not initiated and experience or theory are not readily acquired, a decision process can easily bog down as uncertainty builds on uncertainty.[6]

For example, Figure 9.2 depicts the approximate location in this conceptual space of three of the cases described in previous chapters compared to several contemporary activities common in Oakland and most city governments. The Council members, faced with community-action programs, had no experience and no theory regarding how to proceed. They eventually began to survey others' experience and to acquire it themselves over the years. Thus most of their movement—or adaptation—was along the experience dimension. Figure 9.2 indicates that from the "critical corner," the shortest distance that will significantly reduce uncertainty lies along the x or y vector. In short, the adaptive strategy would seem to be to concentrate adaptive effort on one component or the other rather than on both simultaneously.[7] Thus far, we have argued that there exists a sequence of natural coping or maintenance tactics. If high order uncertainty is to be effectively reduced, however, learning and/or experience must be acquired as the scheme in Figure 9.1 suggests.

In the case of EDP, city officials began with the belief that individuals did exist who possessed knowledge that could make EDP work effectively. However, it appears that officials in Oakland, at least when EDP began, essentially had little information about others' experience with computer technology in local government. The suggestion in Figure 9.2 is that they moved in the direction of increased vicarious and personal experience through the ten-year history chronicled in Chapter 8. How much more effective might the adaptation to EDP in Oakland have been if the administrators had concentrated on widespread education and training?

The parks-recreation case seems to be a clear example of sequential uncertainty near the edge of the high uncertainty area. Yet there was little indication of adaptive movement to alleviate the highly uncertain situation. It may have been that everyone was waiting for someone else to move; apparently no one thought it was his responsibility—or to his benefit—to work to figure out what was known about or what had been done in similar circumstances. Ironically, it appears that a slight movement in any direction might well have cleared P-R from the shadow of high uncertainty. It may be that the P-R administrators perceived their stake—that is, potential personal loss—to be so great

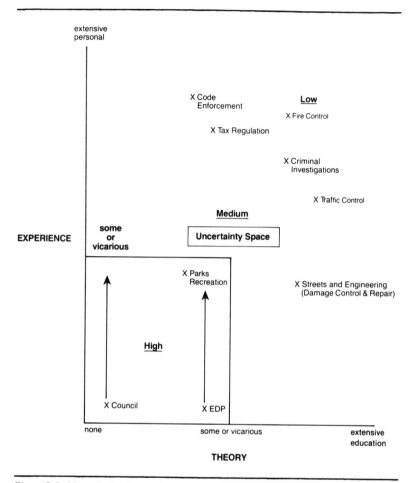

Figure 9.2 Most Activities in the City Remain Well Clear of the High Uncertainty Area

that adaptive activity seemed too costly. It is clear that adaptive action was objectionable to the Council in the case of the community action programs but the decision makers in the Council and EDP cases were so pressed by events that they withdrew from the arena. If withdrawal or immobilism are the coping tactics in effect, adaptive movement is precluded.

In Chapter 3, the ASUO leaders demonstrated that citizens can adapt as well as withdraw from the arena; adaptive movement for citizens who wish to affect local policies is very difficult and expensive.

Nevertheless, the student leaders began with no experience and little knowledge and "moved" considerably along the experience dimension in their attempts to influence school policy in Oakland.

The case of the police administrators in Chapter 5 suggested that each successive chief began with little experience and knowledge of the budgeting tactics necessary to compete successfully for scarce revenues within the city. Each adopted somewhat different tactics, but through time, all learned to act effectively with respect to that complicated, tactically intense process. Similarly, the planners in Chapter 6 indicated that they were surviving and beginning to learn how to be more effective in their ambiguous environment.

Additional Notes on Uncertainty in the Decision Process

The problem of adaptive movement is related to uncertainty with respect to utilities in that certainty about utility derives in part from experience and theory.[8] It is difficult to know what is preferable when one cannot make clear estimates of what is possible. There are yet other wrinkles in regard to adaptation.

Meltsner and Bellavitta (1983) point out that language is an intervening variable in adaptive or coping behavior. Language often has an effect on strategies that are adopted and like the bluffing tactic, it can be manipulated to increase others' confusion, anxiety, and uncertainty. In situations such as those faced by the Council, ASUO, or EDP administrators, people often have differing world views and/or do not understand and cannot communicate. Differing world views may engender conflict and, thus, delay or avoidance behaviors while failure to understand clearly increases uncertainties and may affect coping tactics. At this point, it seems likely that, all things being equal, the coping tactics adopted in situations of mutual misunderstanding would follow the coping model depicted in Chapter 1. More generally, emerging connectiveness or interdependence among objectives or social organizations implies that consequences will be quite difficult to estimate because they are not well-identified. If connections and interdependencies change faster than reservoirs of experience or technical/theoretical knowledge can be built, then movement out of the high uncertainty space becomes impossible.

Before anyone sinks in a sea of despair, however, please note the examples of several city activities that are depicted in Figure 9.2. While administrators differ substantially on the mix of experience and theory they rely on to perform such functions, they tend to scatter around a relatively narrow band between medium to low uncertainty. This is not to say that a situation cannot occasionally develop in any of these service areas that may be considerably more uncertain for the officials in question, but their activities in Oakland from the 1950s through the 1980s were not commonly characterized by feelings of or strategies associated with high-order uncertainty.

Is there utility in this embryonic exposition for someone attempting to move out of the high uncertainty space? The first and most obvious product is that organizing a problem in such a framework encourages one to think through the nature of the uncertainty he or she faces. If the individual can roughly place him- or herself in the uncertainty space, then some paths of attack will be suggested. The second point is that there are several kinds of activities that seem more sensible—more likely to be usefully adaptive—depending on where one finds him- or herself in the space. If the natural coping tactics presented in the first chapter could be ordered and selected to complement adaptive movement, the experiences of policymakers confronted by great ambiguity may be significantly improved.

For a long time now, a certain method of solving problems— especially complex problems—has been widely accepted as both more effective and efficient than others. The most important characteristic associated with the superior method is that of beginning with several possible solutions, each of which can be falsified. The biologist, J. R. Platt (1964), has called this the habit of complex thought. True, the ghost of the so-called scientific method may be perceived in this brief description. Should a problem-solving approach that has a surprisingly good track record be dismissed simply because it has traditionally been associated with laboratories, experiments, seemingly incomprehensible symbols, or unintelligible language?

This habit of complex thought may offer an effective, yet practical, beginning point for an attempt to develop a method successfully to accommodate great uncertainty; think, then, in terms of a set of complementary tactics for subduing a very ambiguous situation.

Beginning the Adaptive Process:
The Wisdom of Doing Nothing

The chronology of these cases, most spanning several years, suggests that most decision problems in city hall can be postponed for a time with little chance that they will explode on the decision maker's desk. It is very difficult to determine if an information search can be helpful unless some estimates of knowledge likely to be needed are made and obvious places are scanned to see whether data are available that, on the face of it, appear likely to be helpful. Before actually commencing a search, the costs of data acquisition relative to the resources available must be estimated. At this point a decision maker may begin to get a sense of his or her level of uncertainty with respect to a new problem or problem-set confronting him or her. If the decision maker finds him- or herself in the middle- to highly uncertain area, then continuing a common search is not likely to be fruitful. This does not mean, however, that one cannot begin adaptive motion; there is no reason to believe at this point that interminable delay—perhaps in the hope that a problem will dissolve— is the best, a good, or even a neutral strategy. In fact, the foregoing research suggests that decision activity will continue under conditions of high-level uncertainty, though it is likely to be slowed by delaying and other coping tactics. Undue delay can be crippling; a strategy is needed that can guide initial adaptive steps when it seems that a reasonably informed decision cannot be achieved within the limits of time and energy available.

Intuition: An Important Aid in the Adaptive Process

If municipal officials, administrators, and local leaders, confronted by high-level uncertainty, were more trusting of and paid more attention to their intuition, they would find it a helpful tool and an important element in developing adaptive strategies from coping tactics. Intuition, carefully defined, does not connote a semimystical clairvoyance but rather very sophisticated, semiconscious problem-defining, alternative-formulating, and probability-estimating processes. Choices based on intuitive estimates are no more likely to be timely, correct, brilliant decisions than choices identified by many other decision processes; however, they may be better in a situation of high-level uncertainty than dated, rigidified guides from professional training, or poorly understood analytic techniques and technologies.

Though heroic characters in novels may rely on intuition despite considerable physical evidence that challenges their intuitive solution, most of us do not trust it to that extent. Thus initial choice, based on intuitive judgments, is likely to be easily reversible. In other words, most regard this kind of decision as a tentative step and do not expect that it is the best possible choice, only that it is, under adverse conditions, an intelligent beginning.[9] In fact Michael Polanyi (1958: 130-131) argues that "seeing" the solution to a tough problem in a momentary illuminative flash offers no final answer but a starting point from which a solution is firmed and tested through a series of explicit, logical operations. Polanyi (1958: 260-261) goes on to say that discovery or problem solution is a complex process in which the actor shifts his or her confidence continually between intuition and formal reasoning, never letting go of either. Original discoveries change one's interpretive framework, and, thus, it is simply impossible to generate an original solution solely by diligently applying any existing, specifiable procedure. One must cross the logical gap between a new problem and its solution on the crest of considerable emotional or psychic energy (Polanyi, 1958: 149). In other words, intuitively based adaptive movement will be emotionally taxing, but would it be more taxing and less satisfying than day-to-day life in a highly uncertain context?

Finally, there is less chance that there is a large personal or professional investment in such a provisional judgment and, therefore, a reduced probability that a potentially dangerous reinforcement tactic will be maintained as an adaptive strategy. Using intuition as a first step implies openness to feedback and willingness to make corrective decisions. The expectation that constant search for evaluative information and frequent correction actions are necessary should reduce the incidence and intensity of surprising consequences.

Increasing Intuitive Capacity:
Mid-Career Education

The intuitive process may be an important aid, but simply giving more attention to and placing more faith in it is not sufficient to adapt to unfamiliar, complex problems. If intuition is a semiconscious problem-solving technique, it is logical to conclude that it would become more reliable and more helpful the richer its substantive base. Formal education and direct and vicarious experiences form the foundation for this process.[10] It has been argued that under conditions of great ambiguity experience, by definition, will not be a good guide and relying on outdated formal education or training, though useful for coping in the short run, can become dysfunctional if there is no attempt to construct adaptive strategies that can supplant the initial coping tactic. When it is not followed by adoption of adaptive strategies, this limited response is like the condition Robert Merton (1968: 252) labeled "trained incapacity." Merton, borrowing from Weblen, argued that if an individual's response, under changed circumstances, is based upon training and skills that may have been appropriate in the past but are no longer suitable, serious maladjustments can result. In short, the very soundness of past training may lead to the adoption of the wrong procedures.

It may be that those, like the ASUO leadership and the deviant P-R administrator, who are closer to their formal educations will more readily develop an intuitive grasp of a problem despite slight on-the-job practice or information. This suggests that continually updating one's formal education supports or feeds the intuitive process and that it is another important element in any set of strategies intended to increase administrators' adaptive capacities. The idea of education "up-grading" or "retooling" is not new, but this recommendation is for a particular sort of education as an integral part of a set of adaptive strategies. This is not an exhortation for education in the sense of refresher or technical retraining like that for a career change. Rather, it must—to serve the needs outlined here—encourage increased perspective on, perception of, and ability to think in general terms about the milieu in which a person has been and will be working.

Most municipal officials and administrators today have college degrees and new administrators increasingly are urged to acquire graduate education, but it is also evident that even the best formal or professional education can become quickly outdated.[11] This means that, in addition to acquiring a thorough grounding in the principles of physical, natural, or human behavior and the processes for locating, codifying, and shaping bits of information in order to clarify and resolve problems, municipal officials must return to school periodically in order to review their perspective.[12] Such midcareer leaves also would provide opportunity for an official to put his or her particular job experiences in a broader frame. Mid-life education is becoming increasingly available and, if this argument is near the mark, it will soon be a common, relatively inexpensive method for improving intuitive capabilities and updating professional or technical ideas so that a fall-back tactic is more likely to be functional for long-term adaptation as well as a natural near-term coping tactic.

An Installment Plan for Increasing
Adaptive Capability

Mid-career education can also be viewed as a strategy for expanding the library of information available to decision makers. In this way, the very high cost of an extensive knowledge base can be paid in a palatable, long-term way. The decision to pay continuously decreases the likelihood that administrators or other public officials will find themselves confronted with problems for which their backgrounds are so deficient that the cost of acquiring information in the short run is prohibitive.[13] The strategy hedges against future requirements or insufficiencies. Moreover, periodically refreshing one's education will tend, on the average, to hold uncertainty levels lower for decision makers.

Homework Is No Fun—But It Helps

More study is another important piece of the puzzle. Those challenged by problems in a context of high-level uncertainty cannot rely completely on experience or professional education regardless of how recently acquired or refreshed. They must expect that considerable homework—the emphasis is on home here—will be necessary if they are to develop a good intuitive grasp of a problem area. Generally, the evidence indicates that few individuals caught in dilemmas such as the ones described in the foregoing chapters set about doing any homework regarding the problems that weighed on them. Few performed even a cursory search for potentially helpful professional publications, basic texts, or other related writings. Again, only among ASUO leadership and a few deviant administrators do we find any who had taken the time and trouble to inform themselves about issues related to the topics of this research. The implication is that the research process, generally thought to be for academics and a few staff specialists, must become part of the municipal officials' way of life (see Landau, 1973).

This does not mean that officials in city hall should dissolve their screening processes and attempt to become expertly informed about all the governmental operations for which they are responsible. If they will assure themselves of a solid, up-to-date foundation and are willing to do some research when an unusual problem penetrates the screening processes, then the leadership in city hall will be better able to reach a successful accommodation to highly ambiguous problems. This comparatively simple set of complementary strategies, suggested by the previous analyses, is not a panacea for frustrated citizens or harassed public officials. But if the lessons drawn from those sketches are near the mark, the set of adaptive strategies just outlined—delay, intuition, education, professional fall-back, and persistence or homework—might enable quicker, more functionally adaptive movement in the face of unusual disruptions. Their purpose is not to eliminate risk from public decision making but to lower the level of uncertainty. Still, it is unrealistic to suppose that municipal officials will not be disagreeably surprised or find themselves in distressful situations even if they follow this strategic blueprint.

Summarizing briefly, if the coping tactics observed in the previous chapters are as broadly common as this research suggests, it is obvious that they fit into a natural sequence that has demonstrated effectiveness. These coping tactics, other than perhaps avoidance and withdrawal, must be seen as interim or maintenance actions. For the most part, they will not reduce the uncertainty level associated with the particular problem facing a policymaker. In order for him or her to adapt to any unusual ambiguity in his or her decision-making environment, the policymaker must begin to build thoughtful, positive actions from these natural coping responses. Thus delay, intuition, education, and the like are compatible with instinctive responses and appropriate to the requirements for adaptive movement; such a complementary set of strategies is not contrary to ideas of responsible or professional decision making and would serve to enable useful adaptation or reduction of unusual uncertainty.

At this point, the question becomes the following: Did the decision makers and administrators in the previous cases have the capability to enlarge their perspective and field of operations so that, guided by a strategic map, they could adapt more creatively in situations marked by considerable uncertainty? In view of the constraints most of us feel—particularly in traditional administrative settings—a set of enabling policies is necessary that will permit and perhaps encourage administrators to pursue a deceptively simple strategic course like that outlined in the preceding paragraphs.

The foregoing chapters clearly indicate that policymakers are constrained by investment in a particular organization or career ladder, available personal or organizational resources, insecurity, and the natural inclination to avoid pain, to name a few. When one is facing a choice problem under conditions of great uncertainty, such constraints work to inhibit adaptive movement. This is particularly true where the administrative leadership is rooted in an ideology of pure rationality. In other words, when administrators believe that it is both desirable and possible for them to approach any administrative choice problem dispassionately adhering only to a rigidly logical calculus, then they must understand such behaviors as those documented in the foregoing chapters in terms of weakness and threat to the organization.

Apart from the obvious psychological strains and tensions for individuals suggested by a belief that individuals can decide—on a regular basis—without considering personal resources, inclination, career position, or the like, an ideology of rationality intervenes between natural coping tendencies and subsequent adaptive strategies. Thus until a person's attachment to an ideal type rationality is weakened, the following policy recommendations cannot be adopted and pursued because they cannot be defended. Despite a pervasive idea of pure rationality in our culture, the foregoing cases did not weaken our hypothesis that, under conditions of high-order uncertainty, the widespread ideas of rationality do not dominate a decision process.

Continuing with this hypothesis, it follows that changes in perspective and action with regard to decision-making behavior would result from the increased understanding and acceptance of decision making based on subjective concerns. Such changes would enable decision makers to develop and to experiment with strategic approaches to ambiguous decision problems. They complement natural coping techniques and imply that, in addition to surviving despite considerable ambiguity, persons can resolve ambiguity if they do not feel that by doing so they are inviting personal disaster.

POLICY RECOMMENDATIONS

Reduce the Cost

In many cases, such as Planning, Parks-Recreation, or EDP in city hall, more creative adaptive response and more effective reduction of high-order uncertainty can be encouraged by reducing the cost or potential cost of trying new ideas. In other words, the opportunity cost and psychic price for trusting an intuitively derived choice must be lessened. This would diminish the pain of deciding incorrectly; alternatively, a context rooted in an ideal rationality intensifies personal cost and pain.[14] This recommendation implies, for example, that those who have the best understanding, whatever the reasons, of an unusual policy or situation should be offered incentive for inventing and forwarding alternatives.

The question always arises of how can the cost of experimentation be reduced in practice. There is no way other than for the leadership to adopt such a policy, stick to it, and educate others to it. Clearly, this requires some restructuring of the configuration of rewards and sanctions commonly practiced when the ideology of sure rationality is dominant. If useful adaptive movement is intended, leadership must not punish incorrect or dysfunctional choices or reward do-nothing behavior in an ambiguous context.

Open the Alternative Formulation Process

If an organization is to benefit from a policy that encourages invention, investment, and multiple attempts with respect to choice under conditions of high-order uncertainty, the senior leadership must be open and receptive. Here, again, the usual tendency is to stress administrative control rather than openness, though students of executive styles long have argued that the senior leader's primary function is to receive and send information. It will do no good for alternative suggestions to flow upward through an organization if the top leaders are unable or unwilling to think seriously about them and to implement them. This is not to say that attempts must be made to implement every alternative suggested, only that each must be received and considered by receptive policymakers.

Under conditions of great ambiguity, the executive style cannot be focused on reduction of uncertainty through control. It must be open and tolerant of the ambiguity as policymakers encourage their organization through the difficult adaptive process. This is not an exhortation to top-level policymakers to abdicate responsibility. Actually, a policy of openness requires more subtlety and emotional and psychic energy than is demanded by a culture based in an idealized rationality. Moreover, the senior leadership has the crucial responsibility of recognizing error and dysfunction in the process of adaptation.

How bad must a situation become after observing a change or adopting a new technique before the decision makers become skeptical of the assumptions that led to a certain choice? When things go awry, the decision maker must probe for the basic, often unspoken, initial premises underlying his or her estimates of a particular "state of nature" or reality. In regard to social organizations especially, this is far more easily said than done. Perhaps it is because we are human and therefore know something about human motivation or behavior that we tend to act as though we know the essentials about any social system. We make no such assumptions about inanimate physical or natural orders. We often are surprised by new insights or findings regarding the behaviors of atomic particles or molecular structures. This research reiterates that there are times when we cannot estimate what effect a change or innovation will have in a social context. Policymakers must discipline themselves to look at social settings in such a way that surprise is to be expected. Furthermore, surprise must not be regarded as crippling so that the energy generated by it can readily be directed toward asking new questions and admitting new possibilities.

Raise the Pain Threshold

Another way to encourage creative response would be to raise the pain threshold. David McClelland (1961: 223) identifies a set of personality characteristics that he calls entrepreneurial. He maintains that people who share these attributes—entrepreneurs—are relatively more self-confident the more "unknown the situation." Screening potential line administrators for entrepreneurial characteristics might be worth considering. Another way of increasing the managers' tolerance for high-order uncertainty would be to require that all middle-level managers receive training for coping with and adapting to nonspecific, high-level ambiguity. Such training could be developed in-house or acquired in prepackaged, modular form.

Consultants Can Provide Alternatives and Inform Choice

Consultant groups could serve to generate alternative possibilities in highly uncertain situations. This approach circumvents many of the difficulties raised by intraorganizational sanctions but raises those of reputation and repeat business for a consultant. However, these latter obstacles could be removed during contract negotiations when expectations are molded, revised, and formalized. Few if any, private-sector consultants regularly provide such a service at present and certainly those encountered in these studies did not. There is no evidence that they were hired for any such purpose. In fact, it seems they were expected, as consultants often are, to strengthen or confirm the intentions of those who hired them. Still, there is—and increasingly will be—a need for consultant groups to serve as a temporary staff offering technical expertise, research capability, and broader experience and perspective in order to create more complete alternative sets and better probability estimates regarding outcomes.

Most of these suggested changes in expectations, role perceptions, and behavior among the municipal leadership, staff aides, or consultants are not impractical or impossible. But neither are they easily accomplished or guaranteed to end all problems in political or administrative life. Certainly part of the problem for any official is to realize and to admit when he or she does not understand a problem; once again, that is primarily a matter of adopting a nonpunitive policy, following it, and educating others to act in accordance with it. Elected officials must realize that the cost of unwillingness to admit ignorance and to work to reduce it can easily be greater than the cost of confession and homework.

The Bottom Line: The Pain Constant in Ambiguous Situations

The problems described in the preceding chapters were difficult, serious ones that often resulted in unhappy consequences for decision makers. It is important to remember, however, that life and government in Oakland continues more or less quietly, smoothly, and effectively. It has not disintegrated from the impact of white-flight, low-resource pressure politics, reorganization, increased or diminished federal-city programs, new technologies, or any other of the many problems, that have confronted local decision makers in recent years. In this city, most survived, but the price in dollar cost, provision of effective service, and personal or psychic discomfort often was high. What is to be learned from these experiences of high uncertainty so that, where possible, they may be avoided?

The Planning, Parks-Recreation, and Electronic Data Processing cases suggest that great uncertainty may follow when simple expectations are held in the face of an unusually complex organizational reality. Alternatively, we learned from the ASUO-school board and Council-community action examples that considerable ambiguity can result when a simple organization is challenged by an unusually complex problem or situation. The concept of a complementary set of strategies is a good one in a situation of simple expectations or overload because the set approach will enrich the natural tactics.

In the second instance, exemplified by the ASUO, the Council, and community action, the predicament cannot be so readily resolved. These cases were particularly complicated in that the intervention of an ideological dimension other than rationality seems to have increased the level of frustration and perceived danger. The rise of pathological symptoms, such as conspiracy theories and paranoia, was evident. If the Council, for example, had adopted the strategic set approach, it might have helped but it is not clear that this approach would have been sufficient to alleviate its problems. The ASUO, Council, and School Board were simple, largely undifferentiated organizations that were overtaxed in normal circumstances. The leadership simply did not have the capacity—time, training, or staff—to deal with the uncommon stresses that were affecting them.

Certainly one important lesson learned from Oakland's experience is that one never gets something for nothing. A price must be paid for greater efficiency, access, control, or revenues; and at least in these cases, the actual marginal cost of these "commodities" far exceeded the marginal reward. Naturally such an imbalance was neither intended nor expected, but no one had estimated the high added cost of adapting to situations characterized by high-level uncertainty. Moreover, dealing with great ambiguity not only seems to cost more, but looking at the adaptive process from the perspective of adherents to the idea of pure rationality, it apparently leads to less than expected return on the investment.

In short, the indications are that situations likely to be attended by high-level uncertainty in the near term will not yield appealing dividends.

It is all well and good to counsel avoiding costly mistakes, but everyone continues to make them. True, if forewarned the tendency is to be better prepared and to proceed more cautiously, but proceed we must. This is true for municipal government as it is for others in society.

This analysis, however, has been concerned with a relatively narrow class of problems. Though it is clear that the bulk of municipal officials' problems will not involve high uncertainty levels, it is to be expected that local officials and administrators will find themselves in ever more complex environments. As a consequence, they will experience episodes of middle- to high-level uncertainty more often. The lesson from this research in Oakland is that policymakers must expand their instinctively based uncertainty management techniques to include thoughtfully constructed tools to facilitate long-run adaptation. If they do not, their experience in situations marked by great ambiguity will be painful, personally costly, and, as long as our administrative culture is rooted in ideologies of pure rationality, dysfunctional for the entire organization.

N O T E S

1. The limits of predictability are mostly practical ones. The more that is known about the personal circumstance of the decision maker, the more predictable his or her response behavior.

2. Paul Peterson (1981: 178-182) argues that delay as a coping tactic tends to be rich and active. Local officials respond by ignoring or screening demands out; making false promises to buy time; rewarding or answering specific complaints while ignoring the overall problem; by concerting demands for redistribution of services to redistribution of power.

3. The term "reasonable" is used here in the subjective sense; the connotation would be "comfortably." See also Mack (1971, especially 122-131), Richard M. Cyert and James G. March, (1963, especially chapters 5 and 6), and J. D. Thompson (1967: ch. 9) for several clear statements of this risk avoidance tendency.

4. See Kantor (1982). Kantor studied 165 mid-level managers in five companies. Her basic questions were what attributes do managers that contribute to innovation share and what factors do innovative companies have in common. She argued that innovative, mid-level managers

- were confident that uncertainties would be clarified; had foresight; and saw unmet needs as opportunities;

- have long time horizons and view setbacks as temporary obstacles in an otherwise straight path to a goal;

- have insight into organizational politics and a sense of whose support can help them at different times. They encourage subordinates to help them, promise a share of the rewards, and deliver on their promises; and

- they persevere, with tact, until they achieve their goals.

Kantor concludes that traditional hierarchical organizations do not encourage innovative middle management. In such settings, managers spend a great deal of their time coping with change; there is an atmosphere of uncertainty that creates opportunities for the very few "risk-takers." Rewards are scarce and promises about rewards are not always kept.

5. Of course a critical node may be encountered in a sequential process and, presumably, would have the same effect as a critical uncertainty encountered in any context.

6. The sequential chain concept is very like the multiplicity axiom in probability theory. However, independence among events is necessary before the multiplicity axiom can be applied, and we can support no such assumption regarding the events in city hall.

7. This scheme does not account for interactive effects that may be present when formal education and experience are mixed. However, at this point, the blend that

provides optimal payoff is not very predictable; so my conceptualization probably offers as good or better prescription for the moment.

8. See Mack (1971: 82) for an expansion of the notion of uncertainty regarding utilities.

9. I suspect that the intuitive process works rather like Bayesian analysis. But a model of an intuitive process based on Bayes' rules would not be appropriate. Bayes cannot be applied unless a complete set of alternatives with estimated probabilities has been specified. See John G. Kemeny et al. (1966: 144-160) and Mack (1971: 63-64).

10. I have observed that children, though very sensitive to mood, role, and behavior, do not have a well-developed intuitive capability.

11. Every council member in Oakland has earned a bachelor's degree and several had graduate or professional education. Similarly, all administrators interviewed, with one possible exception, possessed a bachelor's degree and many held graduate degrees.

12. Don V. Michael (1966) contends that the ever-increasing social and technical complexities of modern organizational life demand constant reeducation.

13. Use of the term "information" throughout this argument implies that it is meant to connote more than a series of facts or raw data. It is used in a broader sense and includes basic concepts, processes, techniques, and strategies for discovering, organizing, and summarizing facts.

14. See, especially, Dennis Slevin (1971) and Anthony Downs (1967: ch. 7). Slevin argues that reducing costs may be the most efficient way to encourage creative administrative decision behavior. Downs implies that administrators will not act creatively if they expect personal retribution. See also J. D. Thompson (1967: ch. 9).

BIBLIOGRAPHY

ALLISON, G. T. (1971) The Essence of Decision: Explaining the Cuban Missile Crisis. Boston: Little, Brown.

ALTSHULER, A. (1965) The City Planning Process: A Political Analysis. Ithaca, NY: Cornell University Press.

ARGYRIS, C. and D. A. SCHON (1978) Organizational Learning: A Theory of Action Perspective. Reading, MA: Addison-Wesley.

BANFIELD, E. C. (1968) Unheavenly City. Boston: Little, Brown.

———(1965) Big City Politics. New York: Random House.

———(1961) Political Influence. New York: Free Press.

BARNARD, C. I. (1938) The Functions of the Executive. Cambridge, MA: Harvard University Press.

BATESON, G. (1972) Steps to an Ecology of Mind. New York: Chandler.

BLEDSOE, M. (1968) "EDP in the auditor-controller's office: a case study." Oakland Project Report, University of California, Berkeley.

BLUMENTHAL, R. (1969) "The bureaucracy: anti-poverty in the community action program," p. 153 in A. Sindler (ed.) American Political Institutions and Public Policy. Boston: Little, Brown.

BORDUA, D. J. and A. J. REISS, Jr. (1966) "Command, control, and charisma: reflections on police bureaucracy." American Journal of Sociology 72 (July).

BRAYBROOKE, D. and C. LINDBLOM (1963) A Strategy of Decision. New York: Free Press.

CLARK, T. N. and L. C. FERGUSON (1983) City Money: Political Processes, Fiscal Strain, and Retrenchment. New York: Columbia University Press.

CRECINE, J. P. (1969) Governmental Problem Solving: A Computer Simulation Model of Municipal Budgeting. Chicago: Rand McNally.

CROWTHER, W. (1968) "Reports on parks and city planning departments." Oakland Project Report, University of California, Berkeley.

CROZIER, M. (1964) The Bureaucratic Phenomenon. Chicago: University of Chicago Press.

CYERT, R. M. and J. G. MARCH (1963) A Behavioral Theory of the Firm. Englewood Cliffs, NJ: Prentice-Hall.

DAHL, P. (1969) "The budgetary process in the Oakland parks and recreational departments." Oakland Project Report, University of California, Berkeley.

DAHL, R. A. (1963) Modern Political Analysis. Englewood Cliffs, NJ: Prentice Hall.

———(1963a) "The concept of power," pp. 39-54 in Modern Political Analysis. Englewood Cliffs, NJ: Prentice-Hall.

DOWNS, A. (1967) Inside Bureaucracy. Boston: Little, Brown.

———(1957) An Economic Theory of Democracy. New York: Harper & Row.

ETHERIDGE, L. (1978) A World of Men: The Private Source of American Foreign Policy. Cambridge, MA: MIT Press.

EULAU, H. and K. PREWITT (1973) Labyrinths of Democracy. New York: Bobbs-Merrill.

FAGIN, H. (1970) "Advancing the state of the art," pp. 133-134 in Urban Planning in Transition. New York: Grossman.

GORDON, G. (1969) "The Oakland survey." Oakland Project Report, University of California, Berkeley, August.

GULICK, L., and L. URWICK [eds.] (1937) Papers on the Science of Administration. New York: Columbia University, Institute of Public Administration.

HOLSTI, O. R. (1976) "Cognitive process approaches to decision making." American Behavioral Scientist 20.

JANIS, I. L. (1972) Victims of Groupthink. Boston: Houghton-Mifflin.

JERVIS, R. (1976) Perception and Misperception in International Politics. Princeton, NJ: Princeton University Press.

KANTOR, R. M. (1982) "The middle manager as innovator." Harvard Business Review (July-August): 95-105.

KATZ, D. and R. L. KAHN (1966) The Social Psychology of Organizations. New York: John Wiley.

KAUFMAN, H. (1960) The Forest Ranger. Baltimore, MD: Johns Hopkins Press.

KEMENY, J. G., J. L. SNELL, and G. L. THOMPSON (1966) Introduction to Finite Mathematics. Englewood Cliffs, NJ: Prentice-Hall.

KRAMER, R. (1969) Participation of the Poor. Englewood Cliffs, NJ: Prentice-Hall.

LANDAU, M. (1973) "On the concept of a self-correcting organization." Public Administrative Review 33, 6: 533-542.

————(1969) "Redundancy, rationality and the problem of duplication and overlap." Public Administration Review 29 (July/August): 346-358.

LaPORTE, T. R. (1969) "Organized social complexity as an analytical problem: an introduction and explication." Space Science Laboratory Working Paper no. 113. University of California, Berkeley, December.

LERNER, A. W. (1976) The Politics of Decision-Making: Strategy, Cooperation, and Conflict. Beverly Hills, CA: Sage.

LINDBLOM, C. E. (1969) "The science of muddling through." Public Administration Review 19 (Spring): 79-88.

LONG, N. E. (1958) "The local community as an ecology of games." American Journal of Sociology (November): 251-261.

LUCE, D. and H. RAIFFA (1957) Games and Decisions. New York: John Wiley.

LYBRAND, R. B. and MONTGOMERY (1969) "Communication to the city." November 20.

MACK, R. P. (1971) Planning on Uncertainty. New York: Wiley-Interscience.

MARCH, J. G. and J. P. OLSON (1983) "Organizing political life: what administrative reorganization tells us about government." American Political Science Review 77, 2: 281-292.

MARRIS, P. and M. REIN (1967) Dilemmas of Social Reform. New York: Atherton.

MAY, J. V. (1969) "Two model cities: political development on the local level." ASPA paper, September.

McCLELLAND, D. C. (1961) The Achieving Society. Princeton, NJ: Van Nostrand.
McFARLAND, A. S. (1969) Power and Leadership in Pluralist Systems. Stanford, CA: Stanford University Press.
MELTSNER, A. J. (1971) The Politics of City Revenue. Berkeley: University of California Press.
———(1970) "The politics of local revenue." Ph.D. Dissertation, University of California, Berkeley, tables 2-3.
———(1968) "Oakland project report." University of California, Berkeley, September 22.
——— and C. BELLAVITA (1983) The Policy Organization. Beverly Hills, CA: Sage.
MELTSNER, A. and A. WILDAVSKY (1970) "Leave city budgeting alone," in J. P. Crecine and L. H. Masotti (eds.) Financing the Metropolis. Beverly Hills, CA: Sage.
MERTON, R. (1968) Social Theory and Social Structure. New York: Free Press.
MICHAEL, D. V. (1966) "Some long range implications of computer technology for human behavior organizations." American Behavioral Scientist 9 (April).
Montclarion (1968) "Students are serious about goals." November 20.
MOYNIHAN, D. (1970) Maximum Feasible Misunderstanding. New York: Free Press.
Oakland City Finance Department (1971) "Computer utilization report." April.
Oakland City Planning Department (1972) Zoning Regulations. Oakland, CA: Author.
———(1969) Options for Oakland. Oakland, CA: Author.
———(1966) Oakland Central District Plan. Oakland, CA: Author.
PETERSON, P. E. (1981) City Limits. Chicago: University of Chicago Press.
PERROW, C. (1970) Organizational Analysis: A Sociological View. Belmont, CA: Brooks/Cole.
PLATT, J. R. (1964) "Strong inference." Science 146 (October): 350.
Playboy (1969) "Jesse Jackson, a candid conversation with the fiery heir apparent to Martin Luther King, Jr." 16 (November): 86.
POHLE, V. S. (1969) "Planning for progress: an operational analysis of the limitations of long-range, comprehensive planning." Oakland Project Report, University of California, Berkeley.
POLANYI, M. (1958) Personal Knowledge. London: Routledge & Kegan Paul.
PRESSMAN, J. L. (1971) "Preconditions of mayoral leadership." American Political Science Review 66: 511-524.
———and A. B. WILDAVSKY (1973) The EDA in Oakland. Berkeley: University of California Press.
RABINOVITZ, F. F. (1969) City Politics and Planning. New York: Atherton.
ROSE, R. (1974) Coping with Urban Change. Beverly Hills, CA: Sage.
San Francisco Chronicle (1969) "Black board members outcry at white critic." August 27.
SAVAGE, L. J. (1954) The Foundations of Statistics. New York: John Wiley.
SHAPIRO, P. (1969) "City planning department: budgetary process." Oakland Project Report, University of California, Berkeley.
SILBERMAN, C. E. (1964) Crisis in Black and White. New York: Vintage.
SILVA, W. (1969) "A study of the depth and adequacy of the Oakland Tribune." Oakland Project Report, University of California, Berkeley.
SIMON, H. A. (1976) Administrative Behavior. New York: Free Press.
SINDLER, A. [ed.] (1969) American Political Institutions and Public Policy. Boston: Little, Brown.
SLEVIN, D. (1971) "The innovation boundary." Administrative Science Quarterly 16 (December).

STEINBRUNER, J. D. (1974) The Cybernetic Theory of Decision. Princeton, NJ: Princeton University Press.

STOCK, R. (1978) "The uses of decision theory in public program and program management." Institute of Public and Urban Studies, San Diego State University, California.

SUNDQUIST, J. (1968) Politics and Policy. Washington: Brookings Institution.

SYKES, G. (1958) The Society of Captives: The Study of a Maximum Security Prison. New York: Atheneum.

TANNENBAUM. A. S. (1968) Control in Organizations. New York: McGraw-Hill.

THOMPSON, D. J. (1967) Organizations in Action. New York: McGraw-Hill.

THOMPSON, V. (1961) Modern Organization. New York: Alfred A. Knopf.

U. S. Department of Housing and Urban Development (1970) Municipal Information Systems. Washington, DC: Government Printing Office.

VETTER, D. (1968a) "The impact of the city planning department on resource allocation in Oakland, California." Oakland Project report. University of California, Berkeley.

———(1968b) "An analysis of the budgetary process in the city planning department of Oakland, California." Oakland Project Report, University of California, Berkeley.

VON NEUMANN, J. and O. MORGENSTERN (1944) The Theory of Games and Economic Behavior. Princeton, NJ: Princeton University Press.

WALKER, R. A. (1950) The Planning Function in Urban Government. Chicago: University of Chicago Press.

WILDAVSKY, A. (1975) A Comparative Theory of the Budgeting Process. Boston: Little, Brown.

———(1963) The Politics of the Budgetary Process. Boston; Little, Brown.

ABOUT THE AUTHOR

Jay D. Starling, a member of the Oakland Project for almost four years, served on the faculty at Southern Methodist University. At Southern Methodist, he was Director of the Urban Studies Programs, Director of the Graduate Program in Public Administration, and Associate Professor of Political Science. He served for many years as a naval officer and aviator. He also has worked as a consultant to business and government; staff director of a committee in the House of Representatives; and major projects administrator for the Atlantic Richfield Corporation. Presently, Starling is working as a project administrator on a team building a new solar photovoltaic manufacturing facility for ARCO Solar, Inc.